The Second Leg Down

The Wiley Finance series contains books written specifically for finance and investment professionals as well as sophisticated individual investors and their financial advisors. Book topics range from portfolio management to e-commerce, risk management, financial engineering, valuation and financial instrument analysis, as well as much more. For a list of available titles, visit our Web site at www.WileyFinance.com.

Founded in 1807, John Wiley & Sons is the oldest independent publishing company in the United States. With offices in North America, Europe, Australia and Asia, Wiley is globally committed to developing and marketing print and electronic products and services for our customers' professional and personal knowledge and understanding.

The Second Leg Down

Strategies for Profiting After a Market Sell-Off

HARI KRISHNAN

WILEY

This edition first published 2017
© 2017 John Wiley & Sons, Ltd.

Registered office
John Wiley & Sons Ltd, The Atrium, Southern Gate, Chichester, West Sussex, PO19 8SQ, United Kingdom.

For details of our global editorial offices, for customer services and for information about how to apply for permission to reuse the copyright material in this book please see our website at www.wiley.com.

Library of Congress Cataloging-in-Publication Data is available:

ISBN 9781119219088 (hardback) ISBN 9781119219019 (ePDF)
ISBN 9781119219002 (ePub) ISBN 9781119219064 (o-bk)

Cover Design: Wiley
Cover Image: © HTU/Shutterstock

Set in 9/11 and SabonLTStd by SPi Global, Chennai, India.
Printed in Great Britain by TJ International Ltd, Padstow, Cornwall, UK.

SKY3674D6E6-8732-4775-A5CB-CB590F5E967A_030521

To Sudarshan and Kailash

Contents

Preface

There have been times when I have looked into the abyss as a portfolio manager, yet found a way to avoid disastrous losses. My trading accounts have weathered the 2008 crisis, the 2010 Flash Crash, the European Crisis of 2011 and the volatility spike from nowhere in August 2015, with varying degrees of success. Things have not always gone as well as I had hoped, yet I have always come away with a collection of new tactics for survival. For a fund manager, it is about survival after all. Aside from the money, your reward for decent performance is another year of money management. You don't want to take the path of boxers, who only decide to retire after a series of devastating knockouts. It is nice not to have to go out on your shield. This book has been inspired by the various crises I have faced as a money manager and the techniques I have learned and devised for managing through them. As every crisis is somewhat different, finding the most efficient hedge is a never-ending quest. I do hope that readers will find something that they can use to avert catastrophic losses.

The style of this book is casual and conversational, yet it attempts to be as accurate and realistic as possible. I have been asked who the ideal reader of this book might be. The best answer I can give is me, 20 years ago. This is a more pedestrian effort than Rilke's *Letters to a Young Poet*. Still, if I had followed the roadmap laid out in the pages that follow, I would have avoided numerous mistakes over the course of my career. More pragmatically, the book is targeted at a wide range of potential readers. Pension fund managers might find value in the discussion of duration hedging, bespoke trend following and roll down as a source of return for bond portfolios. The introductory options sections are designed to give a buy-side perspective on a topic that is usually discussed in terms of arbitrage, precise replication and stochastic calculus. I try to address *why* someone might want to use particular options structures. I also highlight specific structures that portfolio managers actually use and what might predicate a certain trade.

It is common for portfolio managers to hide their best ideas. In some cases, they might even publish strategies that didn't quite work, for implementation reasons. This leads to a situation where people who don't have any money management experience write extensive books about investing, while those who have the most to contribute are relatively silent. How is it possible to provide some valuable content without giving too much away? In this book, I have tried to veer from the norm. By focusing on hedging, rather than alpha generation, I have been able to go into some detail about specific strategies, without pretending to offer a cook book for making money. These have actually been battle-tested in the markets, for institutional clients.

Acknowledgements

The following people have had a profound effect on the contents of this book. I would like to thank them directly.

My wife Lalitha (using her considerable literary talents) edited large sections of the book and improved the flow of the writing.

Diego von Buch provided the initial impetus for the book, calling me from his French chateau and offering a hedging mandate just as market conditions were deteriorating in 2007.

Jerry Haworth deserves a great deal of credit for introducing me to the subtleties of long-dated options and his imprint can be found in Chapter 5.

Marc Malek exerted a large influence on the regime index and trend following sections.

Roy Niederhoffer also played an important role, as a source of original ideas about trend following strategies.

Michael Howell's insights into the relationship between "funding liquidity" and the market cycle were the inspiration for Chapter 8. I can only hope that I have not watered down his ideas to the point where they are unrecognisable.

Pablo Carbajal also deserves special thanks, as he has been the sounding board for many of the ideas presented in this book.

I hashed out many of the ideas in this book with Lee Collins, who encouraged me to put things in simple and concrete terms. His way of talking about trades had a large impact on Chapter 3.

Alex Manzara and Aaron Brown were kind enough to read the entire manuscript, providing valuable perspective on options execution in extreme market conditions.

My mother and father-in-law supported me by selflessly taking care of the boys and freeing up time for me to slog through the manuscript.

Others who provided valuable advice and inspiration for the book were (in no particular order): Jasper McMahon, Ben Paton, Nick Denbow, Norman Mains, Niels Kaastrup-Larsen, Pertti Tornberg, David Murrin, Karthik Bharath, Thomas Hyrkiel, Steve "explain things in a nutshell" Crutchfield, Dan DiBartolomeo, Lee Cashin, John Mallet-Paret (lean and mean writing style) and Izzy Nelken. Finally, I would like to thank my parents for encouraging creativity and independent thinking since I was a young boy.

Hari P. Krishnan is a fund manager at CrossBorder Capital in London. He specialises in global macro, volatility and hedging overlay strategies. Previously, he managed a CTA strategy for a multi-family office based in London and was an executive director at Morgan Stanley. Hari also worked as an options trading strategist for a market-making firm at the CBOE and as a senior economist at the Chicago Board of Trade. He holds a PhD in applied math from Brown University and was a post-doctoral research scientist at the Columbia Earth Institute.

The Second Leg Down

CHAPTER 1

Introduction

Finance is full of colourful stories and the most exciting ones tend to involve someone on the verge of collapse. We feel a mix of thrill and *schadenfreude* when we read about the traders who blew up or the elite hedge funds that had to liquidate after failing to meet their margin calls. In a moment of panic, investors can do the strangest things and this can make for great theatre. Arrogance and overconfidence are punished by the markets, which seem to have a life force of their own. Many shrewd investors have completely lost their way in a moment of crisis. There are numerous stories of portfolio managers who have patiently extracted profits from the markets for years, then had a large and unexpected loss. It might have been advisable for them to exit the position ("cutting their losses") and try to claw back using their core strategy over time. Yet, the temptation is to put all the chips on black in an attempt to make the money back quickly. In principle, this is a wretched idea, as the profit from a long series of rational trades over time may be overwhelmed by a single irrational bet.

THE AIRPLANE TICKET TRADE

The legend of the airplane ticket trade is an extreme example of bad judgment under pressure, yet it is sometimes presented as rational decision-making. The story goes as follows. A trader has been losing money and is unlikely to collect much of a bonus this year. So the trader decides to dial up risk in an attempt to make it all back in one go. This backfires horribly, leading to further losses. The trader expects risk to be cut at any moment now, so he does two things. He makes a very large short-term trade that will either make or lose a large amount and he simultaneously buys a ticket to South America. It's a tactical play, with little edge but lots of risk. The trader then goes to the airport and repeatedly checks his price feed in the lounge. If the trade goes in his favour, he closes the position then goes back to the office. If it goes belly up, he buys a bottle of vodka from the duty free then takes the flight. The trader's behaviour might seem reasonable at 30,000 feet. In the best scenario, he gets a large bonus; in the worst, he takes a long tropical holiday. There doesn't seem to be much downside and one could argue that from the trader's standpoint, he is long an option. But would you want to be that trader at the moment of crisis? If the position is going slightly against you, are you willing to hang on for dear life, with no conviction that you are making the right trade? If it is your own money, do you want to risk everything on a roll of the dice? If you are a fund manager, how can you rationalise what you have done to clients if it all goes wrong?

THE BULL CYCLE

In reality, most institutional losses and disasters are not caused by trading reminiscent of the Wild West. Rather, they are caused by somewhat predictable behaviour through the market cycle. In bull markets, portfolio managers tend to increase exposure in an effort to chase the market and outperform competitors and benchmarks. Ten basis point differentials in performance seem important. By the "market", we mean risky assets such as stocks and corporate bonds. Investors eagerly buy into every dip in the market, dampening volatility. As the value of collateral increases and volatility declines, banks lend more and the market eventually becomes overextended. This applies to equities, corporate bonds and other risky assets. When risky assets appear to be vectoring toward infinity, we would argue that it *is* a good time to hedge. Risk embedded in the system has increased, yet the market is practically giving away insurance. The painful memories of the last crash have been erased, making investors particularly vulnerable to a random shock.

Investors who chase returns after a large sustained move tend to have relatively low pain thresholds. They worry that they have missed the move, but are equally likely to bail out at the first sign of trouble. So long as the rally persists, the cost of insurance (i.e. options) tends to be low. The latecomers to the market do not want to erode their return by hedging and the longstanding bulls are complacent. You could sensibly argue that if the market continues to rally, hedging costs should be more than offset by profits in the rest of the portfolio. Yet there is a natural human reluctance to "waste" money on insurance when everything seems fine.

As the animal spirits take over, investors attempt to rationalise their behaviour in a variety of ways.

- "This time it's different." There is a central bank put on the market, as monetary conditions will be eased whenever there is a risk event. Regulators can prevent extreme intra-day moves by disqualifying trades that occur very far away from recent prices.
- Calm periods are persistent: they tend to last for a long time. Not very much happens from day to day, suggesting that there is plenty of time to prepare for the next correction.
- Over the long term, hedging is largely unnecessary. For example, some institutions don't hedge their currency risk. Over the long term, they assume that currency moves will wash out. Buying insurance on risky assets such as equities is a losing strategy over the long term. According to academic theory, hedging must have a negative risk premium, as it reduces the non-diversifiable risks in your portfolio. Insurance companies are generally profitable because they sell individual policies that are statistically overpriced. So long as the policies are relatively uncorrelated, insurers are able to collect more than they pay out over the long term.

If you are not careful, you can convince yourself that *selling* insurance is an unbeatable strategy. Short volatility strategies tend to perform magnificently in back-tests, without much parameterisation. All you need to do is persistently sell downside protection on equity indices, risky currencies and corporate bonds, or so it would seem. When volatility is low, these options appear to be slightly but consistently overpriced. It is tempting to conclude that you can make small but very steady returns in this environment. As volatility rises, your profits become less reliable from day to day. However, this might be more than compensated for by an increase in the premium you collect when volatility is high. Most active management strategies are short volatility in one way or another. Whether you buy equities, take long positions in risky bonds or engage in spread trades, you will tend to perform better in flat to rising markets than highly volatile ones. The vast majority of hedge fund strategies are structurally short volatility. The incentive structures for many hedge funds and proprietary trading desks favour collecting pennies in front of the bulldozer. However, this does not imply that selling volatility universally has a positive expected return. Once you put a back test into action, you are vulnerable to large jumps that may not have appeared in the sample past. As soon as you introduce leverage, you are vulnerable to risk and margin constraints that can force you out of a trade at the worst possible time. Markets don't usually collapse because investors want to sell, but because they *have* to. Liquidation is forced, in the presence of margin calls. We will examine the effect of margin constraints on short volatility strategies in Chapter 4.

THE RENEGADES

There is a small but dedicated group of defensive, bear market managers in the investment universe. The financial media trots them out every so often, typically after a market sell-off. However, in rising markets these managers are largely invisible or the subject of criticism. Profiting from panics, bankruptcies and liquidations requires patience and does not necessarily win you many friends. When equities are ramping up, bear-biased managers spend more time banging their heads against the wall than raising assets. The cost of insurance is steadily declining, yet there are no takers. The inveterate bears write long and engaging manifestos in an attempt to identify cracks in the financial system. In rising markets, the potential end users of these products generally can't or don't want to buy them. Some institutions take a crude "line item" approach, where they rank their funds according to recent performance and periodically redeem from underperforming managers. This approach seems oblivious to the idea of marginal risk, i.e. how much you can improve the risk-adjusted performance of an existing portfolio by adding a new asset or strategy. In reality, if you can find a strategy that performs strongly during crises yet doesn't lose too much over a market cycle, it can have a dramatic impact on portfolio performance over the long term.

Uncontaminated bear strategies have a hard time competing in a world where allocators believe that emerging markets, high yield bonds and carry trades are "diversifying" investments. While it is true that these asset classes can reduce realised volatility during normal market conditions, they typically amplify losses when conditions become extreme. Some strategies, such as the FX carry trade, seem innocuous during bull markets. They grind their way upward with low volatility. However, it is categorically *not* true that a strategy with relatively low volatility in a bull market will dampen risk during a crisis. If the strategy collects premium while taking extreme event risk, the opposite is in fact true. A manager who combines carry strategies with a modest number of equity index puts will often appear to be over-hedged most of the time and severely under-hedged when the protection is most needed.

In rising markets, dedicated bears have to overcome time decay as well as markets that are moving in the wrong direction. The portfolio manager who takes the opposite side of the trade by selling insurance has an optical advantage. Investors seem to prefer a sequence of returns of the form {+1%, +1%, +1%, +1%, +1%, −5%} to {−1%, −1%, −1%, −1%, −1%, +5%}, even though the compounded return of the second strategy is a bit higher. In the first scenario, you can always say to your client that you are an alpha manager who had a few issues with risk control that have now been resolved. This cynical approach may well salvage the mandate. Even the most dedicated bears are incentivised to scale down their hedges when threatened with redemptions.

The best time to buy outright volatility is when it is low, in a counter-cyclical way. You want to swim against the tide of short-sighted overconfidence. Investors are more than happy to sell volatility when they are feeling confident. However, implied volatility *is* low precisely because there is virtually no demand for hedging or long volatility strategies in general. Hence, long volatility managers struggle to raise assets in situations when the best risk-adjusted returns are available. Our book acknowledges the perverse nature of hedging mandates. When assets are pouring in, outright volatility tends to be overpriced. We try to identify ways to minimise drag while still offering protection after markets have started to tumble.

CLAWS OF THE BEAR

[T]o borrow the term, your sense of time does change when you are running real money. Suppose you look at a cumulative return of a strategy with a Sharpe ration of 0.7 and see a three year period with poor performance. It does not phase you one drop. You go: "Oh, look, that happened in 1973, but it came back by 1976, and that's what a 0.7 Sharpe ratio does." But living through those periods takes – subjectively, and in wear and tear on your internal organs – many times the actual time it really lasts. If you have a three year period where

something doesn't work, it ages you a decade. You face an immense pressure to change your models, you have bosses and clients who lose faith, and I cannot explain the amount of discipline you need.

– Cliff Asness[i]

Once you put real money behind a short volatility strategy, the situation changes. Now you have some skin in the game and things aren't quite so comfortable. Your margin levels can change dramatically over time, requiring that you cut positions that look very attractive from a valuation standpoint. In Chapter 4, we show that wildly fluctuating margin requirements can force you out of a short volatility strategy at the worst possible moment. A historical series of daily NAVs is devoid of emotion and assumes that you have sufficient capital to keep playing indefinitely. It can't capture gut wrenching intraday moves or account for price action that is different from what has been observed in the past. If the worst 1 day historical loss is –10% and your strategy is down –9% at mid-day, there is no guarantee that losses will be bounded at roughly –1% thereafter. In rising markets, investors are quite happy to sweep latent risk under the carpet as risk and margin limits are never reached. Inevitably, at some point, risky assets take a significant leg down. The "stocks go up in the long term" bulls can no longer buy the dip as they approach their risk limits. Large institutions spend ages deciding whether "this is the one", whether credit and equity markets will plunge further into the abyss. Their portfolios might already be down –5% or –10% on an unlevered basis and they really can't take much more. Do they hang on, cut exposure or hedge?

It has often been remarked that "hope is not an investment strategy". Hanging on is a sign of desperation or delusion. Sometimes, an overconfident investor can become convinced that the market *has* to move a certain way and goes all in. It is almost as though the investor believes it is possible to move the market by force of mind. Solipsism doesn't seem to be a viable strategy, either. Some investors doggedly hold onto losing positions using "fair value" arguments. When combined with leverage, this approach can be toxic. The standard argument is that the expected return of a static portfolio goes up as its price drops, i.e. price and expected return move inversely. While this may be true over long horizons, there is a point at which every institutional manager has to cut risk. Most of us do not have an infinite investment horizon in which to capture a risk premium. There is a saying for the leveraged deep value investors who hang on during crises: "it looks good at 90, looks great at 80, looks absolutely fantastic at 70 and you're out of business at 60". This is the classic value trap that needs to be avoided.

ZUGZWANG

In chess, zugzwang refers to a situation where a player has to move, but every move worsens the player's position. When a portfolio manager's risk limits are hit or losses are thought to be unacceptable, the situation is quite the same. There are two choices: cut risk or buy insurance. Neither seems appealing. If the manager slashes positions, the potential for further losses is reduced. This can be agonising for investors who believe that, given enough time, their portfolio is bound to bounce back. Some portfolios are large and complex, implying that they cannot be liquidated in one go. Finally, suppose an investor has been making small bets for years and now has to divest a large percentage of his or her portfolio. This one action can offset a large number of good decisions and successful trades. Some funds scale in and out of positions almost continuously as risk changes. They generally have sophisticated techniques for sampling volatility and correlation over time. However, even these funds are exposed to gap risk (i.e. when a currency peg is released) or situations where their alpha-generation systems have stopped working.

Faced with the choice of liquidating positions or hedging, institutions finally pick up the phone and contact managers who can protect capital during a crisis. Managed accounts that have not been used for months are reactivated, with a hedging overlay mandate. Assets begin to flow into bear-biased strategies. As the demand for hedging increases, its cost sky rockets. To a patient on the operating table in a life-or-death situation, money is no object. Survival is all that matters. And so it goes for an individual or institution on financial life support, who hedges regardless of cost. The long volatility manager who gets the call is in two minds about it. On the one hand, the manager is more than happy to have a new allocation. It serves as vindication, as well as a new source of fees. On the other, hedging looks expensive now. If only the call had come a few weeks earlier, when there was a wide range of inexpensive hedges to choose from! Previously, an overlay could have been slowly and carefully constructed, with an emphasis on finding inexpensive hedges across a variety of asset classes. Now it's a case of making the best of a bad situation. You have to make sure that the patient survives (i.e. that there is a floor on further losses), while ensuring that you don't spend too much along the way. Once markets recover, your performance will be mercilessly scrutinised. Did you make enough on the way down? Did you monetise enough gains to avoid giving it all back during the recovery?

Whether you allocate to another manager or hedge yourself, the pressures are quite the same. Most of the time, you will be incentivised *not* to hedge, even when you can identify good short opportunities. Indirect hedges, such as buying calls on the VIX to hedge against long exposure to the S&P 500, will generally add to your exchange margin requirements. This reduces the degree to which you can lever the rest of your portfolio. Even if leverage is not an issue, hedging suffers from an optical standpoint. Unless you can bury your hedges in the rest of your portfolio, your supervisors and clients will see long strings of mildly negative returns punctuated by the occasional lumpy positive one. Once things get ugly, you will be asked whether you have hedged *enough*. Are you making money on every little drop in risk assets? Have you put a floor on how much can be lost in the overall portfolio?

THE SCEPTICS

Some investors, especially those with a "stocks for the long run" bias (e.g. Siegel, 1998), might argue that hedging is intrinsically wasteful. The hedging sceptics tend to intersect with the true believers in the equity risk premium. If you are prepared to wait long enough, there's no need to hedge, as equity market returns will exceed inflation. Over rolling 10-year horizons, the S&P 500 has nearly always outperformed CPI inflation on an annualised basis. It follows that, if equities deliver a positive real return over the long term, hedging *must* have a negative risk premium. After all, you are paying a premium to take a short position on the market, is that not so? Theory suggests that you earn a premium for bearing an undiversifiable risk. Conversely, an instrument that offsets market risk should have a negative expected return. Insurance companies are in business precisely because insurance is overpriced on average. Historical back-tests in the markets tend to support this idea. Insurance eats into your long-term expected return. Static options hedges tend to lose money at an alarming rate, with modestly positive spikes along the way. On paper, the appropriate strategy involves *buying into* market sell-offs, as risk premiums go up whenever the prices of risk assets go down. It would seem as though the last thing you want to do is buy options *after* volatility has gone up. If an option was expensive before, it must be egregious after a risk event. Our view is that listed options are somewhat different from insurance policies. While typical hedges are probably overpriced, as there is excess institutional demand for them, options are subject to the same cycles of greed and fear as equity markets.

A SAD TRUTH

Recently, a number of books and articles have appeared covering topics such as "tail risk protection", "crisis alpha" or "extreme event hedging". Many of these are thorough treatments of how institutions think about truncating the left tail of their return distribution. Bhansali (2014) is a thoughtful treatise on the nature of asset class distributions and institutional quality hedging strategies. However, they invariably ignore a sad truth. Almost no one wants to hedge much when the going is good. Institutional investors generally do not pay much attention to the independent economists and hedge fund managers who warn that a new crisis is brewing. In bull markets, articles that focus on doomsday scenarios are viewed as nothing more than fearmongering. Indeed, it is notoriously difficult to predict where the next crisis will come from. Will it be credit derivatives, emerging markets or a change in Central Bank policy?

Several well-known hedge fund managers try to engage in crisis prediction by identifying potential cracks in the system. They typically screen for excessive leverage in some part of the economy and then direct their hedges to the places where danger seems to be lurking. This is a substantial improvement on not hedging at all, but it assumes that extreme events are predictable in place *and* time. If the manager places the doomsday bet too early, there may be a long string of losses before any material gain is realised. In the meantime, investors might redeem from the strategy. If the bet is placed too late, the risk of default may already be priced into the market, reducing potential returns. Most of us don't have the foggiest idea when the next crisis is coming and should be honest enough to admit it. Note that we *will* discuss crisis prediction in Chapter 8. It might seem contradictory that we are taking a stab at a problem as difficult as this. For the purposes of this discussion, however, it is best to assume that predicting financial crises is like predicting earthquakes. We can identify situations (geological fault lines) which are unstable, but can't with any certainty say *when* an event will occur.

Returning to the original problem, let us generalise and assume that investors only want to hedge after risk assets have taken a leg down. Hedging is not going to be cheap, as there is more demand for insurance. So what can you do to protect a portfolio against a systemic risk event, that isn't *too* bad? That is what this book is all about.

COMMON MISTAKES

In the chapters that follow, we identify strategies for protecting a portfolio of risky assets *after* a sell-off. Investors have suddenly become wary and are no longer just giving away protection at discount levels. It is not wise to just go in and buy index puts, as these are bound to be overpriced. Yet many institutions do exactly that. They react to an increase in perceived risk by identifying "plausible" downside scenarios and choosing options that target those scenarios. The risk committee might have a discussion about how bad things could get, before reaching a consensus on what constitutes a tolerable and plausible loss. We believe that this approach is flawed. While it is reasonable to average forecasted returns, taking an average of downside scenarios understates the risk of an extreme event.

If everyone is buying options to cover the risk of moderate losses, those options are likely to be overpriced. Our approach is to find other options to buy. We argue that an option does not have to wind up in the money to be profitable. All that is needed is a *repricing of risk*. Just as the price of hurricane insurance goes up when there is a thunderstorm, the price of extreme event insurance rises when there is a moderate sell-off in the equity market. You can always sell an option back to the market if it reprices substantially. In any case, implausible scenarios can appear plausible after a plausible scenario has occurred. This may sound thoroughly convoluted, but it is not meant to be. Our goal is to be as clear as possible. At first sight, a –30% one month collapse in the S&P 500 seems highly unlikely. Even in October 2008, the peak to trough drop was less than that. But suppose that the index drops –10% in the first week. Suddenly, that –30% drop does not seem so unlikely and investors are clamouring for insurance at levels (i.e. option strikes) far below what could be imagined. This is partly a function of perception. It is also based on the idea that in certain scenarios, markets exhibit positive feedback. A drop cannot be viewed in isolation, because that drop may force others to sell as they hit their risk limits. Sell-offs can occur in cascades.

Another common idea is to hedge extreme event risk using currency options. This is a play on the "Mrs. Watanabe trade", which will be analysed in greater depth in Chapter 2. Mr. Watanabe has a demanding job, so he delegates the family's personal investments to his wife. There is no point in depositing money at a local bank, since the bank rate is effectively 0%. The Nikkei 225 is still well below its peak in 1989 and there is no cult of equities in Japan, as there is in the US. The equity premium puzzle is irrelevant, as there is no premium to speak of. Investors are distrustful that Japanese equity indices will deliver a positive return over the long term. So why not sell the Yen to buy Australian dollars

(AUD) or another high yielding currency? When you buy Australian dollar forwards, you implicitly capture the Australian bank deposit rate. If a 1 year deposit yields 5% in Australia, you gain 5% carry in Australian dollars while borrowing Japanese Yen virtually for free. Theory suggests that the forward rate bias should be offset by an expected −5% annual decline in AUD. In practice, Kritzman (1999) and others have observed that spot exchange rates are not very correlated to yield differentials. If anything, high yielding currencies tend to outperform even in spot terms, as investors chase income. Assuming that AUD does hold its value relative to the Yen, you collect nearly 5% per year. This is a huge source of income in a deflationary environment. Once the carry trade gathers momentum, Mrs. Watanabe's investment club piles into the trade. Things sound rosy so far. Ultimately, the trouble with the trade is that it can become overleveraged and overcrowded. This poisonous combination can cause very steep declines when investors are exposed the most. Eventually, a random shock turns into a major reversal as the investment club heads screaming for the exits along with larger institutions.

Given that carry currencies go up the stairs and down the lift, it seems reasonable to hedge extreme event risk using puts on carry trades such as the Australian Dollar/Japanese Yen cross. More precisely, carry trades are negatively skewed, implying that the probability of downside surprises is higher than the probability of ones that work in your favour. The longer-dated the put, the more time you have to wait for a blow up. However, the shape of the currency forward curve can have a dramatic impact on the performance of a hedge. Once you buy the Aussie put, two forces are conspiring against you. Every day that passes, you lose money on time decay *and* drift as the forward rolls up to the spot. So the currency hedge usually winds up a loser.

IMPRECISE BUT EFFECTIVE

The hedges described in this book are *not* precise. We are not going to tell you to hedge your long position in Apple with Apple puts. While this may be the most accurate way to soften the impact of sell-offs, it is often egregiously expensive. If you really don't feel comfortable with Apple downside, your best strategy is probably to reduce the position. Yet institutional practice often suffers from a literal and somewhat narrow-minded approach to hedging. Many consultants in the pension fund industry seem overly focused on precise hedges. The solvency of a pension fund is often calculated relative to the *present value* of its liabilities. The liabilities are the expected payments the fund will have to make to its beneficiaries in the future. If interest rates drop, the value of those liabilities *today* will increase. This necessitates hedging against rate risk. A common solution is to use an actuarial number called the "average duration" of the liabilities as a crucial variable in the hedge. This is the time-weighted average of expected payments to beneficiaries. It is an imprecise number, based on projections of who will retire and when. Still, consultants often think of average duration as an exact number and offset rate risk with swaps or other instruments that precisely target it. While there may be regulatory reasons for transacting in this way, this approach seems wasteful. In a low interest rate environment, receiving fixed payments does not seem like the best idea. There may be other, slightly less precise-looking hedges that offer greater protection and are likely to cost less in the long term. If your shoe size is 8.5, do you want or need a shoe that is precisely calibrated to size 8?

We focus on overlay strategies as a mechanism for controlling portfolio risk. Our goal is to identify areas where insurance is relatively inexpensive, while recalling the idea that our hedges need to make money in a severe risk event. Most of the strategies involve exchange-traded options in deep and liquid markets, such as equity indices, the VIX, interest rates and currencies. We start with a non-technical overview of options theory. The goal is *not* to price options but rather to express the value of an option in terms of its implied volatility. Focusing on volatility, we can identify different combinations of options in different markets that are relatively cheap at a given point of time.

If an emerging markets index drops from 100 to 90 in a day, a 75 strike put may have a larger percentage gain than a 95 strike put, even though the stock hasn't come close to 75. The implausible scenario (a sudden −25% drop) has suddenly become plausible. As we will see, large moves sometimes beget even larger moves as the market enters a positive feedback loop. When investors start to worry about a major loss, they bid up the prices of puts that are far out of the money. This causes those silly strike options to make multiples of what was initially paid.

HEDGING AGAINST IMPLAUSIBLE SCENARIOS

In Chapter 4, we explore hedges that take advantage of changing investor perceptions. One structure revolves around buying large quantities of options that only pay out for moves that appear ridiculously unlikely. We emphasise that we are not really concerned whether these options have value at maturity. When fear grips the market, investors re-price extreme event risk and the options can explode in price. It's a bit like betting on a long shot team in a football tournament. If the odds are 1000:1 at the beginning of the tournament and the team surprisingly wins the first game, the odds might drop to 500:1. The team is still unlikely to win the tournament, but if you exit now you have doubled your money. You don't need the team to actually win the rest of its games and can move on to other long shot bets over time. While sports betting odds are clearly skewed toward the bookies, financial markets offer a more level playing field. Certain options can become surprisingly cheap when investors are complacent. There also seem to be structural distortions in the options markets that reduce the cost of hedging. Our analysis suggests that investors like to hedge against "reasonable" looking downside scenarios over moderately long-time horizons. They wind up overpaying for options that pay out for moves that seem awful now, but won't account for much in a severe bear market. One strategy is to sell a few of those, while buying a large quantity of options that only pay out if there is a financial meltdown. This approach can work well for the VIX as well as for more conventional assets, as we will find out in Chapter 4.

A BLACK SWAN IN CORRELATION

Over the past 40 years, market crises have followed a familiar script. Stocks and risky bonds have sold off together, with a correlation close to +100%. US Treasuries have soared in the opposite direction, as investors have scrambled for safe havens. The market has operated in the "crash correlation" zone initially described by Hua (1997), with extreme diversification offered by a well-known collection of government bonds. So long as the familiar relationships hold under pressure, you can reduce aggregate risk by sprinkling some US or UK government bonds into your overall portfolio. Markowitz theory will work in your favour. But what if the next crisis challenges the core assumption that Treasuries offer protection against an equity collapse? This may sound like science fiction, but it may not be so far away as some might think. If money pours into products that rely upon asset class diversification, we could see a large-scale liquidation where stocks and bonds go down together. In this case, volatility hedging will be the last chance saloon. Options and volatility indices will become the only assets that can be relied upon for true protection in a crisis. This is one of the main reasons why we focus on options structures in Chapters 3, 4 and 5. Convex hedges are more reliable than diversifying assets. You are not at the mercy of historical relationships that may not hold in the future.

TAKING PROFITS

Suppose that gold prices are falling and you fear a further downside move. You can short gold futures or buy puts on the futures contract. The put strategy offers the advantage of reducing entry timing risk. If gold suddenly reverses, your put will dynamically de-lever, capping your maximum loss. You can only lose the premium you paid. However, losses on the short futures position are in principle unbounded until you cover the position. While the entry point is relatively unimportant, timing the exit from a winning long options trade is vital. If you buy an option and you find that its value has doubled, you wind up holding a much larger position than you started with. The gearing in your option has increased as the market moved in your favour.

In the pages that follow, we argue that the best way to manage a hedging overlay is to rotate across different strategies over time. You always want to have *some* kind of a defensive trade on, but you don't want all of your hedging profits to vanish if markets squeeze upward. Some profits have to be monetised. Otherwise, hedging will improve the mark-to-market performance of your portfolio during crisis periods, but you will never realise any profits from the hedge. If you unwind the entire hedge at some point, you might realise some gains. However, the rest of the portfolio will now be exposed to a further sell-off. So you need to walk the tightrope between maintaining enough protection whilst not holding on to hedges that are now overpriced. "Every dog has its day" is one of the many overused slogans from the finance community, but it succinctly characterises options hedging. No options strategy works all the time and it could equally well be said that, under the right conditions, nearly every hedge can work well. Behind each option is a trading strategy that gears dynamically over time. If the S&P 500 is trading at 2000 and you buy a put with strike 2000 (roughly at-the-money), your position grows as the index drops. You are long downside convexity: profits slingshot in tandem with the market. When you combine different options (e.g. buying the 2000 strike and selling the 1900 strike with a month to go), the return profile becomes more complex.

In Chapter 4, we analyse the back-tested performance of options with different deltas over time. This allows us to create hedges where we sell a small number of persistently "bad" options while over-buying the ones that don't look so bad. We explore the analogy between hedging and market making and demonstrate that buying extreme event insurance is worthwhile even if it never pays out at maturity. Hedging with the VIX is particularly intriguing, as VIX options do not burn off at the same rate as equity index options. They stay lively close to maturity. A VIX call is always in play, as any spike in volatility has a disproportionate impact on short-dated options. We discuss how to overcome time decay and futures roll down while building long options structures on the VIX.

THE GOOD, THE BAD AND THE UGLY

We recall that different types of hedges work in different market regimes: the "every dog has its day" argument. But how do we characterise the prevailing regime in a reasonably precise way? When can we say that global markets are calm and when can we say they are in a state of abject fear? Our approach is to use volatility indices, such as the VIX, as a guide. When the VIX is low, our analysis favours value-buying of volatility. As it rises, we transition to relative-value hedges in various markets. At the extreme, we recommend options combinations that provide significant payouts without too much exposure to volatility. We also explore the merits of trend following as a portfolio protection strategy during a crisis. Of course, this requires a definition of what is meant by low and high volatility. We delve into this question in Chapter 5, toggling back and forth between different types of hedges as conditions change.

This allows us to overcome the question of *when* to take profits in a hedging strategy. So long as the client wants a hedge in place, there is always something we can do. As conditions worsen, we simply rotate out of strategies whose cost is very sensitive to volatility, into other types of hedges. We emphasise that, for options that do not have a long time to maturity, stop losses are *not* an alternative to strategy rotation. Option prices can move radically from one day to the next, as volatility and price change for the underlying asset. They can quite easily crash through any internal profit-taking level you might have set or any price you may have flagged to the market.

THE GREAT ESCAPE

Suppose you are a portfolio manager who applies quite a bit of leverage, e.g. using derivatives. You have sold a large number of puts on an emerging markets currency, based on the idea that volatility is overpriced and the currency is likely to drift higher. Suddenly, there is an air pocket move of –5% down. Your portfolio has lost –10% and you need to meet a margin call. The situation is dire and you feel sick. The natural thing to do is liquidate the position. This frees up margin and caps your loss. However, if you still like the trade, liquidating eliminates the possibility of making anything back. Cutting a bit allows you to stay in the game, but is sort of a halfway house between liquidating and doing nothing, while praying that the market comes back. If you cut the minimum amount, another down move could trigger a second margin call, forcing you to liquidate at an even worse level.

One way around this problem is to buy very short-dated puts on the currency. This allows you to hang on, in a responsible way. The short-dated puts act like a giant piece of duct tape on your portfolio. They contain your losses for a few days, while you regroup. As we will discuss later, you pay a small up-front cost that is not overly sensitive to the level of fear in the market. The gaping hole in your portfolio may be reopened when the options expire. Chapter 5 describes ways to use weekly options as a survival tactic. Weekly options are usually presented as either yield enhancers or lottery tickets. Since short-dated options decay rapidly as function of premium paid, you can capture a huge amount of yield by selling and reloading every Friday. As we will discuss later in the book, we believe that selling weekly options on an outright basis is an awful strategy. For now, we simply accept that many investors do precisely that, which may create distortions in the market. With the lottery ticket approach, you buy short-dated options in anticipation that something big is about to happen. That something may be a central bank announcement, an earnings report or anything else that could have a large impact on the price of an asset. The trouble with buying short-dated options in advance of announcements is that market makers will usually have adjusted the implied volatility of these options to protect against event-driven price discontinuities. You will have to pay up for the lottery ticket in this scenario.

But there is another, vastly more important, way to use weekly options. In the context of a hedging strategy, those weeklies let you live to fight another day. You can put a floor on potential losses in your portfolio at low fixed cost. Although the floor *will* disappear after a few days, it gives you time to reshuffle the rest of your portfolio at a measured pace. You can take that walk around the block before revisiting your positions with some clarity. Weekly option strategies are difficult to back-test, so we take a different approach to justifying their utility. In particular, we review some of the early econophysics research, which tabulated the distribution of stock index returns over various timescales. The beauty of this research is its naivety. It is not burdened by assumptions from traditional economics. We focus particularly on research from the Stanley group at Boston University in the 1990s. While the cutting edge has moved far beyond the early studies, the essential qualitative features of financial time series have not changed that much over time. The Stanley group simply tabulated large quantities of data in search of power law distributions, i.e. situations where the index returns had fat tails. They managed to show that returns over very short horizons (i.e. less than a week) had the greatest potential for outsized returns.

Over short horizons, stock index returns tended to have relatively high serial correlation, suggesting that there could be waves of buying or selling that were not interrupted by value investors. Assuming that the tails are not adequately accounted for in the market, weekly options can offer interesting value-buying opportunities as well as a blanket hedge on your portfolio. Chapter 5 concludes with a discussion of ways you can enhance the return stream of a long weekly options strategy, by trading the underlying as it approaches the strike.

HAVING A PLAN

Money managers typically focus on maximising risk-adjusted portfolio returns. From a psychological standpoint, though, avoiding regret is equally important. You don't want to fall prey to silly mistakes that could have been avoided. Having a plan, a strategy for dealing with any market eventuality, is vital. By definition, systematic funds have a plan for entering and exiting positions. Quoting Yeat's epitaph, models are able "to cast a cold eye on life and death" in the markets. Systematic trading strategies are typically based on data aggregated over a long time period. This implies that they cannot focus acutely on current market conditions. However, they enable you to make decisions in an unemotional way, when asset prices are whipping around. In Chapter 4, we start with a digression on back-testing and model development. We review some research suggesting that fairly simple algorithms can outperform human experts when analysing certain types of data. We also discuss common pitfalls when developing trading strategies, including overfitting and the impact of selecting a strategy from a large number of alternatives.

TREND FOLLOWING AS A DEFENSIVE STRATEGY

One of the nice things about weekly options is that you can be *reactive*. You can wait until things get ugly before taking action. Hedging costs are not very sensitive to changes in volatility and the odds of an extreme event tend to increase after an initial spike in volatility. Most large-scale moves are preceded by choppy price action. You can just plug in a far out-of-the-money short-dated option whenever your position looks vulnerable. Let's take things a bit further. Perhaps the ultimate reactive strategy is trend following, where you are always chasing the market in the direction of an initial move. To clarify, trend following is a style of trading that relies upon buying assets that have already been going up and selling ones that are already moving down. Rather than following the value investing mantra "buy low and sell high", trend followers try to "buy high and sell higher". They make no attempt to identify turning points in the market. Instead, they prey upon situations where there are large-scale price moves, as institutions and leveraged investors reposition themselves. By definition, a pure trend follower wouldn't take a short position in S&P futures until they have already started to drop and will not cover the short until there is a reversal. Since trend followers typically focus on futures, they don't have to pay up for options after volatility has spiked. In high volatility regimes, trend following is a cheap alternative to a long volatility strategy *if* it can provide adequate protection. We examine this issue in Chapter 6.

A vaguely philosophical statement might be in order. It is hard to deduce *why* anything happens in financial markets. The newspaper articles about last week's move tend to be rationalisations, rather than accurate explanations. It's quite amusing to look at last month's, or last year's, research reports, where the recent move was extrapolated in an exaggerated way. The S&P 500 has dropped from 2000 to 1800 and the prophets of doom have come out in force, predicting a move to 1500 and below. In this book, we try to veer away from the financial entertainment industry (media headlines and so forth) and focus on ways that practitioners think about markets. Nevertheless, it is possible to speculate about the mechanisms behind market action. Credit and leverage play a larger role than is commonly recognised and it may be that trends are caused by predictable changes in gearing over time. Let's say you are a speculator who buys and sells commodity futures. You use a lot of leverage in an attempt to goose your returns. If the market is going your way, your credit situation automatically improves, because you can apply your profits to the margin account. This allows you to scale up your position. So if you had bought cotton futures, you can buy some more without damaging your margin situation. Conversely, if a long position shifts from a winner to a loser, at some point you have to sell. There is some threshold at which you will be wiped out and a nearer threshold which can turn you into a nervous wreck.

If the volume in a given asset class is dominated by leveraged speculators, trends are likely to emerge. The speculators have to manage their margin by following the policy of "cutting their losses and letting their profits run". This is tantamount to following trends. It is not always that the specs want to be trend followers. Rather, their style of trading demands it. So trends and ultimately bubbles form when the amount of leverage applied in a given direction increases. In Chapter 6, we take our analysis of trends one step further. Does trend following tend to generate positive returns during market crises? As we will see, the issue is quite complex. Historical studies show strong performance for trend followers during periods of market distress. This is called "crisis alpha" in the recent literature.

However, the relationship between the returns generated by a trend following algorithm and a rolling options structure is at best tenuous. We also take the direct approach to modelling trend following returns as a function of volatility. In particular, we will build our own basic trend signal and see how the signal performs in various markets as the VIX changes. It turns out that trend following probably has a mild correlation to volatility. While we can't rely on it as a hedge, trend following seems to offer real diversification benefits during adverse market conditions. Since the correlation to risk assets does *not* increase when volatility rises, it is a welcome addition to traditional portfolios.

TAKING THE OFFENSIVE

That's probably the best way of making money, to be a specialist in panics. Whenever there's panic hanging in the air, that's a great time to invest.

– Victor Niederhoffer[ii]

It might seem unusual to take investment advice from a manager who suffered damaging losses on two documented occasions. However, the basic idea is a sound one. Risk premia *do* go up after a severe sell-off. You can make more money from a piece of credit per unit of leverage than before. The prospective return for equities is inversely dependent on price. There is a reason why high yield bonds tend to outperform over time: only the most diehard investors are left holding distressed paper. The important thing to understand is that you can *only* invest aggressively after a panic if you haven't overreached beforehand or have a strategy for protecting against a further sell-off. In our view, the strategies developed in Chapters 4 and 5 allow you to snap up investment bargains without fear of blowing up. If you *are* going to specialise in panics, you not only need to know what to buy but how to hedge against disaster. In Chapter 6, we introduce some contrarian strategies for extracting alpha in a jittery market, while reminding the reader that it is necessary to size and hedge these strategies appropriately.

THE PRE-CONDITIONS FOR MARKET CRISES

There is of course, a larger issue. If we could solve it completely, the rest of this book would be largely unnecessary. Is it possible to *predict* the timing of market crises? Our view is that it is possible to identify conditions in the market that increase the odds of a crisis. Those are the limits of prediction. However, getting the timing right is nearly impossible. In the sciences, you can conduct experiments under controlled conditions. In the markets, you can't. A scientific idea can be zany, far from the mainstream, yet will be accepted if confirmed by experiment. In the markets, you need to get the aggregate of investors to agree with you in a reasonable amount of time. In 2008, it is probable that the portfolio managers who first predicted the mortgage-backed securities crisis made less money than other managers who jumped on the bandwagon at the last minute. The early buyers of default insurance were forced to pay a premium for many months before they were vindicated. The best one can do is identify situations that court disaster and hedging structures that have a large bang for the buck, i.e. that offer large payouts with low time decay.

At its core, the volatility cycle is intimately tied to the credit cycle. We will examine this idea further in Chapter 8. As banks lend more, investors become more vulnerable to a market shock. They have debts to pay off. So long as the random shock does not occur, volatility will tend to decline. Yet the system is becoming increasingly fragile. In Chapter 2, we argue that when investors scramble for the exits, seemingly "safe" assets can go down as much as risky ones. This was the case when quantitative equity funds were forced to unwind in August 2007. At the height of the 2008 crisis, investors generally sold whatever they had, including stocks that were usually considered to be defensive.

BANKS: THE GREAT MULTIPLIER

In the chapter on crisis prediction, we observe that the banking failures are responsible for most financial crises. If you think of the financial system as a network with agents at various nodes, the banking nodes are perhaps the most important. Once they are removed, the network collapses. Banks are the great multiplier in the economy. With a small quantity of deposits, they can lend a large amount of money. All of that lending goes into financial assets and the real economy, stimulating growth. The peak of the market cycle is generally characterised by a perverse relationship between volatility and leverage. Volatility tends to be low, as investors are complacent about the near future. The value of collateral (equities, real estate, etc.) has risen, so investors are able to apply more leverage to their overall portfolios. This implies that the risk in the system, the potential for a future collapse, is rising, while observed volatility is declining. Margin requirements at exchanges and prime brokers are low, enabling larger position sizes. Equity indices outperform equity hedge funds, leading some managers to chase the market and cut their hedge.

In order to keep lending, however, banks need access to a revolving credit line from investors and ultimately, from Central Banks. If a bank is overleveraged, the market may react by demanding a higher yield on loans. At some point, the bank has to repair its balance sheet by slashing some of its assets. Every loan that is not renewed has a knock-on effect, as corporations are unable to lend. When you take out a loan, you don't let the money just sit there, accruing negative interest. You put it to use, buying a house or investing in financial assets. Borrowing increases consumption, stimulating growth and increasing the value of risky assets. The amount of credit in the system is more important than the amount of money and deposits, as it is put to use in the economy. In Chapter 8, we develop this narrative more fully. In a non-rigorous way, we describe how bubbles form and burst over the market cycle. We take a multi-disciplinary approach, analysing the fundamentals and price dynamics that lead to market crises.

A CHANGE IN RISK REGIME

Some investors try to anticipate what could go wrong, what could cause a risk event. While many crises seem obvious in retrospect, the triggers take a long time to surface, are thought to be unimportant at the time or come as a complete surprise to investors. Many things *could* go wrong at a given time and one could argue that the most obvious ones are already priced into the market. Trying to understand "why" risk assets dropped on a given day is a game best left to market commentators. While text-based analysis of financial articles can shed some light on investor sentiment, we have deeper and darker problems to solve in the chapters that follow.

ENDNOTES

1 Pedersen, Lasse Heje. *Efficiently Inefficient: How Smart Money Invests and Market Prices Are Determined.* New Jersey: Princeton University Press, 2015.
2 Schulz, Kathryn. "Hoodoos, Hedge Funds, and Alibis: Victor Niederhoffer on Being Wrong." Slate. com, June 21, 2010. http://www.slate.com/blogs/thewrongstuff/2010/06/21/hoodoos_hedge_funds_and_alibis_victor_niederhoffer_on_being_wrong.html

CHAPTER 2

"Safe" Havens and the Second Leg Down

Modern portfolio theory has its formal origins in the work of Markowitz (1952). Here, risk is synonymous with volatility. The wilder the path that your portfolio takes, the greater the uncertainty in the final outcome. There are only two ways a static portfolio can become riskier. Either the individual assets in your portfolio become more volatile or the correlation between them goes up. Volatility and correlation are both encapsulated in the covariance matrix of asset returns. Assume that the entries in your covariance matrix move fairly smoothly through time. It should then be possible to *react* to changes in portfolio risk. You can dynamically reduce your allocation to the assets that have the largest instantaneous impact on portfolio risk. These assets are said to have the greatest marginal risk relative to the portfolio. Many asset managers, particularly quantitative equity hedge funds, argue that they can "target" volatility by seamlessly changing their portfolio weights over time. But how can these funds react to situations where a systematic risk factor moves with practically no warning? The law of large numbers doesn't help you much when all of the assets in your portfolio are exposed to a small number of risk factors. As we will show in this chapter, the nature of risk can change dramatically over time, leaving dynamic rebalancing strategies exposed. Safe looking assets can become risky in both absolute and relative terms. This implies that the classical variance–covariance matrix approach can fail to capture risk at the worst possible time. Our strategy is to focus on a series of examples where risk is not immediately apparent in the historical return series of an asset or strategy. The monster appears out of nowhere. This chapter serves as a teaser for the rest of the book, where we explore practical ways to manage risk in disorderly markets.

During speculative bubbles, volatility perversely tends to decline. The formation of a bubble should serve as a warning sign, but tends to be obscured by investor complacency. As the options markets discount future risk, implied volatility may also drift lower. This all seems very logical to a market newcomer, someone who wasn't there for the last crisis. Over short horizons, volatility seems persistent, yet it is cyclical over the long term. How does this all relate to extreme event hedging? If you can identify the assets that overleveraged investors are holding, you can buy options on them. These options will generally be cheap until the bubble eventually bursts. Realised volatility will not necessarily be a harbinger of potential risk. We provide some anecdotal evidence for contrarian options buying in Chapter 2. We also use the portfolio insurance crisis of 1987 as evidence that crowded rebalancing strategies can be as dangerous as crowded positions in stocks or corporate bonds.

THE MATTERHORN

After the Euro crisis in 2011, the Swiss National Bank (SNB) enforced a one-sided peg on the Swiss Franc (CHF) against the Euro (EUR). Without the peg, the Franc probably would have surged toward parity with the Euro. Investors have long considered Switzerland to be a safe and stable economy relative to some of the "peripheral" nations in the European Union, such as Greece and Portugal. Accordingly, the SNB had no imperative to create easy credit conditions in an attempt to attract investors. By contrast, the European Central Bank, or ECB, was forced to accept low quality collateral from vulnerable banks and sovereign states, in exchange for revolving credit. A lower bound on the EUR/CHF exchange rate was set somewhat arbitrarily at 1.20. Whenever CHF threatened to cross the barrier, the SNB would flood the market with more Francs or create incentives for investors to move money out of Switzerland. This caused a sharp decline in downside volatility whenever EUR/CHF approached 1.20, as in Figure 2.1.

Assuming that the floor was solid, speculators could step in and buy the cross close to 1.20. This would amount to buying the Euro and selling CHF. Since Swiss short-term deposit rates were now negative, buying forwards on EUR might also have positive carry. Assuming that the spot EUR/CHF rate stayed fixed, you would be *paid* to hold a forward on EUR. Other investors reasoned that the Swiss Franc was an ideal financing instrument, as it cost nothing to borrow and was tied to a weak currency. They could essentially borrow CHF for free and deploy the proceeds elsewhere. So long as the peg held, the risks were minimal. But was that a safe assumption? On January 15, 2015, the Swiss National Bank issued a short press release that sent reverberations throughout the global currency markets. They announced that they would be "discontinuing the minimum exchange rate of 1.20", while reducing the interest rate for deposits held at the bank to −0.75%, from −0.25%. The implication was that they no longer wanted CHF to be tied to a currency that was backed by a fragile and structurally imbalanced economy. Conversely, the rate reduction was intended to soften the impact of the announcement by penalising investors who wanted to hold CHF deposits. It did not, however, have the desired effect. Investors smashed the Euro from 1.20 to 0.98 in a matter of minutes.

Through the wider lens of Figure 2.2, we can see how the EUR/CHF cross was trading in a severely constricted range in advance of January 15. It has been suggested[1] that the FX options markets anticipated the possibility of a 1.20 breach before the floor was removed. However, realised

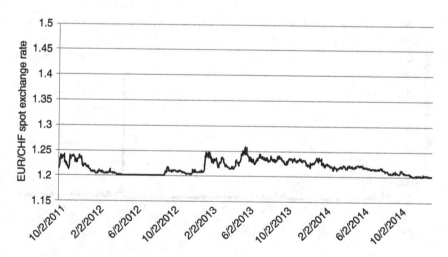

FIGURE 2.1   EUR/CHF exchange rate before the peg was removed

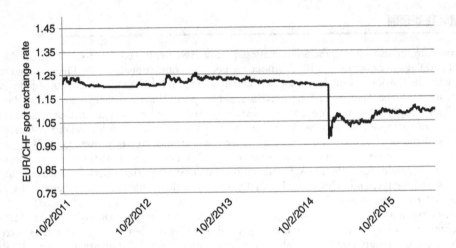

FIGURE 2.2 There she goes

volatility gave no indication of increased risk. On the contrary, it seemed as though volatility was converging to 0.

We can also think of risk in terms of the daily range for the currency. In Figure 2.3, we track the difference between the daily high and low price over time.

For many speculators, the impact was devastating. Everest Capital, a long-established emerging markets hedge fund, was forced to liquidate its flagship strategy after losing a large percentage of its assets on the CHF move. Astonishingly, an order of magnitude $1 billion fund was obliterated in the time it takes to go for a snack break at the office! Leading macro funds and proprietary trading desks also suffered major losses. It is likely that the nearly instantaneous move from 1.20 to 0.98 was amplified by massive deleveraging from the managers who had suffered the most.

Parkinson (1980) has derived a formula that transforms high and low prices over a series of days into a volatility estimate. While the formula makes assumptions about the underlying distribution of returns and does not admit gaps in trading, it is a reasonably simple and clean way to estimate

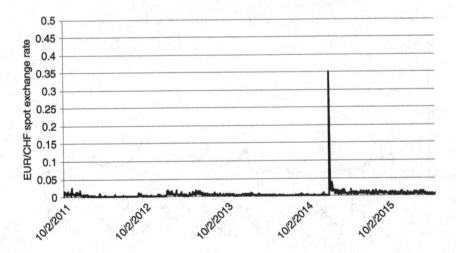

FIGURE 2.3 Daily range of EUR/CHF

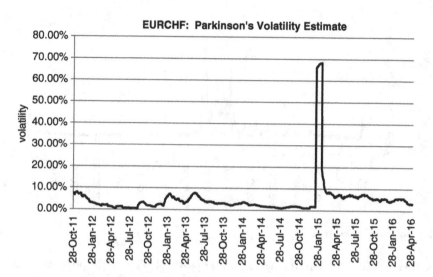

FIGURE 2.4 Parkinson's volatility estimate

short-term volatility. The lookback window can be shortened as we get one extra data point per day. In Figure 2.4, we track range-based volatility over time. The lookback window is 21 trading days.

The combined activity of speculators and the SNB initially caused CHF/EUR volatility to decline and then languish around 1%. Here was a market that could put you to sleep, or so it seemed. Once the peg was removed, range-based volatility jumped toward 70% before settling in the 5% to 10% range.

Given the fiftyfold increase in realised volatility at the extremes, conventional asset allocation models would have been completely caught off guard by the move. We can illustrate this point using a simple and intuitive scheme. The Treynor-Black model is an offshoot of the hugely influential Capital Asset Pricing Model, or CAPM. Treynor-Black (1973) suggests how to allocate to a collection of assets that have "alpha", namely ones that are expected to generate a positive benchmark-independent return. Let's suppose we have an asset whose correlation to some relevant benchmark is 0. According to Treynor-Black, its weight should be inversely proportional to the square of its volatility. As asset volatility increases, the optimal portfolio weight rapidly decreases. Once you strip out benchmark exposure, the allocation process is robust from an optimisation standpoint.

If you had a reasonably high level of confidence that CHF was going to weaken relative to EUR, you would need to assign a massive Treynor-Black weight to the trade. $(0.01)^2$ is a tiny divisor to apply. This would have had terrible consequences in January 2015, as you would have been severely overexposed to a losing trade. Is there any way around the problem, while adhering to modern portfolio theory? One solution would be to eliminate pegged currencies from your system. This is reasonable but not comprehensive. It ignores the fact that other assets can also experience abrupt and unexpected spikes in volatility. You can't close every channel of extreme uncertainty.

Ex post, the decision to remove pegged currencies from a conventional asset allocation model is an easy one. However, there may be other assets in your portfolio that experience unexpected jumps of extreme magnitude. At the risk of repeating ourselves, you can't keep taking stuff out of your portfolio that hasn't worked or else you will run out of things to invest in.

During the 2007–8 financial crisis, LIBOR rates took on a life of their own as shown in Figure 2.5. Volatility jumped to previously unimaginable levels. Observe that LIBOR is an interbank rate for dollar-based loans transacted in London. Qualified banks borrow from each other roughly at LIBOR. The quoted rate varies based on a daily survey. Usually, 1 or 3 month LIBOR varies as a function of the 1 or 3 month US T-Bill rate. There is a spread to account for counterparty credit risk, but it tends to be

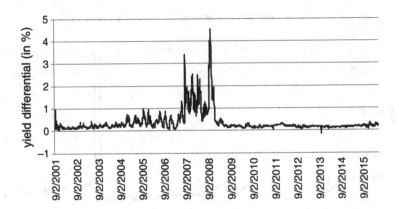

FIGURE 2.5 1 month TED spread

small and sticky. That is, the spread typically has very low volatility. As the prospect of bank failures began to mount, however, the spread became severely unhinged.

MRS. WATANABE'S NO. 1 INVESTMENT CLUB

Non-pegged currencies can also deliver nasty surprises. The FX carry, or "Mrs. Watanabe" trade described in the introduction is a case in point. FX carry is attractive to many investors because it generates a passive return when nothing much is going on. "Time is on your side", as the saying goes. A canonical example is the Australian Dollar (AUD)/Japanese Yen (JPY) cross. These countries are linked by strong bilateral trade agreements, but have starkly different FX risk profiles. While Australian yields have historically been high, Japanese rates have been hovering close to 0 since the late 1990s as shown in Figure 2.6. Many investors have engaged in the FX carry trade, buying AUD forwards while borrowing

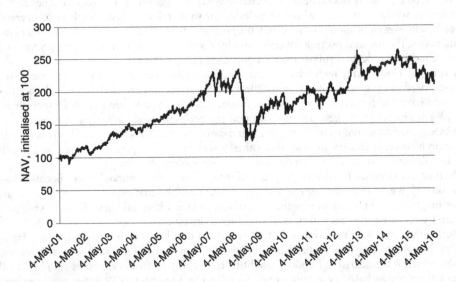

FIGURE 2.6 Up the stairs and down the lift

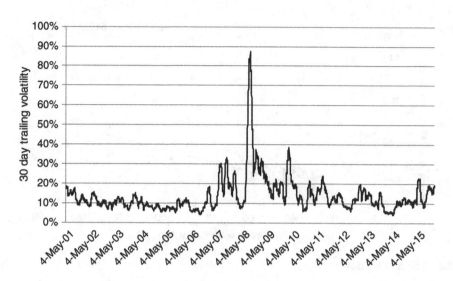

FIGURE 2.7   30 day trailing volatility for the AUD/JPY cross

in JPY. This trade has two sources of return: changes in the AUD/JPY spot rate and income generated from the differential between Australian and Japanese interest rates with the appropriate maturity. In theory, the expected return of the AUD/JPY spot rate should be negative, namely it should exactly offset the carry based return from the forward. Practice suggests that this is not the case. Higher yielding currencies tend to perform considerably better than equilibrium theory would suggest. In risk-seeking environments, the trade chugs along, generating consistent profits. Leverage is easily applied to currencies and the strategy eventually becomes overcrowded.

The series usually drifts up, punctuated by sharp and sudden drops every now and again. Over the 15-year sample set shown in Figure 2.6, the distribution of returns has a negative skew of –0.5. This implies that negative surprises are far more likely than positive ones. As can be seen in Figure 2.7, 30-day trailing volatility is very jumpy.

The move from 10% to nearly 90% volatility in 2008 came with practically no warning. Only a very nimble risk system would have been able to adjust the position size enough to avoid damaging losses.

THE RISK OF WHAT OTHERS ARE HOLDING

In this section, we provide a concrete example of the second leg down concept. We analyse the two stage drop in September and October 2008 and describe the unexpected cross-sectional behaviour of stocks in the S&P 500 in October. We need to make a few introductory comments before analysing the data. We start with a contentious statement, partly for effect. The risk of what others are holding tends to increase when academics get involved. The trouble is that institutions are prone to using academic papers as "validation" of a given strategy. The notion that market conditions can change, partly as a function of money flowing into a particular strategy, is not always addressed. Ironically, the academic ideas tend to be good ones, validated over rich historical data sets. However, ideological group think increases systemic risk. Too many large investors are positioned in the same way. Suppose an investor has to liquidate positions after a margin call. If the investor has a large inventory to sell, prices can move to the extent that other investors have to liquidate the same position. This can lead to a cascade of losses, especially if the amount of leverage in the system is high. When things get really bad, there is

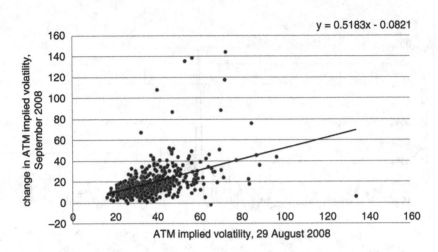

y = 0.5183x - 0.0821

FIGURE 2.8 The first leg down

no such thing as a "safe" stock. In the following example, we illustrate how blue chip stocks can become extremely risky in the teeth of the storm. Value investors might argue that, if you extend your investment horizon enough, the blue chip stocks are still safe. At the extreme, you might be buying a stock whose market capitalisation is lower than its liquidation value. This implies that the share price should eventually come back. Over monthly horizons, however, your conservative-looking investments can have a surprisingly large impact on portfolio risk.

Here is a teaser, a short case study from the financial crisis of 2008. Figure 2.8 depicts changes in implied volatility for stocks currently in the S&P 500, in September 2008. On the x-axis, we track the ATM implied volatility for each optionable stock in the index at the end of August. On the y-axis, we show the absolute change in implied volatility for each stock in the index in September.

The slope of the regression is roughly 0.5. This means that implied volatility for the risky stocks increased roughly 50% more than for the conservative-looking ones. This is as we would expect. When volatility picks up, many investors dial down portfolio risk by reducing exposure to high beta names. In such a scenario, high beta stocks can drop even further than their historical beta would suggest.

Now if September 2008 was a bad month, with the S&P 500 declining by –9.08%, October 2008 was the dramatic crescendo (see Figure 2.9). The VIX peaked at 89.53 when Lehman Brothers defaulted. A number of hedge funds liquidated or locked up client money and several investment banks were on the verge of default. The interbank lending market seized up, as no one seemed to be sure how solvent anyone else was. Eventually, the Fed and other central banks stepped in and offered loans in exchange for questionable credit. Strict mark-to-market accounting was abandoned. As John Hussman has remarked (e.g. Hussman, 2013), this may have been a crucial turning point in the 2007–9 financial crisis. Eventually, banks were able to repair their balance sheets and resume their usual activities. Given this historical backdrop, we repeated the September regression in October. Our expectation was that the regression line would remain upward sloping. If anything, we might have to account for an explosion in implied volatility for high beta stocks. This might require a quadratic regression. As it turned out, the results were quite the opposite. While all stocks became toxic, safe-looking ones jumped the furthest in implied volatility terms.

The regression slope is mildly negative, at –0.15. But even if the slope had been 0, you would have been well served to buy options on safe-looking stocks – the Johnson & Johnsons of this world. Your premium outlay would have been much less for the same level of protection. This is not to say that the idea of sector rotation is unreasonable. Short duration assets, such as bonds and high dividend-paying

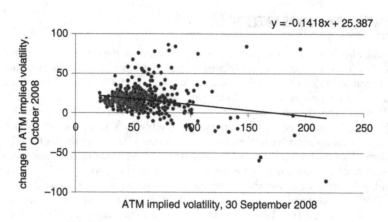

FIGURE 2.9   The second leg down – liquidation time

stocks with strong balance sheets, do tend to outperform in orderly bear markets. Aside from the most extreme cases, the beta of a stock is predictive. High beta stocks perform the worst, while low beta names provide an anchor to the portfolio. It is important to understand that standard models, such as CAPM, are reasonable approximations of reality *most* of the time. They might not account for anomalies such as the low volatility premium described in Falkenstein (2012), but they do approximate to how your portfolio is likely to perform during a sell-off. The trouble isn't the duration of extreme events. It is their severity. During mass liquidations, though, investors have a tendency to sell indiscriminately. There is even a temptation to sell the stocks that have gone down the least, in an attempt to avoid crystallising losses. In the meantime, the big losers *might* come back. For taxable investors, Wilcox (2006) argues that monetising short-term gains and allowing profits to run is a particularly bad strategy. Even in the unconstrained scenario, waiting for your losing positions to come back is a form of mental arithmetic. It doesn't do you any practical good. Alternatively, the riskier looking companies may have gone down so much that there isn't much point in selling them. Can we draw any conclusions from the strange-looking dynamics in September and October? To some extent, low beta stocks played catch up during this wave of selling. More intriguingly, sector rotation in September may have been responsible for the strange moves in October. When risk assets first took a tumble, many investors sold high beta stocks and re-invested the proceeds in safe-looking names, on the assumption that they were reducing portfolio risk. In October, it was no longer a question of selective selling but rather panic liquidation. Investors sold *whatever they had*.

How can we use the surprising conclusions in this study? We have not yet developed the machinery to analyse specific options structures in detail. However, we can say that buying options on stocks whose implied volatility has not gone up very much after an initial sell-off is a promising idea. We want to buy insurance on the companies that the market still deems "safe". These options will be relatively cheap, yet are likely to offer significant protection during a major liquidation.

More generally, we can conclude that extreme markets are not straightforward extrapolations of normal markets. Following on from Taleb (2007), traditional statistical methods have a restricted range of applicability. They are unable to characterise the outsized moves that have a disproportionate impact on long-term returns. As market conditions deteriorate badly, a more holistic approach is necessary. We need to combine experience, academic research and our own validation methods in a sensible way. A renegade spirit is useful for idea generation, but needs to be combined with a disciplined approach to testing. We want to understand things as accurately as possible and build on what we know. However, we don't want to be overly constrained. Our main goal is to develop survival tactics for scenarios where formal academic theory does not apply.

THE RISK OF WHAT OTHERS ARE LIKELY TO DO

Systemic risk can also increase if a large number of investors use the same algorithm for exiting positions. Risk is not purely a function of what people hold, but what they are likely to do given a large random fluctuation in the market. Black Monday, October 19 1987, demonstrated how the market's excessive reliance on a single strategy could trigger a short-term crisis. In the midst of a very strong year, the S&P 500 dropped −2.95%, −2.34% and −5.16% on October 14, 15 and 16 as shown in Figure 2.10. Trailing 1 month historical volatility was roughly 19% going into October 14, unremarkable by long-term historical standards. Yet after the moderate 3-day drop, the S&P fell by −20.47% on October 19 alone. This corresponds to an 11 standard deviation 1 day move in the index!

The magnitude of the move is even visible in a long-term chart, spanning five years to either side of Black Monday. Figure 2.11 shows the damaging long-term impact of the move.

In Burr (1997), Bruce Jacobs argues that a portfolio insurance strategy, originally developed by Leland, O'Brien, Rubinstein and Associates (LOR), was a major cause of Black Monday. Portfolio insurance was inspired by Merton's approach to options pricing in the 1970s. Black and Scholes relied upon the Capital Asset Pricing Model as a source of inspiration when pricing European calls and puts. Merton re-derived the Black–Scholes formula using a more intuitive replication approach. At any point in time, an option could be viewed as a mixture of the underlying stock and a short-term government bond. If a market maker sold a call option and the price of the stock went up, he could buy more shares to neutralise exposure of the call to small moves. If the stock became more volatile, hedging costs would rise, hence the call option would become more expensive.

The intriguing thing was that in the Merton framework, an option was *redundant*. In a world where returns were normally distributed and costs were low, you could create an option by dynamically rebalancing between a stock and a risk-free bond. In theory, an investor could participate in market rallies while capping losses, without explicitly having to buy insurance. Later, we will illustrate how the implied volatility of an ATM option tends to trade above its realised volatility. This implies that, if Merton's assumptions were correct, options would be overpriced from a statistical standpoint. On average, it would be cheaper to replicate an option than to buy the option directly. There might be times where rebalancing would be expensive, e.g. if realised volatility turned out to be high during the life of the option and there were frequent reversals. In zigzagging markets, dynamic replication would require that you repeatedly sell at the low and buy at the high. In the long run, however, hedging would be relatively cheap as you would avoid paying up for the (implied/realised) volatility spread. The benefits after a risk event would be pronounced, as you would not be forced to buy options at the moment where demand was the highest.

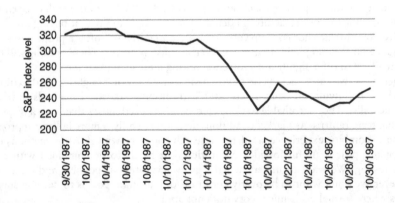

FIGURE 2.10   "Black Monday" in focus

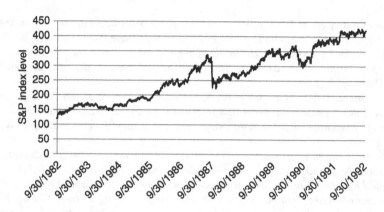

FIGURE 2.11   Black Monday, bird's-eye view

This gave rise to the idea of portfolio insurance. LOR argued that if an index put option could be replicated with a dynamic short position in the index, large institutional portfolios could be protected using a strategy that sold futures whenever the index dropped by a certain amount. The delta of a put increases as the market sells off. In the same way, the LOR strategy would sell enough units of the futures to match the delta of the theoretical put. We suspect that the risk of what others are holding tends to increase when academics get involved. Ironically, the academic ideas tend to be good ones, validated over long historical data sets. The trouble is that ideas originating from the ivory tower tend to be accepted as dogma more readily than those borne out of experience. In turn, it might be said that investment dogma creates systemic risk. Theory became practice when, in 1982, the Chicago Mercantile Exchange (CME) launched a futures contract on the S&P 500. The contract allowed investors to speculate long or short on the index, with low initial cash outlay. As trading volumes increased, large institutions began to use futures as a hedging mechanism against their long equity portfolios. LOR could now implement their portfolio insurance strategy on a large scale.

We can hardly improve upon the Carlson (2006) report about Black Monday[2] and quote it directly below. The report describes the activity of various market agents in a surprisingly lively style. The finger is directly pointed at portfolio insurance providers who kept selling large blocks of futures as the market fell.

> *There was substantial selling pressure on the NYSE at the open on Monday with a large imbalance in the number of sell orders relative to buy orders (SEC Report 1988, pp. 2–13). In this situation, many specialists did not open for trading during the first hour. The SEC noted "by 10:00, 95 S&P stocks, representing 30% of the index value, were still not open" (1988, pp. 2–13); the* Wall Street Journal *indicated that 11 of the 30 stocks in the Dow Jones Industrial Average opened late (1987e). The values of stock market indicies (sic) are calculated using the most recent price quotes for the underlying stocks. With stocks not trading, some of the quotes used to construct market indexes were stale, so the values of these indexes did not decline as much as they might have otherwise (SEC Report 1988, pp. 2–13). By contrast, the futures market opened on time with heavy selling. With stale quotes in the cash market and declining prices in the futures market, a gap was created between the value of stock indexes in the cash market and in the futures market (Chicago Mercantile Exchange, Committee of Inquiry 1987, pp. 18–29). Index arbitrage traders reportedly sought to take advantage of this gap by entering sell-at-market orders on the NYSE. When stocks finally opened, prices gapped down and the index arbitragers discovered they had sold stocks considerably below what they had been expecting and tried to cover themselves by buying in the futures market. This activity precipitated a temporary rebound in prices, but added to the*

confusion (Brady Report 1988, p. 30) . . . with equity prices declining steeply during the last hour and a half of trading. The Dow Jones Industrial Average, S&P 500, and Wilshire 5000 declined between 18 and 23 percent on the day amid deteriorating trading conditions (Brady Report 1988, Study III, p. 21). The S&P 500 futures contract declined 29 percent (SEC Report 1988, pp. 2–12).

In comments following a speech, the SEC Chairman reportedly said that "there is some point, and I don't know what point that is, that I would be interested in talking to the New York Stock Exchange about a temporary, very temporary, halt in trading" (Wall Street Journal 1987f).

This news broke shortly after 1:00 and started rumors in futures exchanges that the NYSE would be closed, prompting further sales as traders reportedly worried that a market close would lock them into their existing positions (Wall Street Journal 1987f).

The record trading volume on Oct. 19 overwhelmed many systems. On the NYSE, for example, trade executions were reported more than an hour late, which reportedly caused confusion among traders. Investors did not know whether limit orders had been executed or whether new limits needed to be set (Brady Report 1988, Study III, p. 21).

Selling on Monday was reportedly highly concentrated. The top ten sellers accounted for 50 percent of non-market-maker volume in the futures market (Brady Report 1988, p. 36); many of these institutions were providers of portfolio insurance. One large institution started selling large blocks of stock around 10:00 in the morning and sold thirteen instalments of just under $100 million each for a total of $1.1 billion during the day.

The deliberate vagueness of the SEC chairman is fascinating to behold. You can almost feel the beads of sweat trickling down his forehead as he discusses possible courses of action. More to the point, risk escalated because nearly all of the "top 10 sellers" were doing more or less the same thing. They were bailing out of the S&P in an attempt to protect client portfolios. As in the second leg down example, our conclusion is that risk is highly path-dependent. If large investors are all wired to react to price moves in the same way, volatility can appear out of almost nowhere. As the financial ecosystem becomes less diverse, the risk of spontaneous crises increases. Many risk systems use similar inputs, such as volatility or the level of cross-correlation in the market. This can produce common exit points and severe congestion as a large number of systems are trying to reduce positions *en masse*. No amount of fundamental analysis can tell you how to avoid these so-called "flash crashes". Flash crashes are dependent on price action and positioning. The adage that the goal of markets is to produce the most pain to the largest number of investors is appropriate here. The only defences for a lower-frequency trader are to avoid leverage or to use options as insurance. The only solution is to maintain some form of cheap insurance in your portfolio *all the time*, acknowledging that the nature of the next collapse is essentially unpredictable. It seems strange that investors don't pay the same level of attention to their short-biased strategies as they do to their long ones. The institutions that had outsourced all of their hedging to an LOR provider probably had numerous managers running their long portfolios, using a variety of methodologies. Even if you can't predict where the next crisis will come from, it is inadvisable to rely too much on a single algorithm when managing your risk.

HERE WE GO AGAIN

Have we learned much from the portfolio insurance crisis of 1987? In some ways, it would seem not. The same ideas get regurgitated through the financial markets every now and again. The new generation arrives, full of confidence and blissfully unaware of the hard lessons of history. The latest flavour of the month seems to be risk parity, which bears an eerie resemblance to the portfolio insurance strategy described in the previous section. A number of leading asset managers have been offering risk parity funds over the past few years. While risk parity strategies have a different objective from portfolio insurance, they generate similar trades to the LOR model. The simplest version of risk parity allocates between two asset classes, stocks and bonds. Commodities and currencies have been added to more recent versions of the strategy. The argument goes as follows. Traditional strategic mandates allocate 60% to stocks and 40% to bonds for very flimsy reasons. The weights were originally chosen because they are round numbers that marginally favour stocks over bonds, in dollar terms. Over time, the 60/40 composite has become market convention. Countless pie charts have been constructed in this way, to the point where investors have become convinced that the underlying methodology must be sound. There are some practices in finance that defy rational understanding. We just get used to them over time and assume they must be correct. The risk parity approach challenges the 60/40 mix, on the assumption that capital is not being used very efficiently and the allocation to bonds in *risk* terms is far too small. US government bonds tend to have less than half the realised volatility of US equities, implying that the performance of a 60/40 portfolio will be dominated by equities. A risk parity portfolio circumvents the problem by gearing the bond portfolio by a factor of 2 or 3 so that bond volatility matches equity volatility.

Figure 2.12 implements the risk parity idea in the simplest possible manner. We assume that S&P 500 futures are a reasonable proxy for equities and that 10-year Treasury note futures are representative of bonds. Next, we consider two cases, using weekly data from 1996 to 2015. The first relies upon a static 60% allocation to equities, with the remaining 40% in bonds. Rebalancing back to a 60/40 mix is performed on a weekly basis. The second case matches the trailing one-month historical volatility of stocks and bonds when setting the weights. The realised volatility of both strategies is roughly 10.5%, yet the risk parity line in black outperforms dramatically. Note that we have set the overall leverage of the risk parity portfolio so that the volatility of the grey and black lines match.

What performance! If we could extrapolate the black line into the future, asset allocation would be a breeze. The trouble is that risk parity might be contaminated by selection bias. We have effectively used a scientific-looking approach to goose up our allocation to bonds. This is not a bad idea from a risk control standpoint. However, with rates at current levels, it seems unlikely that bonds will perform as well in the next 35 years as they have in the past 25.

It remains to describe how a mechanical risk balancing approach such as risk parity can increase the odds of a major sell-off. While a static risk parity portfolio might look quite different from a portfolio insurance overlay, what happens at the extremes can be almost indistinguishable. Let's take the singular limit. In particular, assume a scenario where *everyone* used the same risk parity strategy. In this case, equity indices would probably go to 0. This is sometimes called a death spiral in the credit markets. Assuming equity volatility picked up, the equity component of the portfolio would have to be sold down to maintain risk parity. Since everyone would be selling together, volatility would spike again, forcing even more selling. As long as volatility grew fast enough to offset the shrinking equity weight, there would be no end to the selling. In some sense, this is more toxic than the portfolio insurance

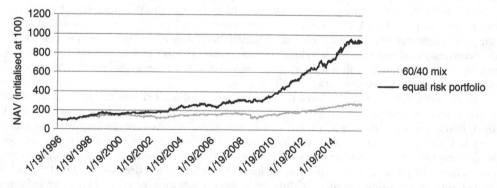

FIGURE 2.12 Historical performance of a bare bones risk parity portfolio

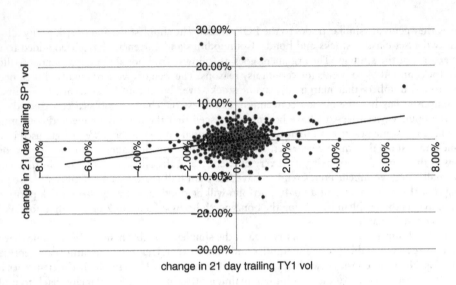

FIGURE 2.13 Historically, US equity and bond volatility have had a mild *positive* correlation

strategy, as volatility can rise more rapidly than prices can fall. We are not claiming that dedicated risk parity strategies have been responsible for any crises that we can point to. We simply observe that the risk parity approach to diversification is a potential source of systemic risk.

In the interests of presenting a balanced argument, we have to admit that there are some statistical factors working in favour of a risk parity solution. Historically, equity index and bond volatility have moved in tandem as depicted in Figure 2.13. We demonstrate this by plotting relative moves in historical S&P 500 and US 10 futures volatility over time.

This implies that the risk parity allocation to stocks and bonds should also be relatively stable. The danger in this analysis is that we are relying upon the idea that the historical relationship between two very different asset classes is likely to persist in the future. However, it is validated by past price action. Risk parity strategies are also likely to benefit if the low growth market regime as of this writing persists into the future. Illmanen (2003) has identified regimes where the correlation between stocks and bonds has been relatively low. Cross-sectionally, across the major economies, stock-bond correlations have increased in tandem with inflation. Focusing on the US, the correlation between stocks and bonds has been particularly low in times of low GDP growth and inflation, and has been decreasing as a function of market volatility. This characterises the developed market economies as of this writing. Since the fall of the Berlin Wall in the late 1980s, the flood of workers to the West has created deflationary pressures on Europe and the US. This is a direct function of the increased supply of goods and services in the post-Communist era. If conditions remain deflationary, with intermittent bouts of market volatility, bonds may continue to provide valuable diversification benefits in a multi-asset class portfolio. However, our original point still stands. If allocations to risk parity strategies become too large, the danger of synchronised mass deleveraging will increase.

The examples above show that overcrowded strategies and asset classes can be a source of risk. You don't want to jump on every bandwagon and can benefit from being a bit out of synch with the market. Randomness can even be a virtue in certain instances. This has been demonstrated for market indices and also applies to managing risk. Most major stock indices (such as the S&P 500) are constructed using market capitalisation weights. The companies whose (share price) * (shares outstanding) is largest have a disproportionate impact on the index. Clare (2013) has demonstrated that if you had allocated to US stocks using a number of different weighting schemes, you would have outperformed the cap-weighted index over time. Equal weighting does relatively well, as well as more fundamentally oriented weighting schemes, such as setting weights proportional to a company's total sales or book value. On average, even random weighting schemes outperform.

Clare (2013) is partly based on an amusing study comparing the performance of 10 million randomly weighted portfolios of US stocks to a cap-weighted index. This required periodic rebalancing to ensure that the random indices would not favour momentum stocks over time. The study showed that the random portfolios outperformed in nearly every simulation. There is an added advantage to random weighting. By construction, you will generally avoid crowded trades. There are legions of analysts who conduct back-tests on nearly every deterministic weighting scheme. The good back-tests often turn into ETFs and the best performing ETFs attract inflows. So even if there has been a persistent anomaly in the past, expected returns can be compressed by excessive inflows. The outperforming strategy also has increased extreme event risk, as the ETF is subject to liquidations.

There are numerous other cases where excessive crowding in an asset class or strategy has triggered a risk event. Khandani (2007) observed that the degree of overlap in quantitative equity fund positions was astonishing when analysing the August 2007 "quant crisis". More examples are to be found in the small province of convertible bonds, which is dominated by geared hedge funds that spread the bond against the underlying stock and other parts of the capital structure. Every few years, a large fund runs into trouble and has to liquidate its portfolio. This can cause collateral damage in an asset class that is surprisingly small and dominated by arbitrageurs. As of March 2016, the total outstanding value of US convertible bonds was roughly $200 billion, equivalent to the market cap of the 15th largest stock in the S&P 500 alone!

How does this all relate to hedging during a crisis? When you see too many people holding the same asset or engaging in the same strategy, you might want to think about the potential consequences of crowded trades, a mob mentality. Whenever money starts flowing into an asset or strategy at an accelerating rate, the risk of a severe unwinding is not far away. It may even be worth chasing the move, *if* you have a strategy for protecting against downside risk. Simply setting a stop loss level below the current price might not be enough, as there is no guarantee you will be filled anywhere near the stop. A safer alternative is to use options as a mechanism for protecting against blood-curdling reversals. Dynamic rebalancing strategies react to price action over some minimal frequency. No matter how sophisticated, they can't protect against "air pocket" declines such as the one in EUR/CHF above. Options have no such limitations. They gear into moves that are practically instantaneous as well as ones that take a longer time to develop.

On a more speculative note, we wonder if the regulator's insistence on using Value-at-Risk in UCITS funds and other fund vehicles may increase systemic risk in the future. UCITS funds have become the vogue as they can be marketed freely to European investors. While there is some flexibility in the way funds calculate VaR, a situation could arise where everyone hits their risk limits at the same time. This could cause a devastating liquidation of assets.

We hope that the reader is now aware of some of the limitations of traditional risk management. Rebalancing tends to fail in precisely those moments where it is needed the most and perversely can be a *cause* of crises. Ideally, investors should have something in their portfolio that provides significant protection against unforeseen risks. That "something" is usually a low-cost options structure. In any case, they should not place excessive reliance on realised volatility when sizing positions. Sometimes, realised volatility can become compressed for structural reasons and it is not possible to identify every case where this might be so. While options-buying during quiet times is the ideal, we acknowledge that there is generally resistance to doing so. At some primal level, we sometimes become too focused on short-term gratification to develop a clear understanding of potential future outcomes. This implies that we need to develop hedges that won't be too expensive even after things have taken a turn for the worse.

In the next chapter, we present some background material on options strategies. The idea is to reach the point where we can make informed decisions about how to choose an appropriate hedging structure from a variety of alternatives. We particularly focus on strategies that are not too expensive even when the demand for insurance is high.

SUMMARY

Risk can appear unexpectedly, based on an exogenous event or synchronised de-leveraging. In extreme scenarios, where investors sell indiscriminately, "safe" stocks or asset classes may perform as badly or worse than the market itself. Options can re-price as quickly as any move in the underlying market and provide the only hard backstop against portfolio disaster. We visit these in Chapter 3.

ENDNOTES

1   Iain Clark, personal communication
2   Carlson, Mark. *A Brief History of the 1987 Stock Market Crash with a Discussion of the Federal Reserve Response.* Federal Reserve Board, 2006. http://www.federalreserve.gov/pubs/feds/2007/200713/200713pap.pdf

An Overview of Options Strategies

Most of the hedges described in this book are options structures. They rely upon buying and selling combinations of calls and puts with different strikes and maturity dates. We are mainly concerned with uncovering strategies that provide protection at low cost. In this chapter, we provide a non-technical overview of options, in preparation for the hedges we will dissect in Chapters 4 and 5. We make no effort to derive Black–Scholes or any other pricing formula. Rather, we will use the Black–Scholes formula as a way to adjust for different strikes and times to maturity. Value will be expressed in the currency of implied volatility. Normalising across strikes and maturity dates can help us decide which options are rich and which are cheap. We start with a bare-bones description of puts and calls, then transition into more complicated structures, such as spreads, butterflies and ratios. Our ultimate goal is to identify horses for courses, i.e. hedging structures that are well suited to a particular market environment. It will take some time before we can delve into regime-specific analysis. This chapter serves as necessary background material. Note that we will primarily focus on exchange-traded futures and options, as they are easier to analyse and trade at an accurate and timely price.

Options contracts have a long and varied history, possibly extending back to ancient Greece and carrying on through to England in the 1600s and the US thereafter. It may be that the options market took off when corporations started to add sweeteners to stock and bond issues. For example, in the 1840s, the New York and Erie Railroad Company issued one of the first recorded convertible bonds. The bonds could be exchanged for, or "converted" to shares if the stock price went up enough. In other words, there was a call option embedded in the bond. This was attractive to the company as the bonds could be floated at relatively low yield. At the same time, investors were keen to own bonds that offered participation in a rising market. New instruments have the greatest chance of success if they generate an active two-way market. There are natural buyers and sellers of the contract. Today, calls and puts represent a tug-of-war: between hedgers who need to insure existing portfolios, and speculators who want to take a directional punt or trade volatility.

THE BUILDING BLOCKS: CALLS AND PUTS

We need to use a bit of math in this section, to make the concepts clearer. Derman (1996) has remarked that Fischer Black wanted an introductory article about the Black–Derman–Toy model to be written without any formulas, with a focus on developing the necessary intuition. While we have fallen short of Black's ideal in this chapter, we will try to minimise our use of complicated formulas and equations. There is an entire industry devoted to exactly that and we have no intention of re-inventing the wheel.

The reader might want to consult Wilmott (2013) for a more mathematically minded, yet pragmatic, treatment of options theory. For now, let's start with calls and puts, as these are the most basic exchange-traded options.

Readers with a strong background in options strategies can comfortably jump to the section "Skew Dynamics for Risky Assets" later in this chapter.

Calls and puts are financial contracts with standardised features. The owner of a call has the right to buy an asset at a predetermined price X at maturity. X is called the option strike. The owner of a put has the right to sell an asset at the predetermined price X. However, in either case, there is no *obligation* to do so. In practice, you would only buy an asset at price X if the market price $S(t) > X$. Otherwise, you could just buy the asset at a lower price in the market. In effect, you are hoping for a rally above the strike. Similarly, you would only sell at X if $S(t) < X$. Viewed in isolation, calls represent bullish bets and puts represent bearish ones. Outright call owners would like nothing more than for the price of the underlying asset to skyrocket from now to time T. This would allow them to buy at X and then dump the asset into the market at a much higher price. The payout of a call at maturity is given in Figure 3.1.

Puts generate a positive payout for whenever the spot drops below the downside strike as shown in Figure 3.2.

It's worth reflecting on the hockey stick payouts for a while, as the bendy part of the curve is what makes options interesting and important. In both cases, the discontinuity in the slope of the curve occurs at the strike X. While options traders generally do not hold to maturity, the terminal payout has a large bearing on the way a call or put evolves over time. We use calls as our base case for now. The value of a call at maturity is $C(T) = max(S(T) - X, 0)$. You receive the higher of the asset price minus the strike and 0. This quantity is also called the terminal payout of the call. This implies that, once you have bought the call, your maximum loss is 0, while your potential gain is theoretically unlimited. This does *not* mean we are suggesting that you will always make a profit from the trade. You need to overcome the initial cost of the call to bank the profit.

Similarly, the value of a put at maturity is $P(T) = max(X - S(T), 0)$. The kink in the payout at X introduces a non-linearity into the payout curve. Why is this important? It allows the owner of a call or put to benefit from large and unexpected market moves. The wider the range of outcomes for $S(T)$, the greater the payout potential of a call or put. Since losses are strictly bounded, put and call prices should increase in tandem with uncertainty. In the unorthodox and evocative language of Taleb (2012), puts and calls are "anti-fragile". They profit from disorder. The wilder and more unpredictable $S(T)$ becomes, the better. We can illustrate this idea using a simple example. The example relies upon a single "binomial" outcome, generated by the flip of a coin.

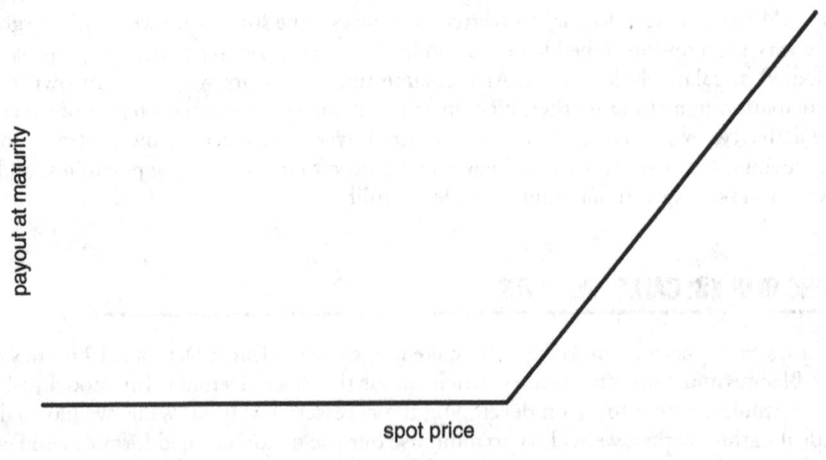

FIGURE 3.1   Payout shape for a call option at maturity

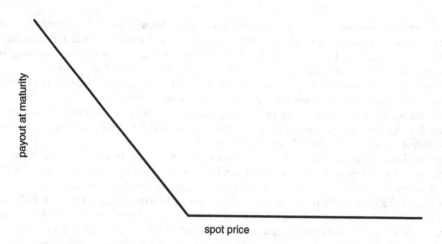

FIGURE 3.2   Payout shape for a long put at maturity

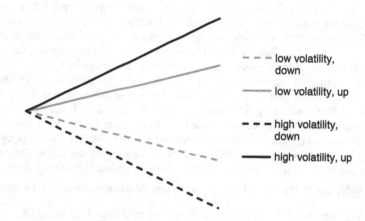

FIGURE 3.3   One-step binomial model with variable volatility

- Suppose we buy a call option on a stock currently trading at 100 and make some assumptions about where the stock can go.
- There are two scenarios. In the first, there is a 50% chance that the stock will land at 90 and a 50% chance the stock will land at 110 at time T. In the second, the spread is wider. There is a 50% chance that $S(T) = 80$ and a 50% chance that $S(T) = 120$. In Figure 3.3, we sketch the two scenarios in tandem.
- The expected value of $S(T) = 100$ in both cases, e.g. $E[S(T)] = 0.5 * 90 + 0.5 * 110 = 0.5 * 80 + 0.5 * 120$. However, the call is worth $0.5 * max(80 - 100, 0) + 0.5 * max(110 - 100, 0) = 5$ in scenario 1 and worth 10 in scenario 2. Scenario 2 has a higher scenario-averaged payout for the owner of the call and hence should be worth more.

This strongly suggests that call and put prices go up as the perceived range of outcomes increases. If we replace the discrete price tree with a continuous return distribution, the situation is identical. Let's take the simplest continuous case, where returns are normally distributed. Recall that a normal distribution is completely specified by two parameters, its mean and standard deviation. Returns fall under the classical "bell curve" after repeated experiments. In this case, uncertainty is completely encoded in the parameter σ. If we normalise the standard deviation appropriately, to adjust for variation over different time horizons, we wind up with something denoted by σ. σ is familiarly called the volatility of returns. It is an extremely important quantity, as it measures risk at the most basic level. The price of both a call and put is increasing in volatility. Without demonstrating anything, we have graphed the payout curve of a call option for different volatility levels in Figure 3.4.

For the sake of concreteness, we have focused on German Bund futures options in Figure 3.4. A call option on any underlying would have the same qualitative payout profile.

Since the payout profile of a call or put is going to converge to a piecewise linear function at maturity, it needs to become increasingly curved at the strike X along the way. Note that a piecewise linear function is just a collection of straight lines glued together.

The non-linear payout creates some complexity. An option can respond in a variety of ways to small changes in $S(t)$, depending on where $S(t)$ is relative to X. If $S(t)$ is far below X, a call will display almost no sensitivity to the spot. The payout curve is simply too flat there. On the other hand, if $S(t)$ is far above X, the call will move nearly in tandem with the underlying price. Later, we will discover that the variable exposure in an option can cause the dynamics of a hedging structure to change quite dramatically over time. We need to understand the chameleon-like characteristics of basic or "plain vanilla" options before we can come to grips with more complicated hedging structures.

The way that a fixed option responds to changes in price and time to maturity can be highly variable. How can we quantify the amount an option will move if we perturb $S(t)$, σ or other factors that might determine the price of an option? Perturbing S means that we are only moving it by a small amount. It's a mathematical term with far ranging implications. If you slightly change the parameters in a system, does it matter? The direct approach to perturbation analysis involves calculating the so-called "Greeks". The Greeks *locally* measure the sensitivity of an option to various factors. For larger moves in the spot or another quantity, option prices can move far more than the commonly used Greeks would predict. Assume that we have a formula for pricing calls and puts. Later in this chapter, we will introduce the Black–Scholes pricing model, but any formula will do for now. If we use a different convention from the market, our Greeks might be different from the market's, but they will still be well-defined. If we want to estimate sensitivity to $S(t)$, we just perturb $S(t)$ then re-price the option to calculate the slope of the payout curve at $S(t)$. This tells us how much our call is likely to move for a small change in the price of the underlying. This slope is called the option delta, in particular,

$$\Delta = \frac{(C(S + dS) - C(S))}{dS}.$$ dS is the size of the perturbation. Mathematicians like to supply emotional content to seemingly dry functions and equations and we take their lead here. The reason that Δ is unambiguously defined is that C is "well-behaved" as a function of S, at least until maturity. The slope of C as a function of S never blows up, no matter how small dS might be. Analogously, we can estimate

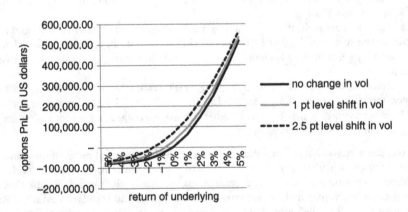

FIGURE 3.4 Sensitivity of Bund calls to changes in volatility

C's sensitivity to σ. We have already seen that puts and calls benefit from confusion, disorder and uncertainty and quantify this notion below. σ, the volatility of S that is agreed upon by the market, compresses these diverse notions of risk into a single number. If we rewrite $C(S)$ as $C(S, σ)$, we can define *vega* by perturbing σ for fixed S, then calculating the slope. Theta, θ, refers to the time decay of an option. It is formally defined as $θ = (C(S, t + dt) - (C(S, t))/dt$ for a call and $θ = (P(S, t + dt) - P(S, t))/dt$ for a put. The convention is to set dt equal to 1 day, so that θ measures how much you will lose in a day if nothing happens. For most options, delta, vega and theta play a significant role. At the extremes, other Greeks can come into play. Close to maturity, gamma can play a large role. Gamma, γ, is sometimes called the "delta of delta", as it measures the degree to which delta changes for a small change in the spot. In particular, $γ = (Δ(S + dS) - Δ(S))/dS$.

If γ is small, the payout function is locally quite straight. Risk varies almost linearly as a function of the spot price. Conversely, the profit/loss in a high gamma option can change quite dramatically as the spot moves. Short-dated options that are close to ATM have relatively high gamma, as we can see in Figure 3.5.

As time to maturity increases, the importance of gamma diminishes. Long-dated options have fairly flat payout profiles across all spot values. Rho, ρ, takes the place of γ as a significant Greek. Specifically, ρ measures the sensitivity of an option to changes in the discount rate.

The reader may wonder why we have made no mention of other higher order Greeks, such as volga (the sensitivity of vega to small changes in implied volatility). Since we are only dealing with combinations of calls and puts in this book, most of the higher order Greeks are tiny. We are avoiding bank creations such as barrier and knock options, where there can be a discrete jump in the payout at maturity. From a hedging perspective, we don't need to have a very precise handle on the Greeks. We only require that our hedging structures have enough kick for a large move in the underlying.

An option is European style if you are only allowed to exercise at maturity. It's American style if you can exercise at any time up to and including maturity. This has nothing to do with *where* the option or underlying asset is based, e.g. options on German Bund futures have American style delivery. Stock indices and the VIX generally have European style exercise, while options on futures or individual stocks tend to be American. This is not entirely arbitrary. The cash settled options are the European ones. Otherwise, exchanges would have to issue official settlement prices for every index on a daily basis. The settlement prices would determine how much would be credited or taken away from

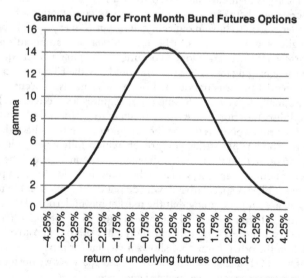

FIGURE 3.5 Bell-shaped gamma curve as a function of underlying return

a client's brokerage account. This would be cumbersome and subject to manipulation. There is also the question of valuation. At first sight, it seems reasonable that an American call or put should be worth more than a European one with the same strike and time to maturity. You have the freedom to exercise whenever you want. This "optionality" should be worth *something*. In other financial contexts, it generally is. For example, Silber (1991) has estimated that a restricted stock should trade at a roughly 50 basis point per annum discount to an equivalent stock that can be traded freely.

Here, it turns out that (in the absence of dividends or other technical factors) the American exercise feature is generally worthless. Imagine that you own an American style call that is in the money, i.e. $S(t) > X$. You could exercise the call if you wanted to, receiving $S(t) - X$ after selling the stock back into the market. The trouble with this strategy is that the call should be worth more than $S(t) - X$ at the time of exercise. The position is equivalent to a long position in the spot, with a purchase price of X, combined with a long put struck at X. Since the embedded put has positive value, you would be well served to sell the call back into the market rather than exercising the option.

WHY BUY A CALL OR PUT?

"Why" can be a dangerous question to ask in many contexts, but is an important one here. There are numerous reasons to buy a call or put, with varying degrees of sophistication. The most basic reason to buy an option is that you *have* to. You either need to block out unpalatable scenarios in your core portfolio or you want to add a new position, but are unable take on too much additional risk. Buying puts on the S&P 500 to protect against further losses in a traditional equity portfolio is a forced move. You want to maintain your existing portfolio but need to hedge against disaster. Buying puts on the target stock in a potential merger, on the assumption that the deal won't go through, is something entirely different. Here, you want concentrated exposure to a low-probability event. If the deal goes through, you only lose the premium you have paid. On the other hand, if the deal breaks, the stock will probably crater. You might then make many multiples of the original premium paid. In these cases, you might not worry or even know whether the puts are overpriced at the time of purchase. All you care about are the payouts under various scenarios.

This can create opportunities for volatility arbitrage traders, who are always sniffing around for mispriced options. Volatility is their currency, not price. If they find something, they will try to extract a profit from the discrepancy between an option and some combination of other options and the underlying asset. Another reason to buy an outright call or put is to express a hybrid view on direction and volatility. You might be able to harvest a bit more alpha by trading an option rather than the underlying. Let's say you want to generate long exposure to emerging market equities. The most liquid instrument available is an emerging markets ETF. You could buy the ETF, buy a call or sell a put. When you buy a call, your potential profit is unbounded but a move needs to occur reasonably quickly. As time passes, the call gradually loses value. Selling a put requires less conviction but an equal dose of courage. If markets stabilise, the short put strategy is likely to perform well. You are betting that any sell-off is going to be more than compensated by the premium you have collected. However, if the price of the ETF crashes through your put strike, you are left with a fully exposed long position. Buying a call is a punchier play, predicated on the idea that the market has underpriced the probability of a large upside move. However, if nothing happens, you lose the premium paid. Buying a put can be a defensive or speculative bear market play. A speculative downside put can be statistical in nature, even if it's not a relative value play. You are simply arguing that the market has underpriced the probability of a move toward the downside strike. If you are really bullish, you can buy a call *and* sell a put. This structure is usually called a risk reversal. Since a long call and short put both have positive delta, the risk in each leg compounds the risk in the other. Figure 3.6 shows a payout for a risk reversal. Since we have sold an OTM put and bought an OTM call, the strikes are spaced apart. As we push the put and call strikes closer together, the structure converges to a forward contract.

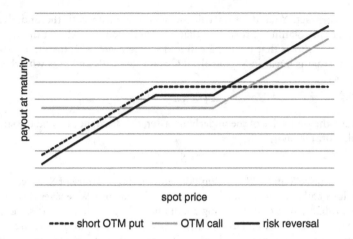

FIGURE 3.6 Construction of a split-strike risk reversal

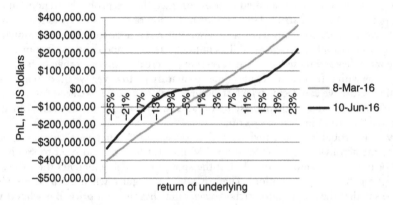

FIGURE 3.7 Evolving payout of a risk reversal on the iShares MSCI Brazil ETF

Figure 3.7 refers to a split-strike risk reversal on the iShares MSCI Brazil ETF. We sold 1,000 puts and bought 1,000 calls on March 8, 2016 and wanted to get a handle on the payout curve roughly 3 months thereafter. The curve evolves from a nearly linear shape (with delta close to 0.5) to one that is fairly flat in the middle.

Suppose there is a persistent put skew in the market you are trading. Put skews are characteristic of risky assets, such as equity indices, based on asymmetry in the underlying return distribution and excess demand for hedging downside risk. "Risky assets" have a positive expected return over the long term (at least according to theory), but may be exposed to large negative downside surprises. When there are more large negative surprises than positive ones, the underlying distribution is said to be skewed to the downside. You then collect premium if the put and call strikes are the same distance from the ATM strike. In other words, you get paid up front to hold the structure. Alternatively, you can construct costless risk reversals where the put strike is considerably further away from the money than the call strike. By "costless", we mean that you collect the same amount of premium from the put as you pay for the call. In the limiting case where the call and put have the same strike, you have effectively bought a forward contract. Your position will move contiguously with the underlying price and is insensitive to changes in volatility. It turns out that vega in the put cancels out the vega in the call. The put–call parity formula shows that buying a call and selling a put with the same strike and maturity generates a structure that is linear in S. Namely, if C and P are calls and puts with the same strike and time to maturity, then

$$C - P = S - e^{-r(T-t)}X,$$

where S, r and X are the spot price of the underlying asset, the discount rate and the strike, respectively. We can rewrite the formula as

$$C = P + S - e^{-r(T-t)}X$$

Since the current price S and $e^{-r(T-t)}X$ don't depend on the volatility of S, we can essentially create a forward with a long call and short put (i.e. risk reversal) structure. Whenever there is a liquid futures contract, there is probably no point in buying a call and selling a put with the same strike. Given the proliferation of options on ETFs that have no equivalent futures, however, there are many cases where building a synthetic forward is a reasonable idea. The forward allows you to apply leverage as well as minimise interest and dividend income.

Forwards, as we know, are "delta one" instruments. There is no kink in the payout curve, hence vega is always 0. Whenever there is a liquid futures contract, there is probably no point in buying a call and selling a put with the same strike. Given the proliferation of options on ETFs that have no equivalent futures, however, there are many cases where building a synthetic forward is a reasonable idea. The forward allows you to apply leverage as well as minimise interest and dividend income.

Once we move beyond these basic structures, we can create a diverse range of hedging structures by mixing options with different strikes and times to maturity. However, we need to have some notion of relative value before we can decide which structures look promising. We need some way to place all of the available options on a single underlying on an equal footing. This motivates our discussion of the Black–Scholes equation in the next section.

For now, it is probably worth reviewing the concept of "money-ness" for an option. We will repeatedly use the acronyms ATM, ITM and OTM in what follows and need to specify what these mean. A call or put is at-the-money, or ATM, if the spot price roughly matches the strike. Why do we use the word "roughly" in a definition? There is some ambiguity when defining money-ness. One approach is to say that the ATM option strike *exactly* matches the spot price. But what if we are dealing with an option on a futures contract? The Black 76 formula prices calls and puts using the current futures price. This suggests the alternative that an ATM option's strike should match the equivalent maturity forward. A third definition, which closely matches the forward price one, specifies that the strike whose delta is closest in magnitude to 0.50 is at-the-money. Once we have decided what we mean by an ATM option, out-of-the-money OTM and in-the-money options follow naturally. OTM calls have a strike higher than the ATM strike and OTM puts have a lower strike. Generally speaking, OTM options have no intrinsic value. They would expire worthless if the maturity date were today.

THE BLACK–SCHOLES EQUATION AND IMPLIED VOLATILITY

In 1973, Fischer Black and Myron Scholes published a landmark paper called "The Pricing of Options and Corporate Liabilities". The paper appeared in the *Journal of Political Economy* (1973) , of all places. They derived a partial differential equation for the value of a "warrant", or call option, using two different approaches. One approach relied upon replicating the option using a dynamic hedging strategy. The other applied the Capital Asset Pricing Model (CAPM) to map risk onto expected return. As it turned out, this equation was solvable, leading to the Black–Scholes formula. Black was able to draw upon his technical background and identify the equation as one that models the diffusion of heat through a metal rod.

Countless books and articles have analysed the Black–Scholes equation from a mathematical and historical perspective and we will make no effort to reinvent the wheel. We simply point the reader to the original paper and Mehrling's fascinating biography of Fischer Black (2005) for further details. Haug (2009) is also worth consulting, for an alternative history of option pricing. Specifically, the price of a European call option is given by

$$C = C(S,X,r,T-t,\sigma) = N(d_1)S - N(d_2)Xe^{-r(T-t)}, \text{ where}$$

$$d_1 = \frac{1}{\sigma\sqrt{T-t}}\left(\ln\left(\frac{S}{X}\right) + \left(r + \frac{\sigma^2}{2}\right)(T-t)\right)$$

and $d_2 = d_1 - \sigma\sqrt{T-t}$.

Here, $N(d_i)$ gives the probability that a normally distributed random variable is less than d_i and takes values between 0 and 1. Recall that a European option can only be exercised at maturity. Options with more complicated features usually can't be priced using a simple analytic formula.

We call the reader's attention to a comment about the formula in the original paper. (Note that the expected return on the stock does not appear in (the) equation. The option value as a function of the stock price is independent of the expected return on the stock.)

The comment almost looks like a throwaway, but it would be hard to overemphasise its importance. If C depended on the expected return $E(S)$ of S, the Black–Scholes formula would contain *two* unobservable quantities, namely $E(S)$ and σ. Note that S and r have unambiguous market prices and X and $T-t$ are explicitly defined by the option contract. They are all known precisely. Since $E(S)$ has no impact on C, we can uniquely solve for σ given a market price for C. This allows us to view Black–Scholes as a powerful translation device, converting option prices into implied volatilities. Options with different strikes and maturities can be placed on an equal footing. German Bund futures, for example, have hundreds of listed options at any given point in time. The same is true for major equity indices, short rates, commodities and individual stocks. For each underlying asset, there is a multitude of different strikes and maturity dates. If we try to compare their prices, we will get hopelessly lost. So how do we specify which options might be relatively cheap and expensive? This is where the Black–Scholes formula comes to the rescue.

We observe that C and P are *increasing* in σ. All things being equal, the higher the volatility of an asset, the higher its option price. The reason for this is straightforward and has been touched upon previously. When we buy a call, our payout at maturity is $max(S(T) - X, 0)$. While there is lower bound on the payout, potential gains are unlimited. Our loss is capped at the premium we have paid. As volatility increases, the range of outcomes also increases. This raises the odds that $S(T) - X$ will be large and positive, implying that the expected value of $max(S(T) - X, 0)$ should go up. This means we can solve for σ uniquely given the market price of a call or put. In particular, $\sigma = \sigma(C,S,X,r,T-t)$ or $\sigma = \sigma(P,S,X,r,T-t)$ for a call and put, respectively. Volatility is a deterministic function of the option price, spot price, strike, risk-free rate and time to maturity. This allows us to compare options with different strikes and maturities in a sensible way. It is hard to develop a visceral feeling about the *price* of an option, i.e. what does it mean for a 1-month 2050 put on the S&P 500 to have a price of 25? How much of the price is intrinsic value, how much is premium and how does the premium scale as time increases? (Note that the intrinsic value of an option is the amount it would be worth if it expired today.)

However, if someone told you that the implied volatility of that put were 14 (really 14%, though volatility is usually quoted in percentage points), you would have something solid to go by. Is the implied volatility higher than 30 day trailing realised volatility? Is it much higher than ATM implied volatility? Where is it trading relative to 3-month implied volatility? These sorts of questions allow us to say something about the fair value of the 2050 put, in relative terms.

THE IMPLIED VOLATILITY SKEW

When we use the Black–Scholes equation to convert the price of an option into an implied volatility, there is some model misspecification involved. Black–Scholes assumes that the volatility of the underlying asset is constant, i.e. independent of time and level. It prices options based on some kind of average volatility of the asset over the life of the option, with no regard as to where volatility is likely to be if the asset drops –20%. Yet, when we derive different implied volatilities for options with different strikes, we are contradicting the model by saying that volatility *is* level-dependent after all. Does this obviate the possibility of using the model at all? Most practitioners would argue not. As we discussed above, the model provides a powerful method for converting option prices into a quantity that we can understand and trade. Suppose that the S&P 500 is trading at 2100 and the implied volatility of the 3-month 1750 put is 10 points higher than for the 3-month ATM put. The market is warning us that volatility will go up quite dramatically if the index gets anywhere near 1750. We can think about this in another way. Investors are coming up with realistic OTM option prices by fudging the only unobservable quantity in the formula. It is only natural that financial engineers wanted to put this on a firmer foundation over time. What started as a back-of-the-envelope calculation has progressively become more sophisticated. The idea of converting option prices into forward risk estimates is encapsulated in the concept of local volatility. We will not cover local volatility in this book and point the reader in the direction of Gatheral(2006).

For our purposes, level-dependent volatility is important as a mechanism for generating fat tails in the return distribution. If volatility jumps whenever an index drops below a threshold, the probability of even larger moves from that point will be greater than a normal distribution might predict. This may be related to contagion effects in the market, which we explore in Chapter 8. Here, we make no effort to solve the so-called "inverse problem", where we infer market expectations about volatility from the price of various options on the underlying. As crisis hedgers, we are not operating in the domain of accurate calibration and prediction, but in the world of survival. Precise relationships can break down when the market suddenly shifts into a risk-off phase.

HEDGING SMALL MOVES

Suppose you have sold a call. The position is exposed to a sharp rise in the spot. You can hedge this risk in various ways. The same ideas apply if you've sold a put and the spot craters. There are two basic ways to manage risk if you have sold a put or a call. You can delta-hedge with the underlying asset or you can hedge the option with other options. In this section, we focus on delta hedging. Let's say you have sold an equity index put. For simplicity, the index doesn't pay any dividends and interest rates are 0. Then the put price P depends on the index price S, the strike X, the time to maturity $T-t$ and the implied volatility σ. In other words, we can write P as $P(S, X, T-t, \sigma)$. There's no reason to worry about how to price P for now. We can simply assume that the Black–Scholes formula is valid. It's then possible to calculate the *delta* of the put. The put delta tells you how much P is likely to move if the index S moves a bit. You can approximate the delta by repricing the put for a slightly different index value delta_S then calculating $(P(S + delta\_S, X, T-t, \sigma) - P(S, X, T-t, \sigma))/delta\_S$. In mathematical terms, you're calculating the partial derivative of P with respect to S. So if the put has a delta of –0.50 (traders would say this is a 50 delta put), you expect to lose 50 basis points if the index goes up by 1%. The delta of a put ranges from –1 to 0 and the delta of a call falls in the range from 0 to 1. Practitioners usually multiply by 100 when they tell you what the delta of an option might be. For example, a put with a delta of –0.50 would be called a "50 delta" put. It's clear that the delta must be negative, since we're dealing with a put. This implies that, for every 10 options you are short, you should be short 5 futures to immunise your position. On average, the profit from regular delta hedging should be dependent on the difference between the option's implied volatility at time of entry and the realised volatility of the asset. In theory, if you can consistently sell options at a higher volatility than the realised volatility of the underlying asset over the life of the option, you have the basis for a profitable strategy.

DELTA HEDGING: THE IDEALISED CASE

Suppose that you lived in an alternative reality where asset returns had normal distributions and volatility stayed constant. This might be a rough approximation of the way markets operate, but can be wildly off at the worst possible times. Suppose asset prices were driven by a random number generator whose properties could be easily inferred. In other words, the return-generating "machine" operated according to strict rules. You could trade at no cost or market impact and prices vibrated continuously through time. Some academics might equate this to a situation where everything was efficiently priced, as any inefficiency would be instantly stamped out by investors. However, this is not a necessary assumption. Here, we assume that statistical mispricings might still crop up in the options markets from time to time. Suppose we found an option whose implied volatility was higher than the constant realised volatility of the underlying. This might occur if the historical volatility of an asset over some interval were higher than the "true" volatility of the asset, by random chance. In this case, implied volatility might be linked to the abnormally high volatility in the past and hence overpriced. We could then turn an almost certain profit by selling the option and delta hedging with the underlying. The underlying asset would typically move less than the option predicted. This implies that the net asset value (NAV) of the delta-hedging strategy would decay more slowly than the premium in the option. It all sounds a bit fancy, so let's take a concrete example. The example is quite extreme, to illustrate the delta hedging concept. Suppose we have a 1-year call option on a stock. The call trades at a fixed 20% volatility, but the stock's realised volatility is a constant 10%. This is a mouth-watering opportunity, so long as the stock doesn't start going crazy. The stock is trading at 100, the call has strike 100 and interest rates are 0.

In Figure 3.8, we track the value of the call against the value of the replicating portfolio over time. Our strategy relies upon selling the call and delta hedging with the stock. In our example, we receive about 8 for selling the call and have to pay roughly 0.55*100 for the shares. Note that 0.55 is the call delta at the moment of sale. This implies we have to borrow roughly 47 from the bank to get the trade going. Over time, the borrow increases if we have to buy more shares and decreases if we sell them

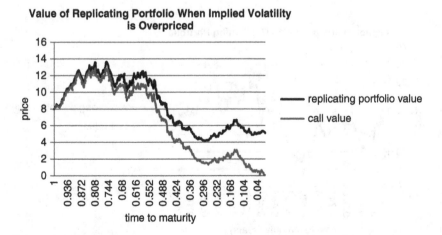

FIGURE 3.8 Extracting alpha from a call that is overpriced in implied volatility terms

down. We can see that, for a representative path, the replicating portfolio decays much more slowly than the premium embedded in the call.

When you sell and delta hedge a call, the largest net profits are realised when the call quickly burns off. This was illustrated in the example above. In this happy case, you quickly gain on the call and subsequently don't have to hedge very much, as the call delta is now low. The delta burns off to the extent that hedging is unnecessary after a while. For a short put that is delta hedged, a rally in the spot is ideal. The less aggressively you need to hedge, the better.

When an option is as mispriced as this one, the odds of locking in a profit are very high. You have a huge margin of error. In Figure 3.9, we simulate the performance of the replicating portfolio, short call strategy over a deliberately small number of paths. The terms are the same as in the example above. The graph tracks average profit as a percentage of the initial option price. After only 10 (!) simulations, our average profit evolves according to a very smooth line. If implied volatility is overpriced and the basic assumptions of replication remain intact, selling then delta hedging options should be an overwhelmingly successful strategy (see Figure 3.10). As we will find out, however, those can be giant "ifs".

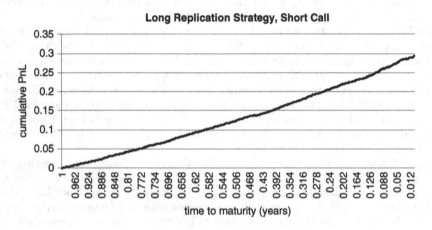

FIGURE 3.8 Arbitrage at its finest when implied volatility is severely mispriced

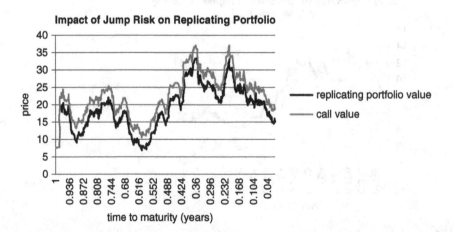

FIGURE 3.10 Impact of jumps on P&L

PRACTICAL LIMITS OF DELTA HEDGING

Once we loosen our assumptions a bit, it becomes harder to delta hedge with accuracy. We can't just sell options that appear to be overpriced and expect to hedge away all of the price risk in the underlying. Changes in volatility, discrete jumps and variations in price dynamics according to timescale will eventually lay siege to our plans. Physical time may appear to move continuously forward, at a constant rate. However, financial data appears discretely and prices can jump discontinuously (i.e. more than one tick) from one time stamp to the next. Some people equate high volatility to a "fast market" and this description feels about right. Fast markets truly give one a feeling of vertigo, like a roller coaster at the local theme park. When lots of transactions are occurring per unit interval, the perception is that time is actually whizzing along faster than normal. Ané and Geman (2000) have introduced the notion of a stochastic transaction clock to account for this phenomenon. When lots of transactions are hitting the wires, a fixed unit of time can contain an unusual amount of activity. By rescaling time, they are able to transform fat-tailed distributions into more normal looking ones.

Let's revert from a paradigm that vaguely resembles Einstein's theory of special relativity back to standard clock time. Even if we haven't observed a six standard deviation drop in the recent past, the risk of such a move is always lurking beneath the surface. These moves are of great significance, even if they sometimes reverse themselves over time. To an options trader, intraday mega-moves can threaten survival. We can't quietly edit out moments where there is "blood on the streets". Price jumps are a vital part of the signal and, over the long term, can be definitive. They are *not* products of measurement error, analogous to noisy patches on a digital image that need to be smoothed out. A small number of very large moves can have a surprisingly large impact on returns over a long horizon. If, for example, we remove the largest 10 down days for the cash S&P 500 index since 1980 as shown in Figure 3.11, the annualised return of the index goes from 8.26% to 11.17%.

This is quite a remarkable statistic, as these down days only account for 0.11% of all trading days over the entire period! The index might eventually retrace to where it was before the devastating down move, but the damage has been done. Our delta hedging strategy would have been forced into the market, selling the underlying near the low then covering at the original level. In the following example, we show how a single price spike can ruin a delta hedging strategy. We return to the 100 strike call example, with a few modifications. Implied volatility (20%) is only slightly mispriced relative to realised volatility in the observable past. Realised volatility is set at 19%, so there is little margin for error. On average, we can extract alpha from the discrepancy in the idealised Gaussian world with no price impact or costs. However, a single price jump can ruin our plans. What is a "reasonable" price jump to consider? The black swan purists might argue that this is a silly question, with some justification. Once we depart from the world of normal distributions, spectacularly large moves are possible. Unreasonable looking moves can occur surprisingly often. In this section, however, we just want to show that it wouldn't take much of a jump to push the delta hedging strategy offside.

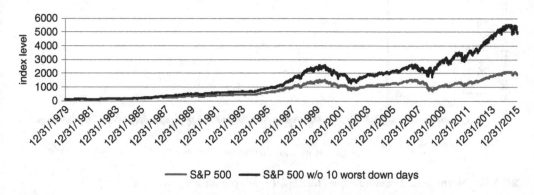

FIGURE 3.11 Impact of removing 10 largest down days from cumulative S&P performance

We start with an example that looks unremarkable from a long-range perspective. Financial historians are *not* likely to look upon October 2, 2015 as an extraordinary day and we have selected it for precisely that reason. The S&P returned +1.43%, which is less than a 1.5 standard deviation 1-day move. Returns of this magnitude should occur about 13% of the time for a normal distribution. These sorts of moves are quite common across equity indices, interest rates, currencies and commodities. Markets had been very turbulent in August and bearish in September. There was a great deal of anticipation for the US payrolls number released at 1:30 GMT. According to market convention, if not reality, this would be an important barometer of the health of the US economy and might also have a bearing on central bank policy. However, there have been many such moments of tension and anticipation in the past. The trouble is that, on an intra-day basis, they cannot be accurately hedged. If you were short a 1-month straddle and kept hitting the bid or offer in an attempt to hedge, there would be large gaps in your fills. If you delta-hedged once a minute, you would miss the move. If you hedged whenever the underlying moved by 0.5 standard deviations, you might only get filled at the tail end of the spike. In either case, your delta hedging profits would be dwarfed by continuous repricing of the short straddle.

Figures 3.12 and 3.13 rely upon two days of historical data, 1 October and 2 October, 2015. On 1 October, we calculate the standard deviation sigma of 1-minute returns from 7 am to 4:15 pm Eastern Standard Time. On 2 October, we take the same time window and divide each 1-minute return

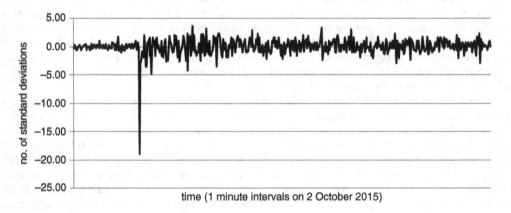

FIGURE 3.12 Normalised S&P 500 1-minute moves, 2 October 2015

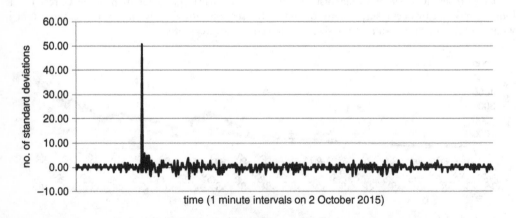

FIGURE 3.13 Normalised 1-minute moves for US 10 year note futures, 2 October 2015

by yesterday's sigma. We have quantified each 1-minute return relative to a 1 standard deviation move on the previous day. The first graph shows 1-minute moves in sigma units for S&P 500 Emini futures.

The second shows normalised 1-minute moves for US 10 year Treasury note futures, over the same period. The scaling mechanism is the same as above.

HEDGING OPTIONS WITH OTHER OPTIONS

It should be evident that delta hedging is not reliable when volatility changes or there are exaggerated jumps in the underlying asset. The problem compounds when we examine options that have outsized gamma or vega. Such options are highly sensitive to unexpected events. As the saying goes, very short-dated ATM options are "gammatastic". They have lots of gamma. Near the strike, delta changes rapidly as a function of the spot price. This forces radical rebalancing of the delta hedge, especially if the spot jumps or oscillates wildly around the strike. At the other end of the spectrum, long-dated options are rich in vega. Changes in risk aversion levels can sometimes propagate far along the volatility term structure. If implied volatility increases, long-dated option prices can jump even if there is no material move in the spot. There is no direct way to hedge changes in implied volatility using the underlying alone. This is especially true when implied and realised volatility do not move in tandem. Does this mean that we should never short options that are very close to or very far from maturity? Not necessarily. We can protect against damaging losses without resorting to dynamic hedging. Haug and Taleb (2007) stridently argue that the most direct way to hedge options is with *other* options. This approach helps you to control all of your Greeks simultaneously. In some sense, it transcends the Greeks, as you can completely eliminate extreme event risk by hedging with options.

Once you sell a vanilla option, you are short gamma and vega. If you buy another option to hedge, some of your gamma and vega might cancel out. Suppose the S&P 500 is trading at 2000 and you want to sell a 1-week 1950 put. While delta might initially be low, it will increase at an accelerating rate if the spot comes anywhere close to 1950. This might force you to bail out of the trade. Alternatively, you could delta hedge the position aggressively, but this would leave you vulnerable to a sudden reversal in the spot. As we will see in Chapter 7, vicious reversals are common in declining markets. A prudent strategy, then, is to buy a lower strike put against the short 1950 put. You might, for example, buy the 1-week 1900 put to cover extreme downside risk. This caps your loss at 50*(contract multiplier), while obviating the need for dynamic hedging.

Once you cover the extreme risk in a structure, you can hold the structure indefinitely without worrying that you will be wiped out. Experienced options traders will affirm that it is easier to extract alpha from a trade you can hold on to. The example above allows you to collect premium with bounded risk. Trading spreads allows you to move away from continuous monitoring of delta, gamma, vega and other Greeks. You don't have to worry quite so much about the path taken by the underlying asset. What is more important is the payout achieved over a given horizon for a range of moves in S and sigma. The tail of the underlying return distribution is now irrelevant, as you have truncated it with the 1900 put. You simply need to decide whether the spread offers good value as a unit.

PUT AND CALL SPREADS

Let's examine option spreads in more detail. They reduce the need for active delta hedging and represent an efficient way to express a targeted view. As above, suppose you think a particular asset is about to go up. This time, however, your conviction level is not quite so high. Rather than buying an outright call or selling an outright put, you can trade a spread. The spread gives you some directional exposure, but does not benefit fully from a large-scale move. To initiate a call spread, you buy a call with a given strike and sell another call with a higher strike. Selling the high strike reduces costs, but also caps your

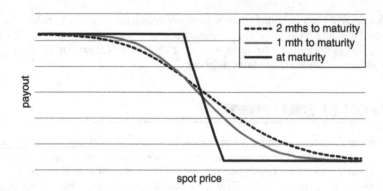

FIGURE 3.14 Evolution of payout curve for a put spread

potential gain, as Figure 3.14 suggests. Selling a put spread has the opposite effect. When you buy a low strike put to cover another put that you have sold, you eat into the premium collected while putting a floor on your loss. In the US, put and call spreads are sometimes called "vertical spreads". The name implies that you buy and sell options at different levels (i.e. strikes), while keeping time, the horizontal dimension, fixed. Call and put spreads can also arise as part of an active trading strategy. You could for example buy a put on a stock index and then sell a lower strike put if the index drops sharply. This allows you to lock in a profit by selling a rich put, while maintaining some level of protection. Conversely, if US 10 year note futures spike and you are short a call, you can buy a further out of the money call to cover your extreme risk. In this way, you can hang on to your original position, with the expectation of a reversal.

In the diagrams below, we can see how the payout of a put spread varies as a function of the spot. The payout curve is initially quite shallow, but steepens dramatically between the strikes as we approach maturity.

STRADDLES AND STRANGLES

In the previous pages, we have analysed structures that combine a view on volatility with a directional view. But what if we want to make a *directionless* volatility bet? Option straddles and strangles serve as an entry point into this space. To construct a straddle, you buy an ATM call and put with the same time to maturity. This structure has a symmetric "V" shaped payout profile, as in Figure 3.15.

Whether you buy or sell a straddle, the position is initially delta neutral, i.e. the call and put deltas offset. For a moment, let's assume that you decide not to delta hedge the structure. Once the spot moves, the delta will move away from 0, as a function of gamma. If you buy an ATM straddle, you are initially delta neutral, with a long gamma profile. In Figure 3.16, we can see how gamma varies as a function of spot for a long straddle. We have based our calculations on an S&P 500 straddle with 30 days to maturity. As we converge on the maturity date, gamma blows up at the strike and approaches 0 elsewhere, with delta jumping to −1 or 1 for the tiniest of moves.

Gamma peaks at the ATM strike. If the spot initially rises, your delta becomes positive. This can generate material long exposure to the underlying asset. If it falls, you pick up negative deltas. As time passes, you start accumulating delta risk at an ever-increasing rate. Short-dated ATM straddles are packed with gamma, hence should not be shorted in a cavalier fashion. The curve looks a bit pointy at the ATM strike, but this is an artefact of our approximation scheme. Gamma should have roughly the same shape as the probability density function for the underlying asset. In a Black–Scholes world, the gamma profile has a Gaussian, "bell curve" profile.

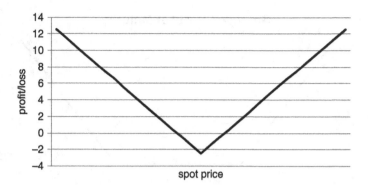

FIGURE 3.15 Profit/loss of a straddle at maturity

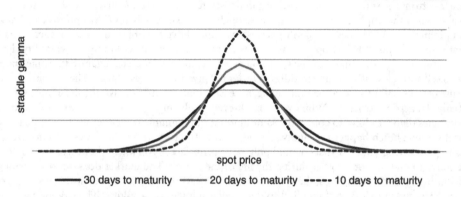

FIGURE 3.16 Evolution of gamma curve for a straddle, as time elapses

We can think of things in another way, from the perspective of a straddle buyer. What you really want is a large move one way or another, as your delta-adjusted position size will accelerate in the direction of the move. As time passes, you need a progressively larger move in the spot to break even. This implies that, if you don't delta hedge a long straddle, you need to time your entry and exit points with precision. You can't wait forever for a move to take place. The problem is magnified for straddles that are relatively close to maturity, where theta is largest. Recall that theta is the time decay of an option. If you *do* decide to delta hedge, straddles transform into a play on the spread between implied and realised volatility. If implied volatility is lower than your forecast of realised volatility, you might buy and hedge a straddle. If it is higher, you might sell and hedge. Since implied volatility usually trades at a premium to realised volatility, selling straddles generally seems to be the more appealing strategy. There are hedge funds and proprietary trading firms that do exactly that. However, if they do not size their positions very conservatively or trade with great skill, they are always in danger of imminent ruin. As we have previously mentioned, large and unexpected jumps in the spot can overwhelm the theoretical edge in a short option position.

Strangles are the close cousins of straddles. You also buy one call and put per strangle. However, for a strangle, the strikes are spaced apart. In particular, you buy a low strike put and a high strike call to construct a long strangle, as in Figure 3.17.

There are a number of reasons to split the strikes and it turns out that some reasons are better than others. Relative to a long straddle, long strangles require relatively low premium outlay. As you push the

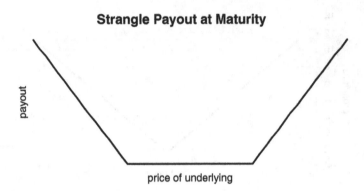

FIGURE 3.17 The "strangler" at maturity

strikes away from the spot, the cost of each leg in the strangle decreases. Conversely, short strangles can offer value when the implied volatility skew is strongly convex (i.e. when OTM options trade at a significant premium to ATM ones in volatility terms). You then have the opportunity to extract alpha from the relative mispricing of OTM options as well as from high levels of ATM implied volatility. There is another rationale for shorting strangles, although we would recommend against it. Some investors choose to sell strangles rather than straddles in order to "give themselves space". The strangle delta isn't very sensitive to small moves in the underlying, at least initially. This can give the illusion of safety in a potentially dangerous structure. While your break-even levels might be further away, you need to sell more strangles than straddles to collect the same amount of premium. You either have to settle for lower returns if nothing much happens or apply leverage to the structure, which increases extreme event risk. The concept of giving yourself space would only be appropriate if you *knew* that there would never be a large move to one side or another during the life of the option. The market does not offer such guarantees. During extreme conditions, the spot can easily crash through one of your strangle strikes, creating more open-ended risk than if you had sold a smaller number of straddles. The payout curve is nice and flat, suggesting that you should make a nearly constant positive return over a wide range of scenarios. However, danger is always around the corner if the structure is not properly attended to.

As we will see in Chapter 4, a wide range of more complex structures also have unbounded risk. By unbounded risk, we mean that there is no nearby limit as to how much you can lose. These include ladders and ratio spreads and may require active delta hedging beyond a threshold. Assuming that you have cut off the extreme downside, however, you can load a position without much active intervention. Sometimes the safe, lazy sod approach is best.

THE DEFORMABLE SHEET

Experienced options traders are able to conceptualise how a given change in short-term ATM volatility will propagate across different strikes and maturities. In our opinion, this is neither voodoo nor special talent, but a learnable skill. The volatility surface moves according to somewhat predictable patterns. Different parts of the surface usually move for logical reasons. For the purposes of hedging, we need to pay particular attention to the "wings", i.e. low delta calls and puts. In this section, we will briefly describe how the option chain for an asset can be converted into a volatility surface. Note that an option chain is the set of all listed options on a given asset at some point in time. The chain spans different strikes and maturities. We then analyse likely moves at the extremes of the surface conditional on changes in ATM volatility. Whenever an option has a reasonable bid and ask price, we can apply the Black–Scholes transformation to the mid price, converting prices into implied volatilities. The mid price of an asset is simply the average of its bid and ask prices. We wind up with an implied volatility grid, with a value for each strike and time to maturity. After interpolating between points on the grid, we can create an implied volatility surface as in Figure 3.18.

It is not necessary to define moneyness by strike. In the analysis that follows, we will usually focus on how implied volatility varies as a function of *delta*. This allows us to adjust for movements in the spot price and volatility over time. There is an ongoing debate over how to model the volatility surface as a function of changes in the spot. We refer the reader to Zou (1999) for further details. In this section, we take a more coarse-grained approach to understanding how the skew might respond to large-scale market moves. The implied volatility surface is difficult to grasp, as it contains so much information. When we start to think about dynamics, the situation gets even worse. There are lots of option prices buzzing around. However, we can sometimes reduce the dimensionality of the problem. If we move one point on the surface a bit, how much should the rest of the surface be expected to move? This is not a purely theoretical question in the context of hedging. In particular, we want to focus on flash points, regions on the surface where volatility is likely to go up the most.

Before looking at dynamics, we can simplify things by looking at static cross sections of the surface. If we focus only on ATM options, we can slice the surface along the y axis. This gives us a curve called the "term structure" of volatility. The term structure reflects market expectations of future volatility over different time horizons. If there is a risk event, short-dated volatility tends to explode, while the rest of the curve moves more modestly. The market is assuming that the event will have diminishing importance over time and prices mean reversion along the curve. Exaggerated moves at the short end can cause the term structure to invert. In Figure 3.19, we focus on S&P 500 options and calculate the beta of changes in ATM option implied volatility for different maturities to changes in 3-month ATM implied volatility. By construction, the beta of changes in 3-month ATM volatility to itself is 1.

If nothing happens after a spike in volatility, short-dated volatility will decline more rapidly than volatility over longer maturities. This is the reverse scenario of what we discussed above. The volatility beta at the short end is relatively high, causing exaggerated movements relative to 3-month volatility. Eventually, the term structure will revert to a more typical, upward sloping shape. Inverted term structures are relatively rare, as bursts in volatility tend to occur infrequently. Bull markets tend to have longer duration than bear markets. However, during prolonged sell-offs, such as in 2008, the curve can remain inverted for quite some time. In summary, short-dated volatility is the dog that wags the long-dated volatility tail. Skew dynamics are more complicated than term structure dynamics, as they are asset dependent. Risky assets, such as equity indices and carry currencies, tend to develop an exaggerated put skew after a market sell-off. Investors are clamouring for downside protection. Other assets

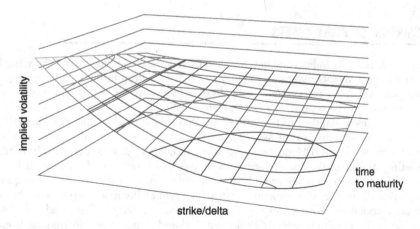

FIGURE 3.18 Qualitative depiction of an implied volatility surface

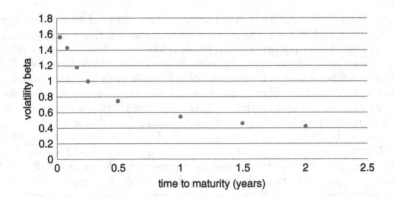

FIGURE 3.19 Variable response of term structure to changes in 3-month implied volatility

can exhibit more complicated dynamics, depending on how the market is positioned and where the need for protection is highest. We examine some of these issues in the next section.

In practice, however, out of the money (OTM) puts and calls are used to construct the matrix. OTM options are generally more liquid, with tighter bid ask spreads. This leads to a more precise implied volatility calculation. OTM option implied volatilities are also easier to calculate in a whippy market, given that their delta is relatively low. As the price of the underlying fluctuates, bid ask spreads for ITM options may not adjust synchronously, causing distortions in implied volatility.

The implied volatility matrix, calculated from OTM options, can be visualised as a surface in three dimensions. The graph below offers a stylised example of an implied volatility surface. The skew is more pronounced for short-dated options and gradually levels out as the time to maturity increases. This is particularly true when we calculate implied volatility as a function of strike, rather than delta. Whereas a 10% OTM put with 1 year to maturity covers moderate downside scenarios, a 10% OTM option with 1 week to go only protects the far left tail. We are effectively looking much further out along the skew when calculating implied volatility for the short-dated OTM put.

From the perspective of long-dated options, strikes that are a fixed distance apart become more similar (in a probabilistic sense) as time to maturity grows. Therefore, the far end of the surface should have a relatively flat skew. In the next section, we give the surface free rein to move, and examine how the put skew for risky assets expands when fear enters the market.

SKEW DYNAMICS FOR RISKY ASSETS

Risky assets, such as equity indices and high yielding currencies, tend to have a put skew. Implied volatility is higher for OTM puts than at-the-money ones. After a drop in the underlying, the put skew tends to steepen, as there is excess demand for disaster insurance. All of this implies that we need to take skew dynamics into account if we want to hedge efficiently.

Figure 3.20 gives a snapshot of the implied volatility skew for Australian Dollar futures in late May, 2016. It is representative of the skew for a risky asset under "normal" market conditions. We constructed the skew using OTM calls and puts with roughly 45 days to maturity. In particular, the implied volatility at each strike was derived from an average of the bid and ask price, using the Black 76 formula. The at-the-money strike was 72. To the left of the ATM strike, volatility rises quite rapidly. This suggests that the market was assigning a fairly high probability to a sharp drop in the currency.

There are a couple of reasons why low delta puts have relatively high implied volatility. On the one hand, risky assets tend to be negatively skewed. The underlying return distribution is more likely to surprise to the downside than to the upside. On the other, there tends to be more structural demand

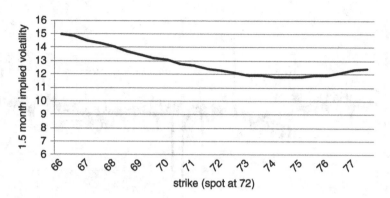

FIGURE 3.20 Implied volatility skew for a risky currency

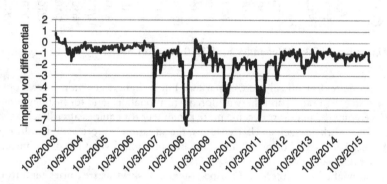

FIGURE 3.21 Negative skewness in the Aussie 25 delta risk reversal

for downside protection. Most investors have a long bias toward risky assets and use options to truncate the distribution of losses in their core portfolios.

Risky assets have more straightforward skew dynamics than squirrely things like Treasury bonds. They typically have a put skew that becomes steeper as volatility increases. The AUD/USD cross certainly qualifies as a risky asset. The Aussie has historically offered high yield, in exchange for commodity and China risk. In Figure 3.21, we track the 25 delta risk reversal (RR) for the Aussie, relative to the US dollar. Here, the 25 delta RR is defined as the difference between implied volatility for the 25 delta call and put. This quantity is related to the eponymous options structure we described in Chapter 3. For the S&P 500, you might sell a 25 delta put and buy a 25 delta call if the put skew is particularly steep.

The dynamics above are quite intuitive. Whenever there is a risk event, the risk reversal drops sharply. Volatility soars across all strikes, with OTM put volatility rising by a disproportionate amount. In other words, the put skew has become elevated. The Aussie tends to plummet during a risk event, with investors nervously paying up for downside protection. Accordingly, we see sharp moves during October 2008, March 2010 and the 2011 European crisis. We also observe that the Aussie RR is nearly always negative. Buying the Aussie is a "yield hog" play. Many investors want a steady source of income. If nothing much happens, they collect. This implies that speculators are biased toward buying the currency and periodically need to buy puts to guard against disaster.

Conversely, if we fix the time to maturity and slice across different option deltas, we get something called the implied volatility skew. The skew is more difficult to characterise than the term structure, as

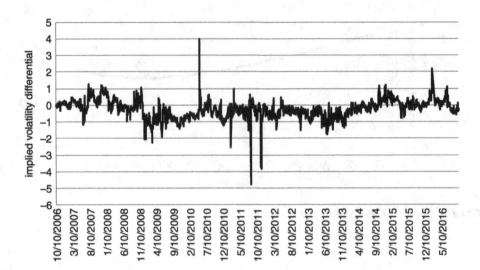

FIGURE 3.22 Unpredictable skew dynamics for US 10-year futures

its shape can vary quite dramatically across markets. Equity indices generally have a put skew, as sell-offs tend to be faster than rallies and there is more institutional demand for hedging long portfolios. It has been observed that the put skew became more prominent for equities after Black Monday in 1987. For sovereign bond markets, such as US treasuries, the situation is more complex. In Figure 3.22, we track the difference between 25 delta call and 25 delta put implied volatility over time, using 1-month US 10-year note futures options.

Ex ante, you might expect there to be a persistent call skew, as treasuries tend to rally during a crisis. As it turns out, the US 10-year skew is a bit of a chameleon, flipping from a call skew to a put skew as risk aversion levels and inflation expectations change over time. When the major risks are inflationary, a put skew might develop. Rising inflation generally leads to rising yields. You can roughly decompose the yield on a bond into one component that measures inflation expectations and another that compensates an investor for bearing duration risk. Conversely, if the market is pricing tough times ahead, a call skew might develop.

THE 1×2 RATIO SPREAD AND ITS RELATIVES

The first skew trade we will examine is the 1×2 ratio spread. This has two varieties, one for calls and one for puts. To construct a call ratio, you buy 1 call that is close to ATM and sell 2 higher strike calls against it. For a put ratio, you buy 1 close to ATM put and sell 2 lower strike calls against it. For example, you might buy 1 US 10-year call at 130 and sell 2 132 calls to build a call ratio. The maturities would generally be the same for both strikes. We will focus on put ratios for now, as they tend to be particularly interesting when analysing the equity index skew. Many traders love to buy 1×2 put ratios when the put skew becomes steep. Market convention dictates that you are long on the 1×2 when you buy the 1 to sell the 2. Suppose the S&P 500 drops sharply. Then, OTM put prices will become elevated, as hedgers enter the market. In all likelihood, the spread between OTM and ATM put implied volatility will increase. In Figure 3.23, we regress levels of the (OTM–ATM) implied volatility spread against the trailing 6-month return for the S&P 500.

A direct way to mine the skew after a sell-off is to buy 1 ATM put and sell 2 OTM puts, while maintaining delta neutrality. For example, you might buy a 50 delta put and sell 2 25 delta ones when

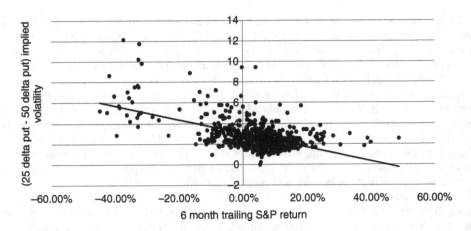

FIGURE 3.23 Dependence of S&P skew on 6-month trailing move

you initiate the ratio. The delta of the "combo" is 0, i.e. $1*0.50-2*0.25=0$. This trade has some interesting properties that are not immediately obvious. In general, you are likely to be a net payer of premium when you enter the trade, yet the structure has *positive* time decay until you get close to maturity. How can this be possible? When you buy an outright put or call, paying premium implies that you are short theta. Every day that passes without incident, some of the premium erodes from your option. Here, the situation is more complex. If nothing much happens, the 2 25 delta puts will initially burn off faster than the single 50 delta one. You are also likely to benefit from a flattening of the skew if the spot hovers around its current level. This suggests that the passage of time will work in your favour until you get close to expiration. While it is true that you will abruptly become short theta close to expiration, the standard strategy is to roll out of the trade before that point. In the graph below, we show how the payout profile for a long 1×2 ratio spread evolves as a function of time. Our example is based on Euro Stoxx 50 puts. In particular, we have bought 100 of the 50/25 delta 1×2 put ratio with about 2 months to maturity. The payout curve is graphed as a function of spot on 3 different dates. The dotted line shows the payout at initiation. The grey "sweet spot" line reflects the time we plan to roll the structure, namely 2 weeks before maturity. Here, the range of positive outcomes is relatively large. For reference, the black line gives the payout at maturity. We have not included the extreme downside in Figure 3.24. However, the structure seems well positioned for a wide range of scenarios.

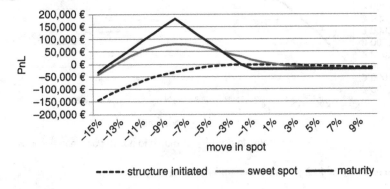

FIGURE 3.24 "Safe" zone for a long 1×2 put ratio

This is a nice-looking trade at some level, but can be fraught with danger. As we will see more acutely in the "Batman" trade section, the trouble is that 1×2 ratio spreads have large vega and extreme event risk. Your loss is essentially open-ended. The 1×2 above is *initially* delta neutral, as the individual legs cancel each other out for small moves. At first sight, it appears to make money for a wide range of moves in the underlying. However, if there is a severe sell-off, your position converges to a long position in the spot. You are potentially facing a large mark-to-market loss and your delta-adjusted position will have grown dramatically. We can see the embedded volatility risk in Figure 3.25. The graph compares the payout curve with 1 month to go in two scenarios. In the first, volatility remains constant. In the second, there is a parallel shift of 10 points in Euro Stoxx implied volatility. This is not an unusually large shock to the skew. If anything, it understates risk, as the skew is likely to steepen if volatility increases across the board. The window of profitability practically disappears and you are left waiting for a sharp drop in volatility before the next potential sell-off.

It might be argued that you can defend against large moves in the S&P 500 because a circuit breaker will be triggered if the futures drop by a large amount. In theory, you could then hedge or exit the structure. This turns out to be a feeble argument. The reality is that options market makers might pull their quotes during a crash, leaving you with no idea as to where the 1×2 should be trading. Volatility may have increased to the point where your structure is severely off side. This brings us to an idea that we will explore later in the book. Since 1×2s seem innocuous but are fraught with danger, it might be worth thinking about *shorting* them. The fact that virtually no one else wants to should serve as encouragement. No one wants to be a plumber when they are young, yet it can be quite a stable and lucrative career. Given the lack of demand, the short 1×2 might be reasonably priced after all. Indeed, in Chapter 4, we will track the performance of a specific short 1×2 ratio spread and demonstrate its effectiveness as an extreme event hedge.

Put and call ladders are similar to ratios, except that you spread the short strikes apart. Rather than buying a 3-month 1×2 2000/1900 put ratio on the S&P 500, you might buy the 3-month 2000/1925/1850 put ladder. More precisely, you would buy 1 2000 put, sell 1 1925 put and sell 1 1850 put. This structure has three distinct legs instead of two, as you buy 1 2000 put and sell 1 1925 put and 1 1850 put against it. You might buy a ladder if you want to spread your short exposure across the skew, rather than focusing on a single strike. In Figure 3.26, we sketch the payout curve of the 2000/1925/1850 put ladder at various points in time.

Conceptually, ratios and ladders are nearly identical and exposed to similar risks. They should be bought with appropriate caution.

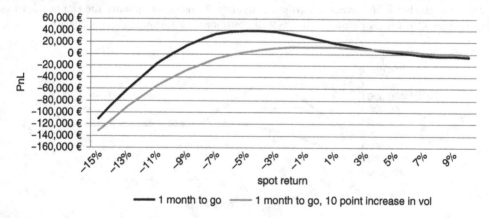

FIGURE 3.25   Sensitivity of 1×2 put ratio to a spike in volatility

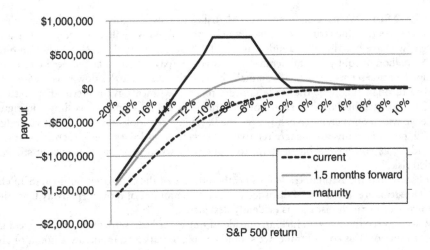

FIGURE 3.26 Put ladder payouts, expanded view

THE BATMAN TRADE

Some trades look pristine from one vantage point, yet very unsightly from another. The 2-sided ratio spread is an excellent example of such a trade. Some traders refer to it as a "Batman" structure, based on the shape of the payout at maturity.

While the Batman logo has changed over the years, Figure 3.27 resembles the original from 1940. The graph below involves buying a 100 strike straddle, while selling 2 95/105 strangles on an asset trading a 100. The structure requires an initial premium outlay and generates a positive payout for moderate up- and down moves.

Let's analyse a concrete example. Suppose we initiated the Batman on November 2 2015, focusing on December 2015 futures options. We might buy a 2095 straddle and sell 2 2015/2145 strangles as a relative value play. The straddle/strangle combination can also be thought of as a pair of 1×2 ratio spreads. We are buying 1 2095 put, selling 2 2015 puts against it, buying 1 call and selling 2 2145 calls

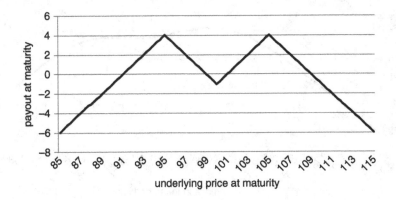

FIGURE 3.27 Payout of 2-sided ratio spread (Batman structure) at maturity

against the ATM call. We have chosen the OTM strikes to have roughly 25 delta at the point of trade entry. This ensures that the structure is initially delta neutral. As we will soon realise, the trade is sized aggressively. We have bought 100 straddles and sold 200 strangles on the S&P 500 E-mini futures contract per $1 million of equity. For moderate-sized moves, the payout on 10 December looks nice and flat. If anything, the trade seems bearish, as you make more if the index trickles down over a 5-week period.

Viewed through this lens, the trade appears to be a winner. Given intermediate returns in the [−6.50%, 4%] range, the expected return of the strategy is strongly positive as shown in Figure 3.28.

Once we widen our perspective, however, the Batman trade looks far less attractive. Judging from Figure 3.29, potential gains are meagre relative to extreme event losses. The structure is "safer" than a naked straddle, as you have a bit of space to work with when hedging. However, it still has severe open-ended risk.

We observe that the Batman trade falls neatly into one of the categories outlined in Taleb's "Anti-Fragile". The structure likes a bit of disorder, i.e. a certain amount of movement away from the middle strike. However, too much disorder is evidently destructive.

Now we can see the dangers lurking outside of our quiet little settlement. If we have a large balance sheet to support this sort of trade, we should be able to harvest a moderate amount of alpha over

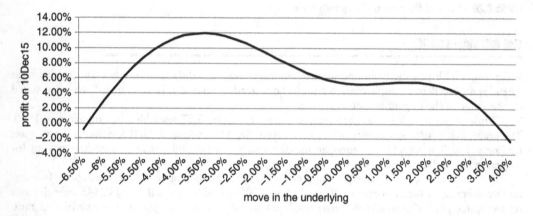

FIGURE 3.28   Profit/loss profile over a range of benign scenarios

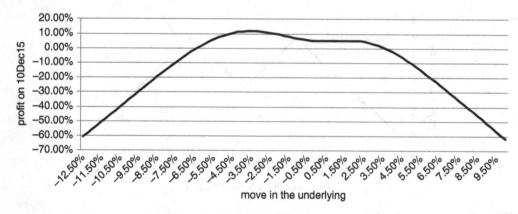

FIGURE 3.29   Batman payout: expanded view – the dark underbelly of ratio spreads

the long term. However, we can't push things too hard. The situation is analogous to covered call writing, which might be more familiar to the reader. Covered call writing is sometimes referred to as a "buy-write" strategy. This is a succinct description, as you *buy* an equity index and *write* a call against it. Writing is synonymous with selling in this context. Buy-write strategies have been served up as alpha generators for many years (Feldman, 2004). However, there is a limit as to how aggressively the call can be sold. Overwriting strategies make for fine back-tests but are not entirely safe. Suppose we own the S&P 500 (see Figure 3.30). We could, for instance, write 2% OTM calls against our long index position. This would allow us to collect some income each month, with limited participation in S&P rallies. In particular, we would capture premium from the short call and up to 2% from gains in the index. In a bear market, our open-ended risk would be the same as the index. However, we would expect to collect a relatively large amount of premium from the call, as implied volatility would be high. This would reduce a string of monthly losses by a small, but ever-increasing amount. The BXM index, which tracks the performance of this strategy, is widely quoted and has outperformed the S&P 500 on a risk-adjusted basis since inception.

What is generating alpha in the buy-write? It *must* be the short call component, as our position is otherwise identical to the benchmark. The short call has negative correlation to the index, as its delta is always less than 0. It also benefits from the tendency of implied volatility to be an overpriced relative to realised volatility, in the absence of an extreme event. This leads to a thought. If the short call is responsible for all of the alpha, why don't we trade it on a stand-alone basis? While tempting, this idea is not a particularly good one. If we start a hedge fund that sells calls willy-nilly, we no longer get the diversification effect from owning the index. We also have to sell a large number of calls to achieve a decent return. In an environment where interest rates are close to 0, there is nowhere to hide. We don't receive any return for excess cash held at our prime broker. As a consequence, we will probably have to use substantial leverage if we want to produce a decent-looking nominal return. The trouble with this idea is that, if equities ramp up, our risks will escalate. We might be forced to buy back the calls at a significant loss. By contrast, if we were simply selling calls against a well-capitalised long position, our delta-adjusted risk would actually drop after a sharp index rally. We might underperform that month, but would have the firepower to reload the strategy indefinitely.

Let's move back to the Batman. Suppose that we only bought 10 Batman structures per $1 million of equity (scaling the trade down by a factor of 10). Then, we might be able to absorb the occasional large drawdown without having to react aggressively. However, this would only allow us to target a return of 50 to 60 basis points every time we loaded the structure. As soon as we force things, adding leverage in an attempt to boost returns, we are vulnerable to short-term price moves in the underlying.

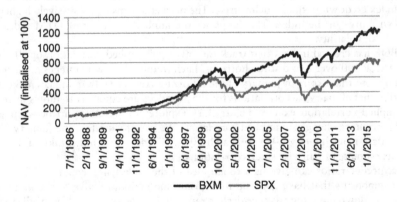

FIGURE 3.30 Performance of buy-write strategy relative to static long position in index

IMPLIED CORRELATION AND THE EQUITY INDEX SKEW

This book unashamedly has a macro bias, based on the author's background and investment philosophy. However, we try to redress the balance slightly here. We have spoken at length about equity index volatility while saying nothing about the volatility of the components of the index. This might seem strange at some fundamental level. Indices would not exist without the assets that underpin them. However, the evidence suggests that stocks move together at moments that matter the most.

A similar question arises in the analysis of fluid flows. Is a wave a collection of water molecules or an entity unto itself? Both modalities are correct and it depends on what you are trying to do. Since our goal is to hedge large-scale market moves, we can usually ignore the fact that equity indices are actually composed of individual stocks. As far as we are concerned, indices move in and of themselves. This idea also features Capital Asset Pricing Model (CAPM) and its various offshoots, where stock betas are calculated with reference to the "market". The market proxy is usually a broad-based stock index, such as the MSCI World. In CAPM, the market is thought of as an exogenous variable, even though in practice it is nothing more than a weighted collection of stocks. So when we measure a stock's beta to the market, it's not obvious that the index is the independent variable.

In severe down markets, this ambiguity should not bother us too much. Systematic risk tends to dominate a stock's overall risk during a sell-off, as nearly everything moves down together. During liquidations, index futures tend to lead individual share moves, as large institutions need to rapidly adjust their aggregate exposures. As hedgers, we are trying to take advantage of those moments of panic when investors are indiscriminate and willing to buying insurance at virtually any price. So, from the standpoint of extreme event hedging, a macro perspective is appropriate. Individual stocks are the cart and indices the horse.

There are times, however, where an analysis of the index components is useful. In this section, we introduce the idea of conditional correlation and suggest how it impacts the shape of the index implied volatility skew. While indices typically have a skew, the components usually have a smile. Implied volatility picks up more quickly to the right of the ATM strike. Large positive moves are assigned a nearly equal probability to large negative ones if a stock is trending sharply up or in advance of a corporate event, such as an earnings report.

It might seem puzzling that the index skew has a radically different shape to an average of the component skews. How can we reconcile component smiles with an index skew? The answer lies in a somewhat nebulous quantity called *conditional correlation*. Let's consider the implied volatility of a 25 delta index put. Roughly speaking, its volatility should depend on the implied volatility of each 25 delta component put, the component weights and the expected average correlation of the components *should* the index go down to the 25 delta strike. The market assigns a progressively higher correlation to large down moves in the index. This amplifies the implied volatility of OTM index puts, while muting OTM call volatility.

The CBOE has created indices that track the "average" implied correlation of 50 representative stocks in the S&P 500 over two distinct horizons. Each trading day, two vintages are listed. Each corresponds to options that expire in January of the following year. The CBOE indices make the simplifying assumption that all pairwise correlations for the 50 stocks are equal. This allows them to solve for the index implied correlation exactly. Figure 3.31 explores the relationship between weekly S&P returns and percentage changes in implied correlation. We have focused on the January 2017 vintage, using weekly data from January 2015 to March 2016. Whenever the index takes a dive, the market ratchets up its estimate of pairwise stock correlations.

Advance/decline ratios can give us a rough idea of the underlying dynamics. These measure the number of components that have gone up in a given time period, relative to the number that went down. On severe down days, the advance/decline ratio tends to be very low. Nearly all stocks go down together. More generally, in bear markets, stock specific risk pales in comparison to the broader macro picture. Cross-correlations are high among the components in an index. Conversely, strong market

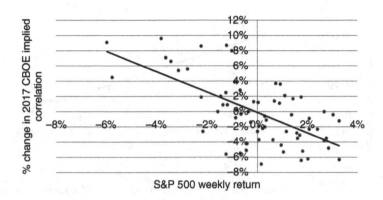

FIGURE 3.31 Implied correlation increases as the S&P declines

rallies can be driven by a fairly slim majority of stocks. In 1999, the NASDAQ composite index returned an eye popping +85.6%. Astonishingly, half of the stocks in the index had an average return of –32%, with the remainder doubling! By this rough measure, the average pairwise correlation between components was low.

We can create a skew out of a set of component smiles directly, as in Figure 3.32. The example is a bit contrived, but illustrates our point. Suppose we have an index that only contains 2 stocks. The stocks have an equal index weight and an identical implied volatility smile. We use the word "smile" rather than skew, as volatility rises in both directions away from the ATM strike.

There is a correlation skew for the two assets, as in Figure 3.33. In practice, we would have to solve for the implied correlation at each index delta, based on the implied volatility of the index and each of the components. Here, however, we assume the correlation skew is known. This simplifies the exposition.

In Figure 3.34, the market is assigning progressively higher correlations to large downside moves. We can then apply the portfolio equation at each index delta, in an effort to approximate the index skew. In particular, assume that asset 1 has implied volatility σ_1 and asset 2 has implied volatility σ_2. $w\_1 = w\_2 = 0.5$ are the index weights and ρ is the conditional correlation. Then the index implied volatility σ for a given delta satisfies $\sigma^2 = w\_1^2 * \sigma\_1^2 + w\_2^2 * \sigma\_2^2 + 2 * \rho * w\_1 * w\_2 * \sigma\_1 * \sigma\_2$.

Each of the stocks has a mild volatility smile, with a symmetric "V" shape around the ATM volatility. Yet the index skew is mildly downward sloping. If rho is large enough, the ATM cross product term

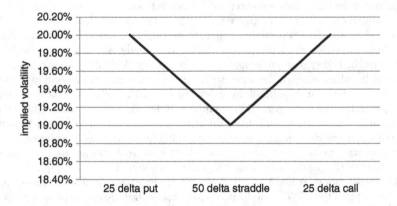

FIGURE 3.32 Symmetric "smile" for each stock in index

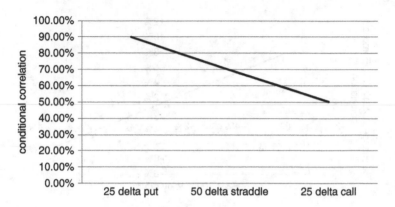

FIGURE 3.33 Hypothetical implied correlation skew

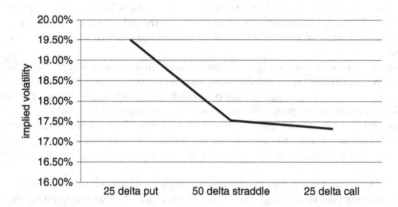

FIGURE 3.34 Component smiles mapped to index skew via implied correlation

$2 * \rho * \sigma1 * \sigma2 * w1 * w2$ in the portfolio equation above can turn a collection of component call smiles into an index skew. Note that we have used the portfolio equation in a somewhat unorthodox way. In the example, we have assumed that there are actually three different portfolio equations, applying to different segments of the skew. This is theoretically "incorrect" in the same sort of way that the implied volatility skew violates the constant volatility assumption in Black–Scholes.

If there is a skew, the market is implying that the average correlation between the components in an index should be dependent on what the index has done recently. After a severe drop, instantaneous correlations should be higher than under normal circumstances. A similar line of reasoning applies to the implied volatility skew, namely, the skew predicts that instantaneous volatility will increase if the index drops. We can test our hypothesis by using the implied correlation indices published by the CBOE (see Figure 3.35). The series goes back to January 2007. We have spliced the CBOE data together to generate a single time series, moving from the front January to the next in mid-November of the previous year. It should be clear that the market assigns high cross-correlations during index sell-offs.

Another important point relates to the madness of crowds during severe bear markets. In the upper left quadrant of the graph, there are several instances where the average implied correlation was above 100%! By definition, realised correlations can never exceed 100%, so this is a theoretical absurdity. Assuming that the CBOE's model is at least a reasonably close approximation of reality, this suggests that index options were severely and irrationally overpriced relative to component options

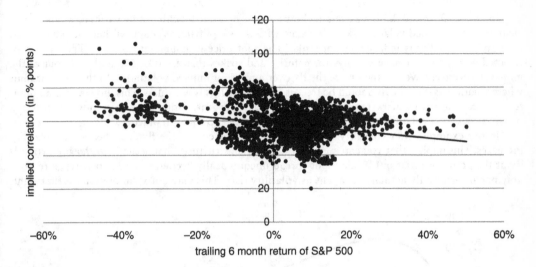

FIGURE 3.35 CBOE implied correlation skew conditioned on trailing return

during the dark days of 2008. Investors were insensitive to relationships between individual pairs of stocks. These were trivial concerns, as the struggle for survival was foremost in their minds.

FROM RATIOS TO BUTTERFLIES

Hopefully, we have discouraged the reader from buying ratio spreads *en masse* and just hoping for the best. The airplane ticket trade mentality we described in Chapter 1 has a nasty tendency to end in tears. You can certainly buy a few, relative to the size of your balance sheet. However, if you want to "back up the truck" with skew trades, non-centred butterflies are preferable. A put fly is nothing more than a 1×2 put ratio with a further OTM put appended to it. This reduces some of the theta in the straight 1×2, but eliminates exposure to an extreme event. Your carry is reduced, but you have added a margin of safety to the structure. We sketch the payout at maturity for a symmetric put butterfly in Figure 3.36. The strikes of the hypothetical fly are equidistant.

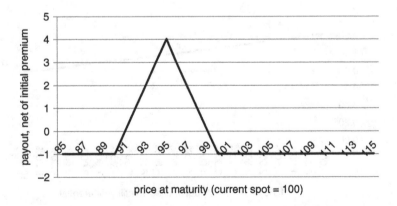

FIGURE 3.36 Hypothetical put fly, payout at maturity

In Figures 3.37 and 3.38, we examine how the cost of a fixed width put fly varies as a function of changes to the implied volatility skew. We start with the simplifying assumption that the skew is flat, i.e. implied volatility is independent of strike. The spot price is assumed to be 100. The fly is constructed with puts that have 30 days to maturity and strikes that are 0%, 5% and 10% out of the money, respectively. We can then price the fly over a range of implied volatilities. In the singular limit where volatility is 0%, the fly should be free, as each of the legs is worthless. This, however, is an uninteresting case, as frozen markets require no hedging. It's more interesting to examine how the cost of a put fly varies for a volatility range that you might actually encounter in practice.

In our example, after volatility crosses 16% or so, the cost of the fly gets cheaper as volatility increases. This implies that you can create mildly bearish structures that actually *prefer* high volatility at the point of initiation! While a put spread unequivocally becomes more expensive, a reasonably narrow-width fly actually cheapens as volatility rises. This may not seem obvious at first sight.

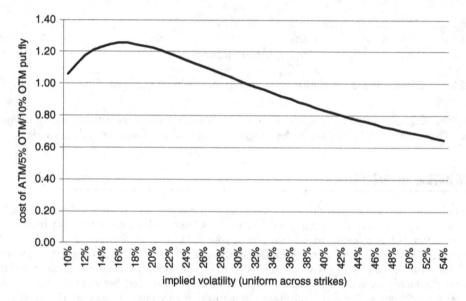

FIGURE 3.37 A defensive structure that actually cheapens when volatility increases

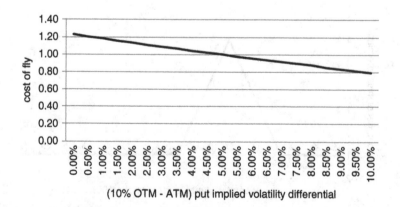

FIGURE 3.38 Impact of steepening skew on the cost of a put fly

After all, you are buying a very far OTM put to cover your risk and this put must be sensitive to the steepness of the skew. However, the far OTM put has relatively little vega. Moreover, the rate of decline in vega is quite rapid at the far OTM strike. If the middle strike is "close" enough, in volatility-adjusted terms, the fly will be net short volatility. Short vega in the middle strike more than offsets long vega at the near and far strikes. Over time, if the spot price doesn't move, vega picks up for the fixed-width fly and eventually becomes positive. Put flies are slow burning hedges. The middle strike starts to lose value and the fly transforms into a proper hedge. The nearby strike put dominates the structure. Near expiration, vega declines somewhat, as the nearby strike loses value. However, you still have a significant amount of protection. In the absence of an extreme down move, you are essentially long an ATM put. You can always unwind the bottom 2 strikes to ensure protection all the way down.

Flies also benefit (in terms of cost) from a steepening of the skew. We show this in the Figure 3.38, where the skew is assumed to depend linearly on strike. We have assumed that 5% OTM put implied volatility is always 20%. Next, we have perturbed ATM and 10% OTM put implied volatility by the same amount, though in opposite directions. For example, if the difference between 10% OTM and ATM volatility is 5%, 10% OTM, 5% OTM and ATM volatility would be 22.5%, 20% and 17.5%, respectively.

Next, we show the impact of a steepening put skew on the cost of the fixed-width fly described above. Our perturbation oversimplifies things a bit, but illustrates the main idea. Put flies cheapen as the slope of the skew becomes increasingly negative. In particular, we assume that the skew is a straight line and show the impact of varying slope on the cost of the fly. The average implied volatility across the 10%, 5% and 0% OTM put strikes remains constant as we vary the slope. In this way, we isolate the impact of steepening on the cost of the fly. We can see that the cost of the fly decreases as the skew steepens, even though the average implied volatility across all strikes has remained constant.

We demonstrate how the vega in a fixed-width put fly varies over time in Figure 3.39. The vega path is appealing in certain scenarios. Suppose you enter the fly after a sell-off. If the down move stalls for a bit, your put fly becomes progressively more defensive until 2 or 3 weeks to go. You have effectively got in on the sly and now have a fairly potent hedge in place.

At first sight, it seems as though we have stumbled upon the perfect "aftershock" hedge. The fixed-width put fly has negative deltas, bounded risk and is trading at a *discount* to its price in a calm market.

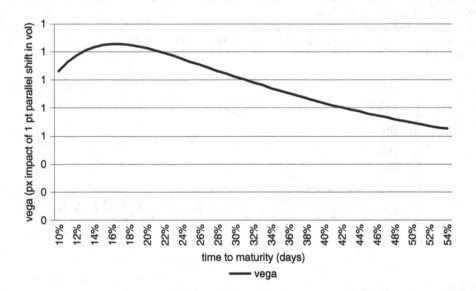

FIGURE 3.39 Vega trajectory for fixed-width put fly

The stars seem aligned. However, we should not jump to a hasty conclusion. It's worth mulling over the structure a bit more. Why should the fly cheapen as risk conditions worsen? The answer lies in the vega profile for a fly where the OTM strikes are not too far away from the spot. The 10%/5%/ATM fly is short vega at the point of entry and only switches to a long volatility profile as we get closer to expiration. This implies that we are not really hedging at all, at least initially. Another way to think about a fixed-width fly is in terms of scaling. High volatility shrinks the distance between adjacent strikes and hence reduces your zone of protection. The market can blow through a bearish-looking fly, compounding your losses. Traders generally think of the fly as a slow grinder. For put flies, you have a moderate bearish bias; for call flies, you are hoping for a modest rise. Even if your put fly starts with a mildly negative delta, you don't want a quick move down. Ideally, the underlying will hang around for a while, allowing the fly to develop into a more defensive structure. Initially, a put or call fly with equally spaced strikes is not much of a hedge. It only turns into one over time. Following this line of reasoning, you might be better served by doing nothing now and buying a put or call spread at some point in the future. However, we should not discard the fly idea too quickly, as it provides a gateway into more secure hedges. We can easily morph a fly into a something that is guaranteed to make money for all downside scenarios. If we move the 10% OTM strike a bit closer, the cost of the fly increases but the structure becomes more resilient. We have converted our put fly into something called a broken fly. The strikes are no longer symmetrically placed. The broken fly ensures that we will at least make *something* if there is a sharp drop in the underlying. For example, if we construct a 100/95/92 broken put fly on an asset trading at 100, we are guaranteed to make at least 2 points no matter how far the underlying drops. This allows us to roll the strikes down, thereby monetising a profit, if the sell-off continues.

In Figure 3.40, we sketch the payout of a broken put fly on the USO with 1 day to maturity. The USO is an exchange-traded fund, or "ETF", that tracks the performance of a rolling long position in WTI crude oil futures. We have chosen the USO as its skew is relatively steep as of this writing. In particular, the fly was loaded on 14 March 2016, with a maturity date of 17 June 2016. The put strikes were 10.5, 9 and 8, respectively. Vega was initialised close to 0, by choosing the strikes appropriately. We can see that the broken fly generates a profit near maturity for *all* down moves of sufficient size. Hence, this is a truly defensive structure, with peak payout for a drop in the –10% range. We acknowledge that, close to maturity, the structure only makes a tiny bit for a drop in excess of –20%. However, the broken fly will be worth considerably more if the drop occurs earlier on. There is still a good chance of reversion back to the –10% range.

Since the cost of a fixed width put fly decreases as a function of ATM implied volatility and skew, it should be possible to construct broken put flies whose price stays relatively constant as a function of implied volatility.

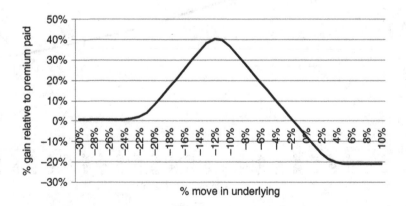

FIGURE 3.40   Payout of a broken fly on the USO close to maturity

The reader may have noticed that we have examined dollar payouts for open-ended structures such as the 1×2 ratio spread and percentage payouts for the fly. This is not inconsistent. We would prefer to calculate percentage payouts for all structures but realise this is meaningless for structures where your *receive* to enter a trade or your premium outlay is very low.

A call butterfly, or "fly", can be created in the same way. You simply cover the risk of a 1×2 call ratio with a higher strike call. While call and put flies are far more common than centred ones, most text books seem to gloss over them. This is a glaring omission, given typical flows generated by the largest hedge funds. There are several reasons why you might want to trade a *non-centred* fly. Suppose you have a directional view but fear that you might be early, with no clear idea as to when the move might take place. Things might take some time to develop. For example, if you are fundamentally bearish on the Australian dollar, you might buy a put fly on the currency. Given the AUD put skew, the initial cost of the trade would be low. However, as time passes, the delta of the structure becomes progressively more negative, hence your potential payout increases. We caution against looking at the maximum payout of a fly. This occurs at maturity, if the spot lands *exactly* at the middle strike. Some sell side researchers advertise flies with 10:1 or higher payouts, relative to initial premium paid. This is a pet peeve of ours, as the payout is effectively unreachable. In most markets, the odds of hitting the middle strike are similar to the odds of a tossed coin landing on its side. The 10:1 payout can only be realised if you hold to maturity. Most traders don't want to take so much short gamma risk, hence roll out of their flies short of maturity. 10:1 is a phantom ratio, belonging to an alternative reality rather than the markets as we know them.

Flies also offer a tactical advantage if you think you can correctly target the value of the underlying at maturity. Targeting equity indices, commodity futures and unpegged currencies within a tight range is nearly impossible. Roughly speaking, these markets evolve according to a random walk, where the range of outcomes fans out quite rapidly over time. The price at maturity can occupy quite a wide range of values with reasonable probability. However, short-term interest rate futures contracts can sometimes be targeted with precision, and flies come into their own in this context. For example, the Fed Funds rate usually moves in increments of 25 or 50 basis points when it moves at all. For reference, Fed Funds futures are based on the rate at which banks can borrow from the Federal Reserve Bank over a 30-day horizon. With short-term rates close to 0, even 25 basis points is a large discrete move in relative terms. Suppose you take the view that the Fed will hike at the next meeting and this is a non-consensus view. You can then construct an inexpensive narrow fly that pays out if the rate does go up by exactly 25 basis points. You can trade the fly as a package, reducing the bid/ask spread on each leg. Close to maturity, it's possible to make a large multiple of premium paid.

The final reason for trading call and put flies is possibly the most important. You want to take advantage of a steep implied volatility skew, with bounded risk. The put skew for equity indices (and other "risky" assets) tends to steepen after a sell-off, as investors bid up the price of OTM insurance. At some point, you might decide that the skew has become overpriced, but are not sure whether the market will continue to drop. You can then buy a put fly, on the assumption that the fly will cheapen if the skew flattens. In the diagram below, we show how the cost of a 1-month put fly varies as a function of the steepness of the put skew. In each case, we buy 1 ATM put, sell 2 puts that are 5% OTM and cover with 1 10% OTM put. By construction, the width of the fly is not dependent on volatility. You can see that, as the skew steepens, the fly becomes cheaper at a fairly rapid rate.

Our conclusion is that off-centred flies can serve a variety of purposes, combining views on direction, landing points and skew. For the sake of completeness, we briefly review the centred, or "iron", butterfly. This trade typically has no directional or skew component. It simply tries to capitalise on the view that the market has overpriced the probability of a large move up or down. Structurally, iron flies are a combination of a short straddle and a long strangle. The idea is to short a straddle, on the assumption that volatility is overpriced and then buy a strangle to bound the risk in the trade. Although the cost of the strangle *is* related to the steepness of the skew, most investors are relatively insensitive to this incremental cost. The main focus is on extracting a return from ATM implied volatility.

We sketch the payout at maturity for an iron fly in Figure 3.41. It is simply a shifted version of the put fly graph earlier in the chapter.

Assuming that the strangle strikes are not too far away and you are not too close to maturity, the payout profile will be relatively flat. This implies that you won't have to delta hedge very actively, if at all. You can always roll into a new centred fly if the underlying price shoots off in one direction or the other. In practice, however, non-centred flies are much more common than iron flies. While they look nearly identical, non-centred flies have very different characteristics from centred flies. The non-centred variety is a *skew* trade. It's a play on the relative price of at-the-money and out-of-the-money options. Note that OTM options become more expensive as the skew steepens. Non-centred flies allow you to sell the skew, with bounded risk. Conversely, when you buy an iron fly, you are effectively a buyer of the skew in an attempt to limit your downside. Risky assets such as equity indices and carry currencies typically have a put skew, while bonds vacillate between a put and call skew. Figure 3.42 tracks the difference between 1 month 25 and 50 delta put implied volatility for the S&P 500.

For US 10-year note futures, the skew tends to track the latest big move, as shown in Figure 3.43. If there is a sustained upward move in the 10 year, a call skew develops, whereas a put skew is formed during sell-offs. We will examine the chameleon 10-year skew at a later point. For now, we simply graph the differential between 25 and 50 delta put implied volatility.

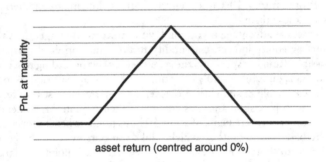

FIGURE 3.41   Iron butterfly payout at maturity

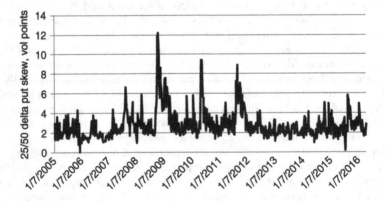

FIGURE 3.42   Historical put skew for the S&P 500

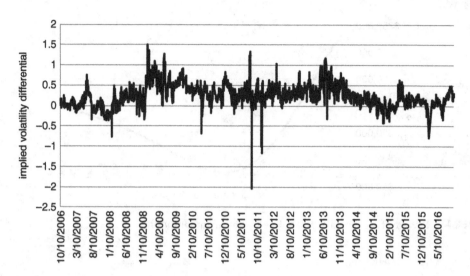

FIGURE 3.43 Historical put skew for US 10-year note futures

CALENDAR SPREADS

Can you construct a trade that is long gamma but short vega? That's a common brain teaser for junior traders. The answer is yes, and it's quite easy to do. You just need to buy a short-dated ATM option and sell a longer-dated ATM option. Conversely, if you sell a short-dated ATM put and buy a long-dated one, you will be short gamma and long vega. It doesn't matter whether you trade a call or put on either side, as gamma and vega are identical for calls and puts with the same strike. You can verify this using the put/call parity formula, which relates the price of a put and call with the same strike to the price of a forward.

Put/Call Parity Argument

Suppose a call and put with strike K and maturity T have price C(t) and P(t) at time t < T. Further assume that the discount (interest) rate r is a constant. S(t) is the spot price at t. Then $C(t) - P(t) = S(t) - K*\exp(-r(T-t))$. Equivalently, $C(t) = P(t) + S(t) - K*\exp(-r(T-t))$. Since S and $K*\exp(-r(T-t))$ don't have any gamma or vega exposure, C and P must have the same gamma and vega. Note that the delta of S is equal to 1, a constant, hence its gamma is 0.

Let's think of this in the context of hedging. When do you want gamma and when do you want vega? Both provide downside protection, though in slightly different ways. This is a crucial question that we will investigate in Chapter 4. The basic intuition is that you want to buy vega before a crisis and gamma thereafter. Once volatility has spiked, it's probably too late to focus on vega. The market may have already priced extreme event risk into the option premium.

We can understand the interaction between gamma and vega more deeply by looking at a specific calendar spread structure (see Figure 3.44). Suppose the term structure of volatility is upward-sloping. You take the view that 5-month options are overpriced relative to 1-month ones, so you sell 100 5-month 25 delta put and buy a 1-month 25 delta one. The trade has "Batman"-type characteristics.

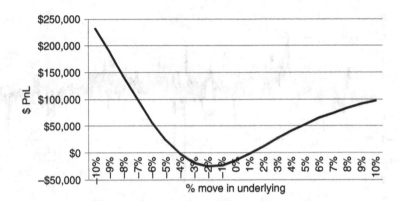

FIGURE 3.44 Payout of a calendar spread, fixed volatility assumption

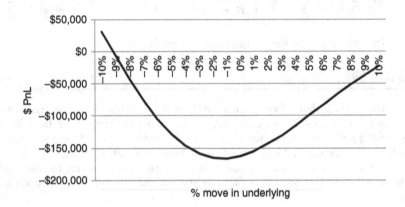

FIGURE 3.45 Profit/loss diagram for a calendar spread, assuming parallel shift in volatility

It looks sublime if volatility remains constant. You harvest a considerable premium, with an apparent margin of safety as you are selling a far-away strike.

Suppose you decide to play this by selling 6-month 25 delta puts and buying 1-month 25 delta puts. The trade looks safe as the front-month strike is much closer to the spot than the 6-month one. But this is a horribly messy structure, as you are simultaneously exposed to skew and term structure effects. There are too many moving parts. But what happens if the S&P rallies in the first 3 weeks and then plummets? While the index might not reach the 1-month 25 delta strike, volatility could rise sharply over a range of maturities. This is bad, as you would make nothing on the front month while taking a massive hit on the longer-dated put. Plotting the scenario payout under a constant volatility assumption gives no indication of the danger in this trade.

Recall that the Batman trade goes from safe to scary when we expand the view, including very large moves in the underlying in either direction. Similarly, the calendar (or "horizontal") spread shows its true colours when we increase volatility (see Figure 3.45). Near maturity, we can't expect to take the trade off at a profit simply because the 1-month strike is closer than the 6-month one. Any increase in volatility will have a large impact on the longer-dated put. The worst scenario corresponds to a repricing of volatility with no material move in the spot. This might result in a large mark-to-market loss as the 1-month put gets close to maturity.

SUMMARY

Your brokers will subscribe to Napoleon's slogan from *Animal Farm*, "four legs good, two legs bad". The larger the number of legs, the higher the commissions. In any case, there is a fairly unambiguous mapping between your view and the appropriate options structure.

- If you are bullish, buy an outright call. If you are bearish, buy a put.
- If you are *really* bullish, you can use a risk reversal as a kind of "Texas hedge". You buy a call and sell a put, doubling your exposure to the underlying, while mining the put skew.
- Conversely, if you are on the cautious side or do not want to pay up when volatility is elevated, you can buy a call spread or a put spread.
- If the put skew steepens beyond where you think it should be, buy a 1×2 put ratio or a put ladder. For equities and risky currencies, the skew will typically steepen after a sell-off, so you are banking on a return to normalcy.
- If one side of the skew seems very steep but you don't want to take open-ended risk, buy a put or call butterfly.
- Don't trade the Batman in size unless you are skilled at managing gamma risk in your portfolio. Even then, tread carefully.

Hedging the Wings

Here, we explore practical ways to hedge against ruin, at relatively low cost. We focus on the short 1×2 ratio spread on equity indices and bonds and the short VIX futures, long VIX calls strategy. Both are designed to provide powerful extreme event protection while collecting premium or benefitting from roll down. Naturally, there are subtleties to every trade that can only be learned by experience. However, this chapter should provide a rough road map to hedging equity and interest rate risk. The structures in this chapter should be broadly applicable to any market where the implied volatility skew moves in a predictable way during a crisis.

TAKING THE OTHER SIDE OF THE 1×2

Hedging the "wings" conjures up the bizarre image of the market return distribution as some sort of bird, a phoenix rising from the ashes, perhaps. Nonetheless, the phrase is widely used. The wings refer to the extremes of the distribution. If the 1×2 is so dangerous, why not turn it on its head? *Selling* the 1×2 is an inexpensive way to isolate the put skew in advance of a crisis. This is not to say that we want to short a ratio spread with the same strikes as the Batman trade in Chapter 3. For extreme event hedging, we typically target lower deltas than the Batman trade does, as we want to profit from a significant repricing of extreme event risk. The hedge is not really concerned with moderate moves in the spot. Figure 4.1 pushes our deltas further out along the put skew.

Short 1×2 Put Ratio Payout

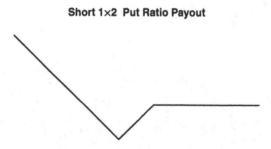

FIGURE 4.1   Payout at maturity for short put ratio strategy

We track the performance of a strategy that sells 25 delta puts and buys 10 delta puts in a 1:2 ratio. The underlying index is the S&P 500. The position is rolled weekly, to re-establish a delta-neutral position.

COMPARING THE 25 AND 10 DELTA PUTS

If we want to build hedging structures, we need to start by identifying rich and cheap points on the skew. We can then buy relatively cheap strikes, while avoiding or even selling the expensive ones. One way to approach the problem is to look for persistent anomalies. Is there excess demand for specific levels of protection? The following analysis suggests that investors have historically overpaid for insurance against moderate moves in the S&P 500, in absolute and relative terms. As we discussed in the introduction, –20% moves seem implausible until the first –10% drop. Investors also do not seem to embrace the idea that you can make a significant amount of money on an option without the spot ever reaching the strike. For a strategy where you do not hold to maturity, what is really needed is a re-pricing of risk across different strikes.

The following example is quite simple but illustrates our point. The results are summarised in Table 4.1. Using roughly 10 years of historical data (ranging from mid-2005 to mid-2015), we have compared the performance of a rolling strategy in 4-week S&P 500 puts, for a range of deltas. We have chosen 10, 25 and 40 delta puts and rolled them weekly. This covers a fairly broad and representative range of strikes and we can be reasonably assured that the implied volatility of each option will be accurate. We have made the simplifying assumption that there is always a "flex" 4 week put with the correct delta. The flex feature allows you to specify the strike and maturity date of the option you wish to trade. We have calculated the Black–Scholes price of the puts using an interpolated implied volatility and repriced them after a week, before reloading into a fresh 4-week put. The "interpolated" number is a weighted average of implied volatilities for traded options with nearby maturities and strikes. We have also normalised the returns of each put strategy so that their volatilities match. If a given week is bullish or uneventful, the price of each put will drop. The 10 delta strategy will benefit the most from a volatility spike, as the skew will have likely steepened. The weekly return is based on the change in the option price divided by the index value at the beginning of the week.

It's worth paying a bit more attention to the 25 and 10 delta puts (Figure 4.2). These are in the area where we want to hedge. Having matched their realised volatility, it's apparent that they perform similarly during the worst 1-week drops in the index.

The 10 delta puts rarely wind up in the money, but benefit from rising volatility and skew steepening if the index drops sufficiently. We re-emphasise that deep OTM puts do *not* have to land in the money to "pop" in your favour. The spot price doesn't need to drop below the strike. Their value simply needs to be re-assessed by the market. Note that we have bought roughly 1.5 times as many 10 delta puts as 25 delta puts, so that the strategies have the same historical volatility. If we track the performance of each delta over time, it becomes apparent that the volatility-adjusted 10 delta puts outperform in quiet markets, yet provide similar levels of protection during extreme market conditions (Figure 4.3).

The 25 delta put strategy requires a greater premium outlay, yet doesn't do much more for you. Superficially, it might look a bit better, as you can tell your clients that you have made *something* when the S&P drops by a small amount. That's about it. Once you conclude that the 10 delta put

TABLE 4.1 Historical performance of S&P puts with variable deltas (volatility-adjusted)

	10 delta put	25 delta put	40 delta put
average weekly return	–0.053%	–0.083%	–0.087%

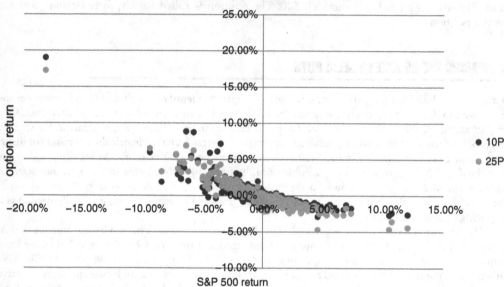

FIGURE 4.2   10 delta S&P puts offer more "bang for the buck"

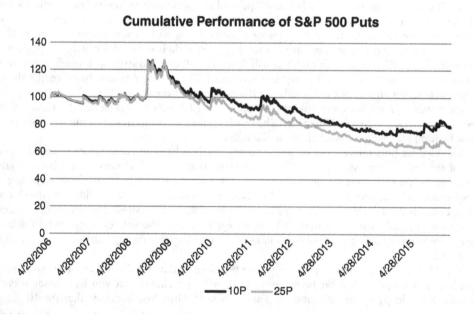

FIGURE 4.3   Relative performance of 4-week 10 and 25 delta puts, constant risk budget

is the superior hedging instrument, you can explore structures where you sell a small number of 25 delta calls and buy a larger number of 10 delta calls. When you sell the 25 delta, 10 delta put spread in a 1:1 ratio, you are trying to extract alpha from the market. Overbuying the 10 delta put converts your alpha trade into a hedge, while retaining some of the attractive features of a short put spread. In particular, it offers significant protection at low cost. In many instances, you can even *collect* to put the trade on, as we see below. Buying and selling an unequal number of puts with two different strikes generates something called a ratio spread. When you overbuy options at the wing, convention dictates that you are short the 1×2. This convention suggests that investors are more inclined to buy 1×2s than sell them. The payout at maturity for the short 1×2 looks a bit like a square root operator, so "square root hedge" is a convenient mnemonic for the strategy. The analysis that follows assumes that we have sold 1,000 1×2 put ratios on the Euro Stoxx 50 index, with roughly 40 days to maturity. Specifically, we have sold 1,000 25 delta puts and bought 2,000 10 delta puts at the point of entry. Note that Euro Stoxx 50 options have a multiplier of 10 Euros.

Before we analyse the short 1×2 in more detail, we provide further evidence that the 25 and 40 delta puts are to be avoided. In this instance, we take a regime-specific approach. The easiest way to split the data is to think of 2008 as a "high risk" scenario and everything else as normal. We'll be politically correct and emphasise that the high risk scenario is not "abnormal" in any way. It can't be expunged from the data. We can then tabulate the historical performance of the 10, 25, 40 and 50 delta puts as a percentage of premium paid.

On a historical basis, all of the above options appear to be expensive. There is no silver bullet in terms of cost. However, some may be more expensive than others. Relatively speaking, the 10 delta put offers decent value. The bar chart allows us to visualise *where* the market implied distribution might be mispriced. In particular, the market seems to be overestimating the probability of a moderate drop in the index. Very small and very large drops are priced more reasonably. Figure 4.4 serves to clarify things.

The implied distribution is relatively Gaussian, though not exactly so. To some extent, the options market does account for large downside jumps. For equity indices, the implied volatility skew predicts that left-tail events will occur somewhat more frequently than a normal distribution would suggest. However, our analysis suggests that left-tail events are still underpriced relative to "typical" down moves. Selling deep OTM options is attractive to investors who have no experience or memory of the last face-ripping sell-off and this compresses the put skew. We need to depart even further from a classic bell curve if we want to accurately represent the data.

We want to avoid buying puts or put spreads where the shaded area is above the black line, while focusing on areas where the excess demand for hedging is relatively low.

In the high risk 2008 scenario, it is fairly clear that lower delta puts generate larger returns, as a percentage of initial premium paid. High delta puts don't provide much extreme event protection,

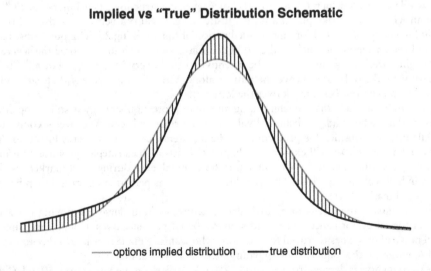

Implied vs "True" Distribution Schematic

—— options implied distribution —— true distribution

FIGURE 4.4 Our view on the differential between "true" returns and those implied by the skew

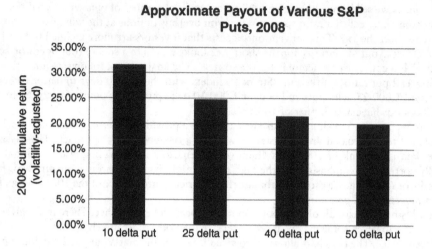

FIGURE 4.5 Punchiness of volatility-adjusted returns for various deltas, 2008

relative to their cost. Obviously, you can buy a larger number of 10 than 50 delta puts on a fixed budget. This can pay dividends in a severe crisis.

To an extent, Figure 4.5 confirms what we have been saying all along. As shown, 25 delta puts on equity indices are expensive. The same analysis applies broadly to other risky assets, such as carry currencies. There are enough instances where 25 delta puts wind up in the money that we can say this with confidence. These are the sort of puts that large institutions like to hold as protection against "realistic" downside scenarios. We can draw another conclusion from Figure 4.5. Buying 1 50 delta put and selling 2 25 delta puts (the left half of the Batman) seems reasonable as an alpha play, if you can guard against extreme event risk. However, selling the 25 delta put and buying 2 10 delta puts has even greater utility in a portfolio context. You wind up with a position that is long extreme event risk, while selling an expensive put along the skew.

Some managers have argued that a rolling OTM put strategy is a decent benchmark for an equity hedging overlay. The 25 delta put is a natural choice when constructing a benchmark, as it's "half way" between an ATM and 0 strike put in a probabilistic sense. It's also a benchmark that no one in their right mind would want to hold for an extended period of time. Rolling 25 delta puts consistently loses money and even mega-events such as the 2008 crisis are not enough to overcome the severe negative carry. Hedging overlay managers would be incentivised to do very little hedging at all if beating the benchmark were the only goal. Leave the patient alone. Virtually any strategy that isn't too invasive will beat the 25 delta put benchmark over the long term.

We can only conclude that benchmarking an equity protection strategy is still an open question. Our view is that hedging adds substantial value if it can roughly break even over a complete market cycle while offering considerable protection during a systemic crisis. This idea is linked to the notion of "crisis alpha", which we will explore in Chapter 6. Crisis alpha strategies promise a bit more than what we have described above. In particular, they try to break even during quiet markets, with outperformance in high volatility periods. This is a difficult target, as performance would then be materially positive over a market cycle.

When discussing the merits of a particular structure, we find ourselves moving back and forth between historical performance charts and scenario-based payout curves. Coming to grips with the potential range of outcomes is crucial for someone who wants to manage risk on a day-to-day basis. In Figure 4.6, we graph the "square root" payout of the short 1×2 at maturity.

The payout curve is derived from 4% and 12% OM strikes, on the Euro Stoxx 50 index. As above, we assume that we have sold 1,000 1×2 put ratios. Is it worth holding the structure to maturity? After

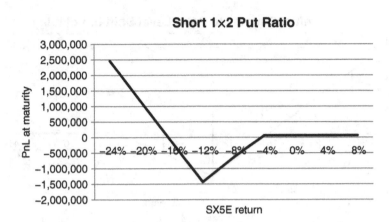

FIGURE 4.6 Profit/loss at maturity for a short 1×2 put ratio on the SX5E index

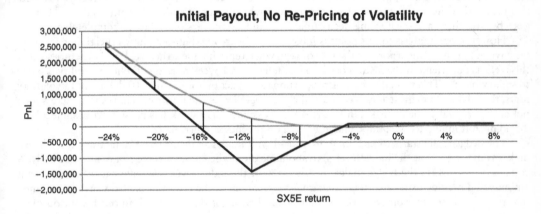

FIGURE 4.7 Payout of short 1×2, constant volatility assumption

all, the square root payout does have some attractive features. Since you are a premium collector in this example, you actually *make* money if the index has dropped less than –4% at expiration. Your profit also crosses 0 and increases linearly as the index drops more than –16%. The trouble is that the hedge actually loses a substantial amount if the index takes a hit in the –10% range, but does not collapse. Moderate down moves are the price you have to pay for the short 1×2. Naturally, you have the option of rolling the structure if it quickly goes in the money. Then you don't have to worry too much about the deep trough in the payout curve at expiration, as Figure 4.7 suggests. We cover a range of instantaneous moves from –24% to +8%, in an attempt to show how much gamma is embedded in the short 1×2. It's worth mentioning that some intriguing trades along these lines did crop up in 2008 and 2009. As equity indices collapsed, several short S&P 500 put ratios went through the market with strikes that seem incredible today. One structure revolved around selling puts with a strike around 700 and over-hedging with puts in the 500 range! In that event, the S&P 500 would have truly lived up to its name. While this sort of structure seemed bizarre at the time, it allowed the buyer to collect a premium while hedging against a Great Depression-type scenario.

At first sight, the strategy only seems to hedge *very* extreme events, at almost unreachable levels. The payout curve doesn't slingshot in your favour until the index drops about –10% intraday.

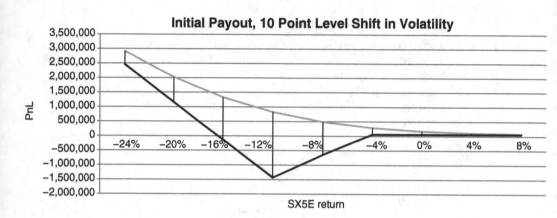

FIGURE 4.8 Payout of short 1×2, volatility "jacked up" by 20 points

At −10%, trading is likely to be halted on a broad-based index. If the curve is correctly specified, this means that there is virtually no scenario under which you can realise a profit on day 1. As time goes by, you then face severe time decay unless the index recovers or collapses completely.

However, our analysis to this point is incomplete. We are missing something crucial. In particular, we have not properly incorporated the role of vega when repricing the structure. For a structure such as this, vega is our friend. If the SX5E goes into free fall over a 1-week horizon, implied volatility is likely to spike violently. This should have a disproportionate impact on the original 10 delta put. In volatility units, the 10 and 25 delta strikes have moved closer together, so the position behaves more like a long put at the original 10 delta strike. In Figure 4.8, we assume that a week has passed. We assume a level 20-point shift in implied volatility, unconditional on the index return.

The hedge really starts to kick in at around −4%. If the SX5E drops by −8% in a week, the hedge makes roughly +2% at the index level. Extrapolating along the curve, if there is a really severe −16% collapse in the SX5E, the hedge makes nearly +5% at the index level. We have cut off a significant amount of downside using a strategy that *collects* premium at the outset. It is also worth mentioning that these estimates are conservative, as there is another factor that can work in our favour during a risk event. As volatility rises, the put skew is likely to steepen and our structure is manifestly long the skew. Implied volatility at the 10 delta strike will increase disproportionately to the 25 delta strike, giving us an extra performance kicker.

It's instructive to see how our short 1×2 put ratio would have done in the past, as proof of concept. Our mindset is changing from that of a discretionary options trader who wants to understand the range of outcomes for a specific structure to that of a systematic investor. Here, we want to check whether repeating the same strategy over and over again would have worked in the past. Our running hypothesis is that moderately OTM puts are overpriced relative to far OTM ones. This is based on excess demand for puts that cover "reasonable" scenarios. It is not immediately apparent whether options that are far OTM are rich or cheap. However, when combined with the statistically overpriced options, it is possible to construct extreme event hedges that are not too expensive. We analyse historical performance and the payoff curve for these structures. The following study is a direct consequence of our previous studies. We have tracked the performance of a short 1×2 put ratio on the S&P 500 over a 10-year window. Specifically, we sold 1 25 delta put and bought 2 10 delta puts, resetting the structure weekly. Both strikes had 4 weeks to maturity at initiation. Our results are summarised in Figure 4.9.

By "NAV", we mean the hypothetical net asset value of the strategy. The short 1×2 is a surprisingly good hedge if transacted cheaply and correctly. It more than breaks even over a 10-year historical window, while providing significant protection during volatility spikes such as the Lehman crisis and

FIGURE 4.9 Historical performance of short 1×2 on the S&P 500, gross of costs

the "flash crash" of May 2010. The average premium outlay for the short 1×2 was 6 basis points per week, or roughly 3.1% per year. This compares favourably to a rolling position in 10 delta puts, which cost roughly 26.3% per year.

The cost reduction is enormous, given that you have completely blocked out the extreme downside for the index. Yet for many money managers, hedging with short 1×2s is unpalatable. They simply do not like the idea of losing money on a hedge when the index drifts down, compounding the loss in their long portfolio. This may be the reason why short 1×2s with low delta strikes have tended to be attractively priced over time. The only players who typically like to hold short put and call ratios are market makers, as they want to hold low delta options to reduce the risk of going bankrupt.

We acknowledge that realised returns would have been a bit lower than the ones in the chart above, as we have not accounted for transaction costs. At first glance, rolling 1×2s every week *must* be expensive and might offset the benefits of the trade. Experience suggests that rolling costs can be kept at a reasonable level if we have competitive brokerage terms and restrict ourselves to the largest and most liquid markets. Our purpose here is not to "give away the shop", but rather to show how interesting and unorthodox hedging structures can be derived from long-term back-tests. One might argue that our back-test doesn't overwhelmingly favour the 10 delta put. The short 1×2 strategy returns are only mildly positive and require intermittent spikes in volatility to stay positive. If there is a long quiet spell, the strategy will not be able to overcome negative drift. Once we broaden our perspective, however, the 10 delta put becomes more compelling. We tabulate the average cost of 10, 25, 40 and 50 delta puts with 1 month to maturity below. Our reference index is the S&P 500, as before. Note that we have overbought the 10, 25 and 40 delta puts so that their in-sample volatility matches the 50 delta put.

The volatility-adjusted 10 delta puts are the cheapest. But do they offer comparable protection, given their cost? Using 2008 as a reference, the answer is yes, according to the following chart.

In a low-volatility regime, the short 1×2 put ratio acts as a particularly powerful hedge. It offers excellent protection against a "flash crash", such as the one witnessed in May 2010. It benefits from acceleration in the spot toward the 10 delta strike as well as dramatic steepening in the put skew. The short 1×2 is also an efficient way to protect against a geopolitical event that may occur in an otherwise benign market. This is where most of the extreme convexity on the rightside of the graph is observable. Figure 4.10 only considers cases where the VIX was below 20 before the structure was initiated.

It is reasonable to ask why the volatility-adjusted short 1×2 offers more bite in relatively quiet market regimes. This is largely a function of the distance between the 25 and 10 delta strikes. When volatility is low, the two strikes are bunched close together. Any lurch down in the index will bring the 10 delta put in play, immediately creating a geared downside payout on the index. We measure the sensitivity of the strike distance to ATM volatility in Figure 4.11.

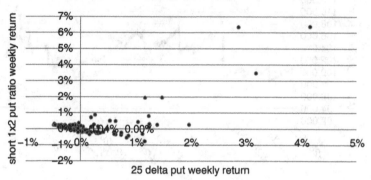

FIGURE 4.10   Convex payout of short 1×2 when initiated in low volatility regime

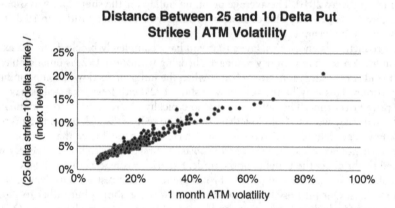

FIGURE 4.11   Distance between strikes in 1×2 increases in tandem with ATM volatility

The strike distance is almost linearly dependent on ATM volatility. However, skew effects create some dispersion around the line of best fit. If the skew is a bit steeper than expected for a given level of ATM implied volatility, the 25/10 distance will be a bit larger than usual.

It's worth checking that the short 1×2 put ratio works for other equity indices as well as shown in Figure 4.12. Here, we track historical performance for the FTSE 100 index.

The pattern of returns is roughly the same as for the S&P 500. At this level of gearing, the strategy makes a tiny amount. This is a good result in a portfolio context, as the strategy NAV shoots up during risk events. Recall that a strategy can have a *negative* expected return yet receive a large allocation in a mean-variance. The beauty of the trade, though, is that a few down weeks are likely to cause a massive shift in the skew. Traders often equate changes in the skew to movements in an oil tanker. It might take a while for the market to react to changes in risk aversion, but once the tanker turns around, there's no stopping it. We will see later in this chapter that risk regimes tend to be persistent over the short term and strongly mean-reverting over longer horizons. The short 1×2 put ratio is something that has been in our arsenal for quite some time. It worked particularly well during the Flash Crash of May 2010, when the put skew steepened dramatically for equity indices and risky currencies.

Our short 1×2 put ratio provides a nice convex payout on the index. It has straddle-type properties. In Figure 4.13, we conduct a non-linear regression of weekly returns for the short 1×2 against

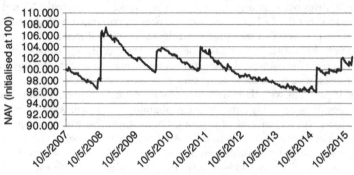

FIGURE 4.12 Short put ratio returns for the FTSE 100, gross of costs

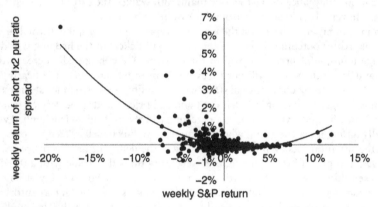

FIGURE 4.18 Convex payout of short 1×2 put ratio spread

weekly S&P index returns. The payout is "non-linear", as it profits disproportionately from large index moves in either direction. We can see that a quadratic function fits the scatter plot of historical returns reasonably well. This allows us to visualise how the short 1×2 benefits from sharp drops, with no ill effects if the index rises.

At some point, you can get more offensive with the short ratio spread. Suppose, for example, that the S&P 500 has been in an extended sell-off. You believe that a recovery is likely, but realise that the possibility of a complete collapse can't be completely eliminated. The index isn't going to stick in place forever. You can lighten up on the 1×2 by selling a 1×1.5 ratio spread or a straightforward put spread. The 1×1.5 should break even if the index blows through the bottom strike, while generating modest income if the market rallies. If we had to choose *one* strategy to cover most situations where equity hedging is required, it would probably be the short 1×2 ratio spread. The spread doesn't require perfect timing and can be traded in size. The cost of the structure doesn't go up very much if there is a parallel shift in volatility, which gives us more time to place the trade. However, the distance between the 25 and 10 delta strikes *does* increase in tandem with volatility. This implies that, if the index drifts down, you will start to fall into a deep well near the 25 strike and may be forced to manage the position aggressively. Managing a position that resembles a long straddle in a high volatility environment can require great skill. The other difficulty with the hedge relates to re-investment risk. Once the S&P

put skew expands beyond a certain point, the short 1×2 becomes prohibitively expensive. This means that 2 units of the 10 delta put start increasing in price at a much faster rate than 1 unit of the 25 delta put. If you manage to short the 1×2 in *advance* of steepening, you profit from relative repricing of the 10 delta put. All is well, as you can take profits on the ratio and roll into a different type of hedge as necessary. But it might be too late to initiate a new 1×2, without having to pay up for the privilege. Once the skew has moved far enough, the structure is too expensive to consider buying.

Some practitioners, who focus on hedging very extreme events, might argue that a 10 delta put is not *that* far away. It pays out well short of a Black Swan event. Suppose we apply the rule of thumb that the delta of an option is roughly equal to the probability that it will wind up in the money. Then, a 10 delta option has a 10% chance of paying out. On average, you will wind up exercising a static long position more than once a year. This is quite often relative to the perceived frequency of extreme events. We can analyse things from a different angle. The 10 delta strike is only 1.6 or 1.7 standard deviations below the index. This would be a mere drop in the bucket from the standpoint of former Goldman Sachs CFO David Viniar, who claims to have witnessed several 25 standard deviation moves in August 2007. This was in reference to the roughly –27% drawdown suffered by the Goldman Sachs Alpha fund from January to August 2007. The absurdity of such a comment was duly observed by several statisticians, including Dowd (2008). Even a 5 standard deviation move would only have been expected to occur on 1 day since the last woolly mammoth walked the earth (i.e. roughly 10,000 years ago). Mammoths haven't been stomping around for quite some time.

If 10 delta puts offer value, based on the way they reprice during a spike in volatility, 1 delta puts should have even greater potential. These are the Powerball tickets of the hedging world. An investor can make a huge multiple of premium paid in the extreme. We conceptually agree with the idea of buying *very* low delta options, but will not focus on them in our analysis. It is nearly impossible to assess their effectiveness using conventional statistics. Modelling skew dynamics at the extreme tails of the distribution is fraught with danger. 1 delta put and call prices need to be derived from bid and ask spreads that are typically quite wide apart, as a percentage of the mid-price. The implied volatility skew will be materially different depending on whether you want to buy or sell a "teeny" option. As we move below 1 delta, the situation gets even muddier. The lower the delta, the greater the probability that an option will have a bid price of 0. There might be several options that trade with a 0 bid and a single tick ask, yet these options can't all be worth the same amount. For buy-side investors such as hedge funds, the 1 delta strategy requires a bit of faith. Market makers are reluctant to absorb a large short position in tiny delta options, as this dramatically increases their business risk. This implies that, under most circumstances, you will be forced to pay up for the "teenies". Back-testing must be performed with great discretion. We are not suggesting that buying large quantities of low delta options is a bad strategy in practice, quite the contrary. If you can truncate the very extreme sell-offs that occur once every 5 to 10 years, your portfolio should compound at a significantly higher rate. However, validating such a strategy is exceedingly difficult and may require a cross-sectional study of extremely rare events.

HEDGING SOVEREIGN BOND RISK

In Chapter 3, we described how to take advantage of large discrepancies between implied and realised volatility. If implied was overpriced, we could sell an option, delta-hedge it and try to lock in the (implied–realised) spread. It follows that the (implied–historical) volatility spread can be used as a valuation metric, a barometer of "fair value". We can use it as a mechanism for deciding whether options on a given asset are rich or cheap. Some long/short strategies rank individual companies according to this measure. In particular, they sell options on companies where the differential is high and buy options where the reverse is true. Note that we do not know what realised volatility will be over the life of the option and need a rough proxy. The simplest choice is to use some measure of historical volatility as a guide. So long as subsequent realised volatility is not too different from our backward-looking measure, our buy and sell signals should have some information content. Another approach is to forecast volatility, using GARCH or perhaps a homegrown model. However, accurate forecasting is

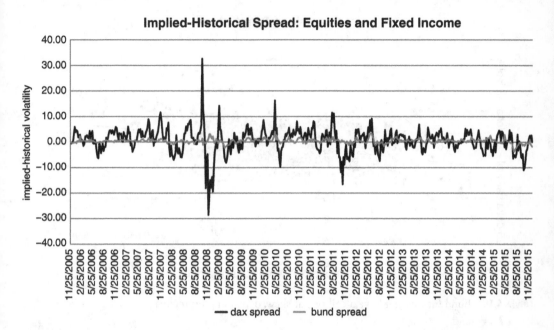

FIGURE 4.14   Spread between implied and historical volatility for Bund futures and the DAX

not easy with any model, so we stick with a historical measure for the time being. Let's simplify things by focusing on ATM options. We can then say that, if the spread between ATM implied volatility and historical volatility is persistently small, then ATM options are reasonably fairly priced. By contrast, if the spread is "all over the shop", it may be that ATM options are subject to cycles of fear and greed beyond what is reflected by spot moves. In Figure 4.14, we can see that ATM Bund options are much more competitively priced than DAX (German equity index) options. We have compared 30-day trailing volatility with implied volatility for a front month ATM put that rolls with 20 days to maturity.

We acknowledge that, on average, DAX ATM implied volatility is 3 or 4 times higher than Bund implied volatility. This accounts for some of the increased volatility in the (implied–historical) spread. However, the largest DAX (implied–historical) differentials are roughly 10 times higher than the largest Bund ones. This implies that DAX volatility is relatively unstable and that DAX options are more likely to be wildly mispriced from time to time. The same basic relationship holds for the S&P 500 *vis à vis* the US 10-year Treasury note. Volatility trading opportunities are relatively abundant in US equity indices.

This brings us to the next question. How does the short 1×2 apply to bond futures? We have a squirrely skew to deal with. OTM puts are not always in demand when volatility picks up. After persistent rallies, a call skew tends to emerge. Severe enough sell-offs appear to trigger a put skew, although we have relatively few instances to work with. Figure 4.15 explores the connection between the degree of trending for Bund futures and the shape of the Bund skew. The x-axis tracks the futures price relative to its 100 day moving average. It is a simple trend indicator. The y-axis takes the difference between implied volatility for a 1-month 25 delta call and put, respectively. We can see that, since 2010, there has been a strong positive correlation between the recent trend and the shape of the put skew. The R^2 of the regression is roughly 0.10. Whenever Bunds have rallied, a call skew has developed. Whenever they have sold off, puts have gone bid. This is significant, as it suggests that investors are unsure as to whether extreme risks lie to the upside or downside.

Testing the performance of options structures on bonds is relatively tricky, as they have been in a relentless bull market for decades. This implies that put-buying strategies wouldn't have worked, no matter how clever they might have been. So where can we find enough choppiness to test our theories? We need at least one instance of a major sell-off. Otherwise, we would be inclined to choose a hedge that has

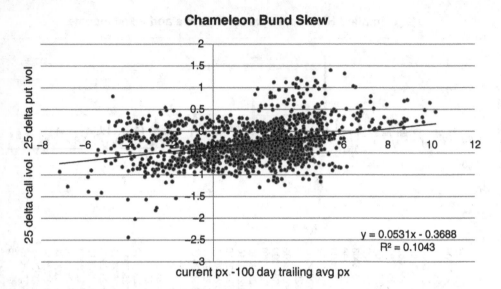

FIGURE 4.15 Bund futures can have a call or put skew, depending on regime

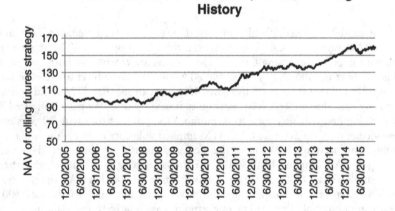

FIGURE 4.16 A relatively long data set with few incidences of sell-offs

relatively low time decay, irrespective of how it might perform during a blow out in yields. "Tail risk" managers are perversely incentivised to do nothing most of the time. So long as nothing too bad happens, they appear to have minimal time decay. Bund futures, while persistently rising, offer the occasional sell off that is useful (though by no means definitive) for our purposes. In Figure 4.16, we graph the performance of a rolling front month strategy in Bund futures, from December 2005 to December 2015. We have chosen our lookback window based on the availability of accurate implied volatility data.

There is one sharp sell-off in the data, from April through June 2015. The reader might observe that there was also a decline in Bund futures in the second half of 2010. However, this move was too shallow for a short-term put buying strategy to capitalise on. The one severe drawdown might not seem like much, but it's about all we have to work with. We magnify the chart for 2015 in Figure 4.17, to emphasise the magnitude and severity of the sell-off.

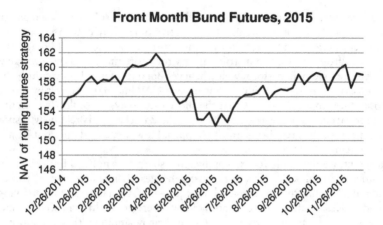

FIGURE 4.17 Close up of price dynamics in 2015

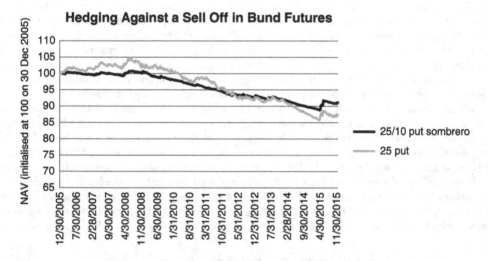

FIGURE 4.18 Relative performance of naked put and "sombrero" for German Bund futures

We want to find an efficient structure that would have made a significant amount during the 2015 sell-off. By "efficient", we mean a structure that doesn't have too much time decay or exposure to the futures roll. A naked Bund futures put would not be very efficient by this standard. If nothing much happened on a given day, your put would lose value based on a combination of theta and forward drift. As we shall see later, bond futures trade in backwardation whenever the yield curve is upward sloping. This pushes the futures away from a downside put strike if the spot (i.e. the cheapest-to-deliver bond) doesn't move.

The consequence here is that you need to overcome term structure effects as well as time decay when buying puts or shorting futures. Our solution is to resurrect the short 1×2 ratio spread as a cost-effective extreme event hedge. If we sell 1 25 delta put and buy 2 10 delta puts against it, our exposure to futures drift will be reduced. We still have to accept that the 10 delta put will burn off quickly at the outset, but are no longer taking the Bund futures head on. In Figure 4.18, we compare the performance of roughly 2 short 1×2 put ratios against 1 long 25 delta put. We have taken some liberties by adjusting leverage on the short 1×2 to match the performance of the long put during the

2015 sell-off. In practice, doubling the size of the short put ratio is sufficient. We have simply matched the performance during a sell-off to highlight the relative time decay in the two structures.

Neither strategy performs all that well over the entire period. How could they? The futures have been rabbiting away from downside put strikes nearly the entire time. What we *can* say with some certainty is that both strategies will perform well whenever Bund futures sell-off viciously. If the frequency of 2015-style moves increases, the steady decline in each NAV line may be offset by intermittent spikes. For our purposes, the important point is that the short 1×2 decays more slowly than the outright put, even adjusting for variations in leverage. To be sure, the 25 delta put is relatively responsive to small sell offs. In other words, the grey line is much choppier. However, this should not be a concern if you are focused on extreme event protection.

Up to this point, we have only focused on hedging sharp falls in bond futures. For equity indices, it is usually sufficient to think in terms of downside hedges. Risk is asymmetric, based on aggregate investor positioning. Most institutions have a long equity bias, with large static portfolios of individual stocks, ETFs and indices. Real money accounts, held by sovereign wealth funds, endowments and insurance companies tend to be particularly static. Given their positioning, they are more worried about equity declines rather than "melt ups". Institutions with interest rate exposure, however, have a wider range of concerns. Bond risk can be two-sided. Bond managers often worry about rising rates, which cause bond prices to fall. Conversely, pension funds worry about a sharp drop in rates. This increases the present value of their liabilities and can render them technically insolvent from an actuarial standpoint. Therefore, it is important to analyse upside call as well as downside put structures. Bonds usually rally during deflationary scares or "flight to quality" events. In a flight to quality scenario, investors are unloading stocks while seeking safe lower duration assets. Cash is king, but investors also have a tendency to stockpile longer duration Treasuries in preparation for an extended downturn. Solvency requirements for banks incentivise the purchase of diversifying assets such as bonds.

We can easily run into difficulty when comparing the historical performance of various upside Bund structures. What was a problem while testing defensive put spreads is still a problem, though in the opposite sense. Nearly every upside trade seems to work in an environment where bonds have been rising and the term structure of futures has been in backwardation. We serve up the 50/25 call spread on the Bund as an example (Figure 4.19). This has been implemented using front month futures options.

From 2012 on, the graph in Figure 4.19 goes up in a straight line. It's the backtester's dream and the market's bait. Isn't that why people go to quantitative investment conferences, to see hypothetical profits that move inexorably upward? Such steady performance is uncommon for a *long* options strategy, which has negative time decay by construction. Here, theta in the call spread is offset by a

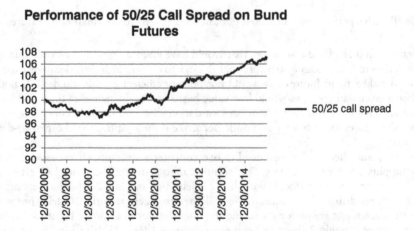

FIGURE 4.19   Historical performance of a call spread buying strategy on German Bund futures

combination of roll down and persistently declining yields. If yields do start to rise and the curve inverts, we should not automatically assume that a call spread will offer protection during a risk event. So long as the term structure is in backwardation, however, the "bleed" of a 50 delta call will be relatively low. You don't lose much from day to day if nothing much happens.

In a steep yield curve environment, call spreads on bond futures do turn out to be elegant hedges, as time decay is partially offset by roll down. We recommend them as "grey swan" hedges against moderate flight to quality events.

SELLING PUT RATIO SPREADS ON THE S&P 500

It's tricky to say whether very low delta puts are rich or cheap, as we don't and in fact can't know the true probability of extreme events. Our research suggests, however, that 1-month 25 delta puts are expensive with a high degree of confidence. So our core square root hedge relies upon selling 25 delta puts and *overbuying* 10 delta puts, i.e. we sell a put ratio spread. This structure sells something that is almost certainly expensive to finance something that has a large potential payout. Many hedge funds tend to think in terms of buying the ratio, but presumably focus on options that are closer to at-the-money. Specifically, our analysis revolves around selling a 1×2.5 ratio of 25 and 10 delta puts, so that our initial position is delta-neutral.

THE HYPOTHETICAL IMPLIED DISTRIBUTION

You can get fancy with the implied volatility surface and try to specify the implied *distribution* of an asset, based on a matrix of option prices. If correct, this distribution would generate the market implied probability of a move of any given size, over any horizon. It would completely characterise the market's collective view on the asset. This idea has been presented by several authors, notably Derman (1999). One way to think of the problem is in the context of binary options. Binaries pay out a fixed amount if the option winds up in-the-money at maturity. Otherwise, they pay nothing. Suppose we have a binary that pays 1 if S(T) lands in the range [S* − delta, S* + delta] and 0 otherwise. Assuming that the drift is 0, the market price of a binary should be equal to the probability of landing between (S* − delta) and (S* + delta) at maturity. In roulette, we face the same sort of payout. We collect a predefined number of chips if the ball lands in the pocket we have chosen and lose our initial bid otherwise. This implies that, if you had a very fine partitioning of strikes, it would be possible to approximate a binary option by a call or put spread whose strikes were very close together. We can label the distance between adjacent strikes as delta_K.

Now we know that, if interest rates are 0, the price of a call spread whose strikes are infinitesimally apart can be approximated by 0.5*delta_K * P(S is between K and delta_K at maturity). Solving for P, we can build a histogram of implied probabilities for the asset. We can then construct relative-value trades by targeting areas where there is a large discrepancy between the options-implied histogram and one constructed from historical data. It's possible to use smoothing techniques to build a continuous implied distribution that is consistent with all prices along the option chain. This circumvents the fact that listed strikes are usually a discrete distance apart.

An accurate implied distribution can give the sell-side a small advantage. In theory, "flow" traders can exploit small irregularities on the implied volatility surface, wherever they might occur. The idea would be to compare the implied distribution of an asset with its historical distribution. A big gap between the two in some regions might suggest a trading opportunity. Note that a flow trader is someone who executes orders on behalf of clients. Flow traders can see order imbalances build up, causing distortions in the skew, and can transact at practically no cost. For buy-side participants, such as asset managers, the implied distribution approach is less useful. Market impact and commissions tend to offset any profits that can be extracted from a minute statistical mispricing across options.

As hedgers, we are more concerned with the dynamics of the skew than with a notion of fair value. We want to buy things that will jump in value if there is a risk event, without paying too much for them today. When we back-test options with different deltas, we can check which ones were liveliest during sell-offs. These are the options we want to hold in advance of a sell-off.

You can see that the 10-year trailing performance of the S&P 500, hedged with a short ratio spread, roughly matches that of the index. Buying a 25 or 50 delta put outright is a significant return drag. However, the volatility of the hedged index is 15.41%, compared with 18.25% for the unhedged index. On a risk-adjusted basis, the ratio spread considerably improves a long-only position.

Relative performance in the second half of 2008 might not be clear from the graph. We magnify performance from July to December 2008 below.

OUR FINDINGS SO FAR

Here is a brief synopsis of what we have found. We have focused on options with a month or so to maturity. We have learned that

- risky assets such as equity indices and high yielding currencies have a persistent put skew
- the put skew tends to steepen after volatility picks up
- 25 delta puts seem to be historically overpriced, relative to far out-of-the-money options.

This implies that we want to buy puts further down the skew for low cost protection. Our basic mechanism for taking profits is to roll the strike down if the market shoots toward our long option strikes.

BACK-TESTS: A CAUTIONARY NOTE

In the last section, we argued that whenever you buy an option, you're buying a trading strategy. Your exposure dynamically scales up and down as the underlying asset moves. Given that an option is equivalent to a trading strategy, we back-tested 4-week puts with different deltas to see which ones would have performed best over time. It turns out that, while the 25 delta S&P put looks particularly bad, none of the puts do all that well over time.

So maybe the right idea is to just short puts? Conceptually, this is not a bad idea, as options tend to be overpriced in the absence of an extreme event. On a historical basis, selling puts also looks promising. In Figure 4.20, we short 25 and 50 delta 1-month puts, resetting once a week. The hedging structure from before has been turned on its head. Both the short 25 and 50 delta strategies generate stronger risk-adjusted returns than a static long position in the index. Whereas the S&P 500 only recovers its 2007 peak in 2013, the short put strategies are onside by 2011.

It seems as though you can achieve an even better return stream by gearing the short 25 put strategy than by selling a single unit of the 50 delta put. We can extrapolate and think of selling 5 10 delta puts rather than 1 50 delta put. However, this sort of reasoning is severely flawed. It invites margin calls and extreme event risk. Gambler's ruin is embedded in this approach, as you are implicitly adding to a losing position on the way down.

When you find a losing strategy, shorting it does not automatically translate to a winning one. At the very least, you need to *scale* the short strategy correctly. Let's ignore costs for a moment. It's mathematically correct that if you invert a strategy whose average return is negative, the inverted strategy will have a positive average return. However, if the drawdowns are large enough, its *compounded* return can be negative. A simple example illustrates this point. Imagine a strategy that loses –50% and makes +40% every other month. The returns follow the sequence {–50%, +40%, –50%, +40%, . . .} and your portfolio descends quickly to 0 with an average monthly return of –5%. If you short this strategy, your return sequence should be an alternating sequence of +50% and –40%. Although the average return is now positive, this sequence also goes to 0, as Figure 4.21 suggests.

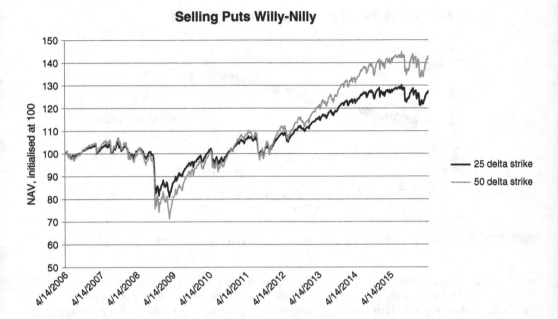

FIGURE 4.20 Superficially, selling puts looks like a fine idea

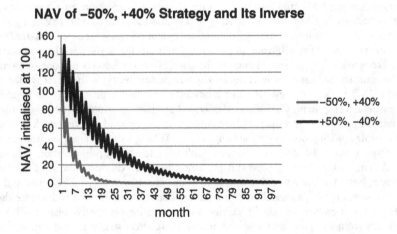

FIGURE 4.21 A strategy and its inverse can both converge to 0 if gearing is too high

Assuming that the {+50%, −40%} *ad nauseum* sequence is guaranteed, we accept that it is possible to transform it into a winning strategy by reducing leverage. In particular, if you hold 50% cash and invest the remainder in the {+50%, −40%} strategy, your NAV will no longer decay to 0. For any cash balance above 50%, the strategy will be profitable. In Figure 4.22, we assume that 75% of equity is held in cash.

For simplicity, we have assumed that the cash return is 0%. Performance is strong, but the essential point is that there is a limit to how much we can do. Readers can delve more deeply into optimal leverage ratios using generalisations of Kelly's Criterion, as in Brown (2011).

Let's drift back to the 1×2 back-test. Some readers might be sceptical of our analysis of the short put ratio. We can't be certain that our back-test is representative of the true return of the hedging

FIGURE 4.22 Inverting a losing strategy does work after dialing down leverage (gross of costs)

strategy. Following do Prado (2013), it might be argued that our verdict suffers from selection bias. The do Prado paper introduces the notion of a "deflated" Sharpe ratio to account for over-fitting and selection bias. Maybe we should refer to it as a manifesto, as it is attempting to overhaul the way systematic strategies are marketed. To a large extent, this is a healthy development. The more configurations you test before arriving at a model, the more you need to penalise the performance of the model back-test. One configuration might be testing a short 1×2 ratio. Another might be testing a short 1×3 ratio, and so on. You also have some flexibility in choosing strikes and the time to maturity of a given structure.

Note that the Sharpe ratio of a strategy is equal to (average strategy return − risk-free rate) / (standard deviation of strategy). After all, from all possible combinations of puts, we have chosen a structure that happened to work fairly well as a hedge in the past. Here, the issue is not one of having over-fit a model. On the contrary, we have not introduced any free parameters into the strategy. But are we guilty of cherry-picking? We take the view that our analysis of the 1×2 is an exercise in hypothesis testing rather than model development. Our initial idea was that many institutions are biased toward hedges that are likely to wind up in the money if there is a sell-off. They tend to over-pay for options that are close to ATM, while ignoring options at the wing. These OTM options can reprice dramatically without ever having intrinsic value. In other words, they don't have to wind up in the money to be profitable. The short 1×2 hedge attempts to exploit this persistent bias. We do not claim that our hedge is optimal in any sense, but have back-tested it simply to show proof of concept. Do Prado and others have argued that it is worth testing a model against simulated data, in an attempt to increase the size of the sample set. However, there are serious difficulties with simulating alternative histories. If you resample individual returns from the past, you lose the precise correlation structure that can lead to trends or other structural tendencies in the data. Even if you resample blocks of data, in an attempt to preserve the relationship between consecutive returns, you might miss the positive feedback loops that drive really large moves. Do Prado is undoubtedly correct when he claims that most back-tests are based on limited amounts of time-varying data. However, the construction of alternative histories is fraught with danger.

We remark that there are glaring examples of selection bias to be found in the investment community. The "stocks for the long run" crowd, referenced in the introduction, claim that equities will nearly always outperform inflation over horizons of 10 years or more. These studies are based on US equity market returns, given the abundance of historical data in the US. This is a reasonable argument, except for one thing. The US is the strongest performing major market over the past 100 years. Success stories are always well documented, in words and numbers. "History is written by the winners", as the saying goes. Going all the way back to 1900, the five largest capital markets were the US, UK, Germany/Austria, France and Russia. If you had applied modern thinking and allocated to each economy, you would have been wiped out in two of them. You can't restrict yourself to data from the survivors when calculating a risk premium, as *ex ante* you don't know who they will be.

Before we get carried away with this argument, it is worth pointing out that tabulating data is not necessarily a bad thing. As long as you size positions cautiously, there is no reason to discard information that you have observed. Suppose you were invited to two dinner parties. One of the parties was hosted by someone you had met a few times and gotten along well with. Conversely, you had only spoken briefly with the other host and left with a bitter taste in your mouth. You don't have much to go by, but if you *had* to make a choice, the first party is obviously preferable. While mean reversion effects need to be taken into account with financial data, the basic principle is the same. There is every reason to use the available data, so long as you do not place too much confidence in what you have found.

A SHORT DIGRESSION: DELTA-NEUTRAL OR COMFORTABLY BALANCED?

You can construct positions that are delta-neutral but highly imbalanced. If you short a large number of straddles that expire tomorrow, you are *initially* delta-neutral, but your position is hanging on a knife edge. The profit from the trade will be highly dependent on your ability to delta-hedge at the right moments. Any trade that induces severe physical symptoms is by definition imbalanced. For winning trades, it is tempting to think, if only the position had been larger. But if you *had* done more, you would have needed to tighten your risk controls to the point where you might not have made any more money. This is a reasonable, if heuristic, argument for sizing open-ended strategies conservatively. We are doing this for your health.

THE 665 PUT

We conduct a small and hopefully amusing *Gedanken* experiment in this section. However, the experiment does have important consequences. Namely, it shows how margin constraints need to be factored into any strategy that incorporates leverage. The year is 2005 and you have a vision. You divine that, however tumultuous markets may become, the S&P will never close below 665. 665 is a rock solid floor. Note that we did not choose 666 as the floor because S&P index option strikes appear in multiples of 5. Nostradamus will not factor in our experiment. The rest of the future is not revealed to you. As you sit mulling things over, you realise that you have a strategy that *can't* lose. All you need to do is sell a 1-month 665 put, wait until expiration, and repeat. If your vision is true, the put will always expire worthless. The worst-case scenario is that you won't collect much premium when the S&P is well above the strike. To an extent, you can adjust for this by maintaining a relatively constant margin-to-equity ratio over time. In master of the universe mode, you aggressively trade according to the following rule in your brokerage account.

- Once a quarter, you decide how many 3-month 665 puts you are going to sell, by setting your margin to equity ratio at 50%. In other words, you have 50% cash to support your positions.
- At the end of the quarter, you cash out any gains from the quarter. These are no longer usable as margin as they have been deployed elsewhere.
- You then sell the appropriate number of 665 puts, with end-of-quarter expiration. This assures that no rebalancing will take place along the way.

Now, let's wind the clock forward to 2015. The thought experiment is about to take a dramatic turn. You sit comfortably in a plush chair bought with the gains you expect to realise now. After all, expectation is a form of wealth. However, your deputy is nowhere to be found. Nonetheless, it is time to review your statements and congratulate yourself on the cumulative result. Your vision was correct, as the intraday low for the S&P was 666 on March 6, 2009. All must be well. As it turns out, there are no statements from 2010 to 2014. You defaulted, in the sense that your account was *liquidated* by the broker in March 2009. How can this be? You had a sure-fire trading strategy. You gave yourself some

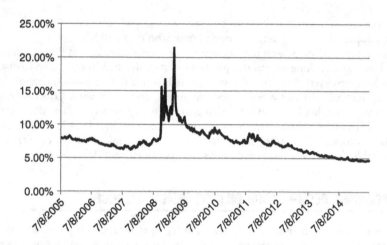

FIGURE 4.23   Estimated margin requirements for short 665 put

wiggle room by leaving 50% of the account in cash, to cover mark-to-market losses. No dice. As Figure 4.23 suggests, the problem was the way you sized positions. Neither your broker not the exchange could give you credit for perfect foresight.

Figure 4.23 estimates the exchange margin requirements for 1 short S&P 665 put. While your broker may require more margin, this is a lower bound on what you need to post. If you short a put listed at the CBOE, the initial margin required is equal to the (put price) + 0.15 * (put strike). In the graph, we have simply converted the margin required into a percentage of the index level. Recall the way we sized the strategy. Sizing is a bit contrived, but instructive. We agree to harvest gains from the previous quarter, to the point where there is a 50% cash buffer at the beginning of a new quarter. The strategy gets knocked out if the margin requirement ever doubles from its initial level at the beginning of the quarter. Can we please remind the reader again that back-tests don't have emotions? It's not simply a question of leverage constraints in the example above. Once you are in trouble, the high probability of a recovery stipulated by your model is not enough to rely upon.

IMPLICATIONS OF THE SQUARE ROOT STRATEGY

We have analysed the short 1×2 put ratio in some detail, as a low-cost hedge against a severe drawdown. Short 1×2 call ratios also have a function, e.g. as an extreme inflation hedge. We might sell a call ratio on a commodity index if a bubble seemed to be developing, i.e. if the move seemed overdone, but might go "parabolic" before reversing. If we wanted to hedge *both* extremes while harvesting some premium, we might wind up with a 2-sided ratio spread, such as the one following.

Figure 4.24 can be viewed as a blueprint for investing and risk taking in general. Our internal code name for the strategy used to be "sombrero", based on the payout profile at maturity. (A "Stockton hat" would have been a more accurate description, but we are no hat experts.) This sent brokers scrambling to the internet when we placed an order, to no effect. They typically had no idea what we were talking about and were afraid to ask. In reality, a sombrero is just a 2-sided short ratio spread. The code name was a concise and amusing way to describe it.

Many, if not most, investment strategies rely on capturing a risk premium of some sort. These include deep value/distressed investing, FX carry, buying the target stock in a potential merger, selling volatility among others. In each case, you are collecting a return for bearing risk that some segment of the investment community can't tolerate. This is all well and good, but if your strategy involves any leverage, it can get wiped out during an extreme event. So it is absolutely vital to include low-cost, low-delta options as

2-Sided Ratio Spread at Maturity

FIGURE 4.24   2-sided ratio spread, payout at maturity

part of a risk premium harvesting strategy. Once you add OTM hedges, your composite position resembles a condor. If you buy the wings more aggressively, you wind up with a short 2-sided ratio spread in spirit. Are these far OTM options rich or cheap? At some level, it really doesn't matter. So long as your hedge-adjusted carry is large enough, the "teeny" option hedges are simply the cost of doing business. Over-buying options at the extreme gives you the opportunity to add to your risky trades as they become more attractive or take some profits at the wings while maintaining a hedged book.

FUTURES VS SPOT

Suppose we take the view that crude oil is about to go up. We want to profit from an increase in price, but don't have the infrastructure to receive, store and deliver physical oil. A natural alternative is to buy crude oil futures. The front-month futures should move roughly in tandem with spot oil prices. By "front-month", we mean the live contract that has the least time to maturity, yet significant open interest. In order to maintain our long position over time, we need to "roll" the contract before it expires. Rolling involves selling front-month and buying back-month futures to re-establish the position. The back month is the next active futures contract along the term structure.

Now suppose that the term structure is "in contango" at the short end of the curve. This means that front-month futures are trading at a discount to the back month. If we want to roll our long position, we need to sell low and buy high. More precisely, we have to pay (front month price–back month price) / (front month price) in percentage terms to maintain our long position. This is our roll yield and in this case is negative. The implication is that roll will materially impact our returns if we wish to hold a position for a long time. As we will see later, cumulative roll yield can have a larger impact on your overall return than changes in the spot price! When the short end of the term structure is in severe contango, it is tempting to think about buying long-dated futures. This offers two advantages. The long end tends to be relatively flat, reducing roll down from one month to the next. In addition, you don't have to roll quite so often. The trouble with this strategy is that long-dated futures can be relatively illiquid and more importantly, they might not respond enough to a jump in the spot price. When there is a supply shock in a market such as oil, front month futures tend to jump. The market prices some mean-reversion further along the curve and the effects can be muted there.

A DRAMATIC EXAMPLE

We start with an extreme case, to highlight the potential impact of roll down. Our opening gambit involves trading the yield curve, which is structurally similar to the futures term structure. Imagine that we stumbled upon a yield curve in the shape of a step function, as in Figure 4.25.

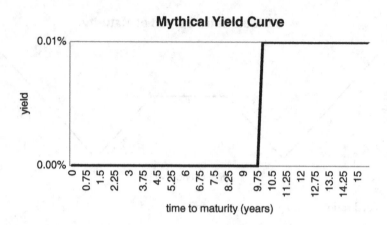

FIGURE 4.25 Mythical yield curve: roll down, rather than absolute yield, can generate attractive returns

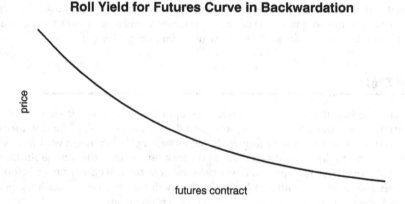

FIGURE 4.26 Maintaining a continuous long position in a market where the term structure is in backwardation

Yields are uniformly low, in absolute terms. From a long horizon asset allocation standpoint, bonds look like a terrible buy. If you hold any bond along the curve to maturity, your annualised return will be less than 1 basis point, or 0.01%. This is unlikely to excite anyone unless the underlying economy slips into a severe deflationary spiral. From a *trading* standpoint, however, there is a fantastic buying opportunity embedded in the curve. It's unimportant that the absolute level of yields is low. All you need to do is buy a 10-year 0 coupon bond. The yield curve is infinitely steep at the 10-year point. Assuming no change in the curve overnight and a par value of 100, the bond reprices from $100*\exp(-0.0001*10) = 99.90$ to 100 in one day. Assuming 252 trading days per year, this corresponds to an annualised return of 29%! The alchemy of a steep yield curve allows you to convert low yields into high returns.

The same logic applies to forward curves, though with opposite sign. Note that bond prices move inversely to yields, so that a steep yield curve favours a bond buying strategy. If you buy futures on a commodity such as heating oil, an *inverted* forward curve creates positive carry. When the term structure is downward sloping, it is said to be in backwardation. Front-month futures are trading at a premium to deferred contracts. The mechanics of maintaining a long position when the futures term structure is in backwardation are illustrated in Figure 4.26.

While our "mythical" yield curve strategy relied upon unwinding a 10-year 0 coupon bond every day, futures are generally rolled once per expiration cycle. Rolling a long position requires selling the front month while re-establishing a long position in the back (i.e. second actively traded) month. So long as the curve remains in backwardation, you can keep selling the front month at a higher price than you buy the back month. This generates a return equal to (front month price–back month price) / (front month price) each time the contract is rolled. Sovereign yield curves tend to be upward sloping more often than not, as investors typically demand compensation for bearing duration risk. This suggests that the roll yield for bond futures contracts should typically be positive.

It is instructive to quantify the long-term impact of roll yield on investor returns. In the next section, we will show that roll yield dominates spot price movements for most physical commodities over long time horizons.

A CROSS-SECTIONAL STUDY

Till (2006) provides concrete evidence that returns from a rolling futures contract on a commodity are distinctly different from returns on the spot commodity itself. This can have a bearing on our decision to take a directional bet in the futures markets. If the inherent roll yield is negative, you need to have high conviction or a short target holding period to justify buying the futures.

Suppose you take a bullish long-term view on gold, on the assumption that central banks will engage in the competitive devaluation of their currencies. You can't buy physical gold, as you neither have a place to store it nor a mechanism for receiving and delivering it. So you wind up buying gold futures and rolling every so often. Also suppose that the futures term structure is in contango, implying that long-maturity futures trade at a premium to short-dated ones.

In order to maintain the gold position, you have to roll the futures, typically as open interest moves from one contract to the next. If the curve remains in contango, rolling is persistently costly. You repeatedly have to sell the front month futures at a lower price than you are buying the back month. In other words, you are selling low and buying high over and over again, so your carry is negative. So when you trade gold futures, you are not really trading physical gold, but a combination of the spot commodity and its cost of carry. This applies uniformly to all futures contracts where the term structure is not completely flat.

Various authors have studied the relationship between physical commodity returns and returns from a rolling futures strategy on the commodity. Over long horizons, it turns out that the shape of the term structure is the decisive factor. Moves in the underlying asset are overwhelmed by roll yield. Figure 4.27 updates the analysis of Till (2006), with minor modifications. We cover 10 of the most actively traded physical commodities, using data from 1995 to 2015. The x-axis gives the average level of backwardation for each commodity. More specifically, if the price of the front and deferred month forwards are F1 and F2, respectively, we calculate (F1 – F2)/F1 for each commodity. We then average (F1 – F2)/F1 over the entire period.

We can draw several meaningful conclusions from Figure 4.27. Most of the dots are to the left of the y-axis. This implies that commodity term structures tend to be in contango. Roughly speaking, contango is more common than backwardation. Secondly, the regression line is strongly upward sloping, with an R^2 around 0.65. The persistently backwardated commodities, namely soybeans and heating oil, have the best long-term rolling futures returns. Commodities in trade in contango in the absence of a supply shock, such as natural gas, have very negative annualised returns. One might argue that there are only 10 points in the scatter plot, implying that the regression is based on a thin data set. We would argue, however, that by averaging the quantity (F1 – F2)/F1 over 20 years of weekly data, each dot is a solid one. The points on the graph are not very noisy.

It should now be apparent that there is a strong relationship between the average shape of the term structure in a given market and realised futures returns. Accordingly, it seems advantageous to roll long positions in markets that are typically in backwardation and to roll short positions in markets

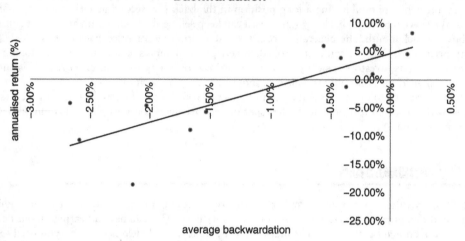

FIGURE 4.27   Impact of futures term structure on long-term returns for various physical commodities

that are in contango. Both strategies generate positive carry over the long haul. Bond futures, stock index futures in a low interest rate, high dividend environment and the odd commodity (e.g. heating oil) are good candidates for a rolling long strategy.

A cautionary note is in order. It's one thing to keep buying a contract that is regularly in backwardation for a definable structural reason. That straightforward strategy seems to work, at least over a long enough horizon. What *doesn't* work is an attempt to jump in and capture roll yield when a curve that is normally in contango suddenly goes into backwardation. For example, natural gas futures may switch into backwardation after a supply shock. Short-term prices rise more than long-term ones, as investors assume that the current shortage will eventually be remedied. However, the futures curve at this point can be very unstable. When you buy front month futures on the assumption that it will be possible to roll at a lower price in the future, you are assuming that the shape of the term structure will not change much over time. This assumption can be a disastrous one after a supply shock. Spot gas prices can decline very quickly, forcing the term structure back into contango. In this case, your implicit curve trade (long front month and short back month futures) will go strongly against you.

In the next graph, we explore the relationship between the level of backwardation of natural gas futures and its 4-week forward return. The graph is based on historical futures data from 1995 to 2015, at weekly intervals. Let's denote the front month futures price by F1 and the deferred month price by F2. The degree of backwardation relative to the front month contract is given by (F1 – F2)/F1. When F2 > F1, the term structure is upward sloping, or in "contango". When F2 < F1, it's in backwardation. We can now compare forward returns over some horizon to the degree of backwardation in the term structure. The results are summarised in Figure 4.28, assuming that we calculate forward returns over a rolling 4-week interval.

Buying natural gas after the curve has inverted is a losing strategy. It is true that long-term performance is primarily driven by an aggregation of negative returns when the curve is mildly in contango. This is the scenario that occurs most frequently. However, the best individual returns occur when the gas curve is steep and the worst returns when it is inverted. It may be that the severe contango returns are based on an implicit value play. The denominator F1 in (F1 – F2)/F1 is relatively low. Conversely, the snap back after curve inversions can be vicious.

How do things stack up on a cross-sectional basis? The results are similar and given in Figure 4.29. We have repeated the natural gas regression for a larger collection of physical commodities. The historical look-back window is 20 years.

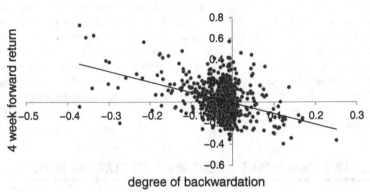

FIGURE 4.28 Prospective natural gas futures returns actually drop when the curve goes into backwardation

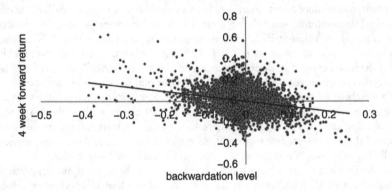

FIGURE 4.29 Cross-sectional dependence of returns on level of backwardation

The results are broadly similar. Most of the points are to the left of the y-axis, suggesting that storage costs and other considerations usually force the term structure into contango. Episodic moves into backwardation should be sold, as the odds favour normalisation of the curve. If roll yield is to be exploited over the long term, it needs to be reliable. Buying front month futures after a supply shock just doesn't seem right. Dedicated commodity traders are always on the lookout for term structures that have gone into backwardation. They usually try and squash the spread by selling front month futures and hedging further along the curve. Anecdotally, these traders tend to make money most of the time. It is debatable whether they take extreme event risk to collect if the curve flattens, but this is beside the point. You are unlikely to make consistent profits by taking a long position in front month futures after a risk event without exceptional timing.

What you really need is a market that is *persistently* in backwardation. So long as the yield curve is upward sloping, Treasury bond futures are an excellent choice. From 1982 to 2015, the US 10-year yield has been higher than the 3-month T bill rate roughly 90% of the time. Given an upward sloping yield curve, 10-year note futures *have* to trade at a discount to the cash bond. Note that we have glossed over several technical details here. For example, there is a basket of notes that can be delivered into the futures contract and they may have much shorter durations than 10 years. However, the rough argument goes as follows. If the futures traded at par to the cheapest-to-deliver cash bond, you could make a guaranteed profit by selling the futures and borrowing money to buy the deliverable bond. Then, you would be flat at maturity, having collected an annualised return of (deliverable bond yield – T bill yield), which is greater than 0. As you go further out the curve, the futures will generally decline in price. The same arbitrage argument applies, with a cheaper cash bond and a greater interest rate differential between the bond yield and the cost of borrow. In the absence of conversion factors, we are applying a larger discount to a cheaper bond. Hence, given an upward sloping yield curve, bond futures should trade in backwardation.

THE "New" VIX: MODEL-INDEPENDENT, THOUGH NOT PARTICULARLY INTUITIVE

At this point, we move into a discussion of what the VIX is actually measuring. From 1990 to 2002, the VIX was calculated in a relatively simple way. The calculation relied upon taking the three closest to ATM options in the front two months, then applying Black–Scholes and doing some averaging. In particular, the three closest strikes would be averaged according to their distance from the ATM strike. The front two months would then be averaged, based on their distance from a constant 30-day-to-maturity window. Note that the original VIX calculation was derived from S&P 100 options, while the new one focuses on the S&P 500.

At some point, model-dependent quantities became *verboten*, no longer tradable according to the regulators. We find this amusing, since the regulators have no hesitation in accepting model-dependent risk calculations based on Value-at-Risk or other methodologies. The current VIX is based upon the pricing formula for a variance swap, as in Carr (1998). A variance swap is a contract that pays out based on the difference between realised variance and the swap "strike". The strike is based on the market's expectation of future realised variance. It turns out that the variance swap strike can be priced directly from a weighted average of market call and put prices, *without* reference to Black–Scholes or any other pricing formula. The contribution of an OTM call or put with strike K is proportional to $1/K^2$. This implies that deep OTM puts (i.e. where K is small) can have a large impact on the price of a variance swap if their prices are not too small. As the prices of calls and puts rise, expected variance goes up as well. The new VIX is just the square root of the variance swap strike.

The updated VIX formula does have some advantages over the original one. In particular, it incorporates all available strikes, which gives a slightly more skew-dependent view of the level of risk aversion in the market. Variance swaps also have a fairly pure design, as pricing does not require any assumptions about the distribution of the underlying asset. It has been shown, as in Hiatt (2007), that the new formula tracks the old one quite accurately. The downside is that the average Joe doesn't understand the intricacies of the new calculation. Tradable quantities probably should not rely upon complicated mathematics. It is not Joe's fault if he is afraid that the more complicated formula might start to wildly diverge in the future, as the extremities of the put skew become distorted.

THE SPOT VIX: OASIS OR MIRAGE?

In theory, the VIX can be an attractive hedge for a number of reasons. The correlation between the VIX and the underlying S&P 500 index (SPX) has historically been very high and negative, in excess of –80% using daily observations. Although mean-reverting, the VIX tends to have more than 5 times the volatility of the SPX. It is far more likely that the VIX will double than that the SPX will drop by –50% over a short horizon. This suggests that a relatively small position can go a long way. Unlike an option, the spot VIX does not have explicit time decay.

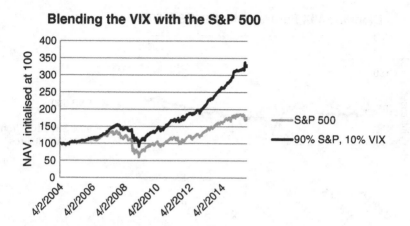

FIGURE 4.30 Impact of 10% spot VIX allocation to S&P index returns

In the introduction, we mentioned that if you could predict crises with perfect accuracy, hedging would be either trivial or unnecessary. The same line of thinking applies to the spot VIX. If you could buy the spot VIX, hedging a portfolio of risky assets would generally be quite easy. Unfortunately, this is a giant "if". You could hold a static long position in the spot VIX against your portfolio of equities or credit. There might be ways to optimise things further, but this would be an excellent starting point. Note that the spot VIX is the number quoted by the media. It has two characteristics that constitute an ideal hedge, i.e. persistently negative correlation to the S&P 500, with no time decay or negative carry. In Figure 4.30, we track the performance of an unlevered portfolio consisting of a 90% position in the S&P 500 and 10% in the spot VIX. A dash of the VIX does wonders for your overall portfolio.

The results are astonishing. The blended portfolio has roughly *double* the compounded return of the index. The NAV (net asset value) virtually moves in a straight line from 2009 to the present. This seems too good to be true. We appear to have stumbled upon a very basic strategy that has enormous alpha. Does the market really give things away so easily? In the case of the VIX, the answer turns out to be a resounding no. When we try to implement a VIX buying strategy, it immediately becomes clear that the returns in the above chart can't be replicated. It is not possible to buy the VIX directly. In practical terms, the VIX doesn't exist; the quoted number is virtually useless for a buy-side investor. It is true that the VIX calculation is based on a weighted average of prices for listed S&P options. However, you would have to constantly rebalance your replicating portfolio as the index moved, to ensure that all of your options were out of the money. You would also have to pay through the bid ask spread for deep OTM puts that can have a meaningful impact on the index. The replicating portfolio would consist of hundreds of OTM calls and puts, creating an awful mess. Rebalancing would be prohibitively expensive from a buy-side perspective.

VIX futures offer a direct way to express a view on S&P volatility over short horizons. They have been listed at the Chicago Board Options Exchange, or "CBOE", since 2004. At maturity, VIX futures have to converge to the spot VIX, so there is a close functional relationship between the two. It is tempting to conclude that you can leave precise replication to the banks and just buy the futures. The impracticality of this approach becomes apparent when we replace the spot VIX with a rolling position in VIX futures in the blended 90%, 10% portfolio above as shown in Figure 4.31.

While the spot VIX materially improves risk-adjusted returns, VIX futures dramatically reduce performance. Buying and rolling VIX futures is an outrageously expensive way to protect against disaster. The difference in performance is astounding and at first sight, surprising. How can this be so? We have simply replaced the spot VIX with the forward VIX in our calculation. The trouble is that the VIX futures term structure tends to be in severe contango most of the time. The VIX is not a deliverable

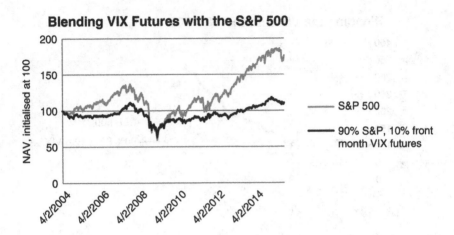

FIGURE 4.31   Impact of adding VIX futures to static long S&P 500 position

commodity and the term structure of VIX futures reflects excess institutional demand for hedging. The structural imbalances driving the VIX futures curve have created trading opportunities that have attracted the attention of yield curve traders and other "arbitrageurs".

We have reached a critical juncture. Why not apply the VIX formula and simply try to replicate it? If replicating an S&P index put with the underlying is dangerous in the presence of jumps, VIX replication is practically impossible for most buy-side investors. As the saying goes, you can't buy the spot VIX any more than you can buy a sunny day. Hedging with volatility turns out to be a challenge after all. Reasoning from the VIX formula, you would have to own every OTM put and call with open interest and rebalance whenever the ATM strike moved. On average, you would have to rebalance several times a day, as the following order of magnitude argument suggests. Suppose the S&P 500 is trading at 2000. S&P options strikes are typically 5 points apart or 0.25% of the index. In quiet market conditions, a 1 standard deviation 1-day move is roughly 1%, implying that you would have to buy and sell large quantities of options several times a day. The costs would rack up, given that you would also have to rebalance daily to maintain a constant 30 maturity profile.

To understand the impact of negative roll yield, we need look no further than the data. In Figure 4.32, we track the front-month VIX futures premium over the spot VIX, as a function of time. While the spread between futures and spot has been quite volatile, we can see that the average futures premium has been very high, at around 6%. The difference between the front month futures price and the spot is commonly referred to as the basis.

The traditional basis is of concern if we hold to maturity. For perpetually rolling strategies, we are more worried about the spread between front and second month VIX futures. This will determine the cost of maintaining a long position. In Figure 4.33, we track the average level of contango at the short end of the VIX term structure. This is a different convention from the one used by Till and Eagleeye (2003). We are now thinking of the *cost* of maintaining a long futures position, rather than the risk premium collected for contracts that are in backwardation. Specifically, we trace the evolution of the quantity (second month futures price–front month futures price) / (front month futures price) from 2006 to early 2016.

The straight grey line is an in-sample average over the entire period, with dire implications. We would have had to buy roughly 10% fewer contracts in the back month each time we rolled, assuming we didn't add cash to the position. This suggests that our volatility hedge would have simultaneously lost money and withered away over time. The implication is that we do not want to take the VIX head on. Maintaining a long volatility position by mechanically rolling VIX futures is simply too expensive. One thought is to buy OTM call options on the spot VIX, on the assumption that roll down exposure is relatively indirect. The trouble with this idea is that, although the calls *settle* based on the spot VIX at

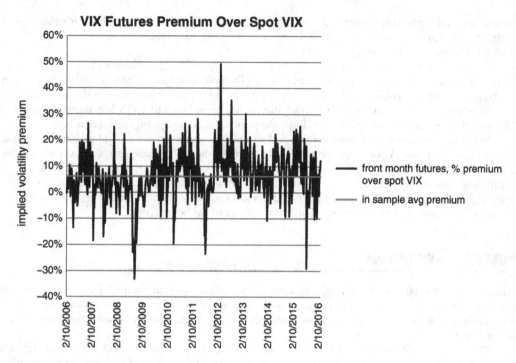

FIGURE 4.32 Historical VIX futures premium over spot VIX

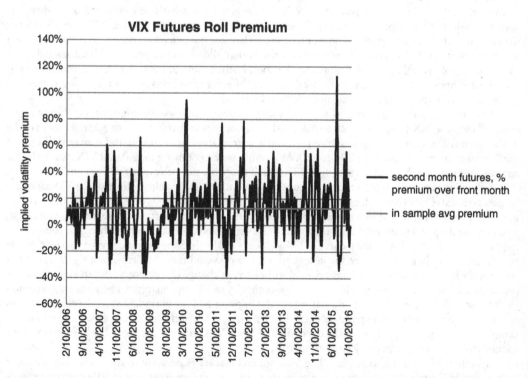

FIGURE 4.33 Front month VIX futures premium over second month, historical perspective

expiration, they *trade* with reference to the VIX futures. Your instantaneous roll down is equal to (call delta) * (roll yield of equivalent duration futures). So you still have fractional exposure to roll down, which is compounded by time decay in the call.

Whether in futures or options form, the VIX is not a buy and hold instrument. You have to finesse or time it in some way. But if you *could* market time VIX futures or options, why would you need them in the first place? You could simply exploit the high structural correlation between the VIX and S&P 500 by selling an appropriate number of S&P futures whenever you had a VIX buy signal. This would give you similar (though perhaps less explosive) exposure, while eliminating roll down.

Structural challenges are one of the things that make investing interesting and perhaps we should view things differently. A potential solution is to revisit the short S&P ratio spread idea, with a twist. Rather than trading a ratio spread, you can sell VIX futures while overbuying OTM VIX calls. Selling a call ratio spread turns out to be sub-optimal, as 10 delta VIX calls do not offer value to the extent that 10 delta S&P puts do. Before investigating the short futures, long calls strategy, we need to analyse the peculiar properties of VIX options. This is the subject of the next section.

MIGRATING TO VIX OPTIONS

This section culminates with a strategy that provides a convex payout on the VIX, at relatively low cost. The strategy turns out to be particularly useful during risk off regimes, when standard hedges are invariably overpriced. We first need to discuss some of the intricacies of VIX options, before constructing our hedge.

We have observed that, while VIX options settle with reference to the spot VIX, their price depends upon a VIX *futures* contract with the appropriate maturity. For example, if you bought a September VIX call, you would plug the September futures price (rather than the spot VIX) into Black–Scholes to value the call. This is logical. September VIX futures give the market's best estimate as to where the spot VIX will land at September expiry. What makes things complicated is that VIX futures do not depend upon the spot in a purely deterministic way. They are not priced according to a standard cash and carry formula. Indeed, there is no simple formula that allows you to price the VIX forward curve as a function of prevailing interest rates and the spot. Rather, they reflect supply and demand dynamics for S&P options and the futures themselves over different time horizons. In this respect, they are qualitatively different from physical commodity futures.

This suggests that long-dated calls may not appreciate as much as one might expect during a risk event. If the spot VIX jumps from 20 to 50, we should not expect that a 3-month 50 strike call will be at the money. The futures term structure prices in a degree of mean reversion and it may well be that the 3-month futures are closer to 20 than 50. As a result, we can't rely on long-dated VIX calls to hedge against intermittent, short-term risk events. They will probably not be responsive enough.

An obvious alternative is to focus on front-month options. In principle, short-dated VIX calls can be powerful extreme event hedges. However, you face multiple headwinds when buying VIX calls that are close to maturity. Roll down tends to be highest at the short end of the term structure. As a result, you face the double whammy of high time decay and severe roll down. However, there are compensating factors. At the very least, short-dated OTM VIX calls are lively. Suppose you buy 1-month S&P 500 put. If the index rises +10% over the course of a few weeks and then suddenly drops −10%, the put will usually lose money. Time will have passed without a net change in the spot. Close to expiration, the put delta will have fizzled away. However, a 1-month VIX call will probably make a sizeable return as the VIX will likely be much higher than it was at the beginning of the period. Out-of-the-money strikes remain in play late into the expiration cycle. Over a modest horizon, the VIX is much more likely to double than the S&P is likely to decline by −50%. Hence, VIX calls are far more likely to jump in the money than S&P puts, especially close to maturity.

Structural issues are also at play. The VIX options market is perverse in the sense that it almost encourages VIX futures to overshoot fair value. In particular, the open interest in VIX options exceeds

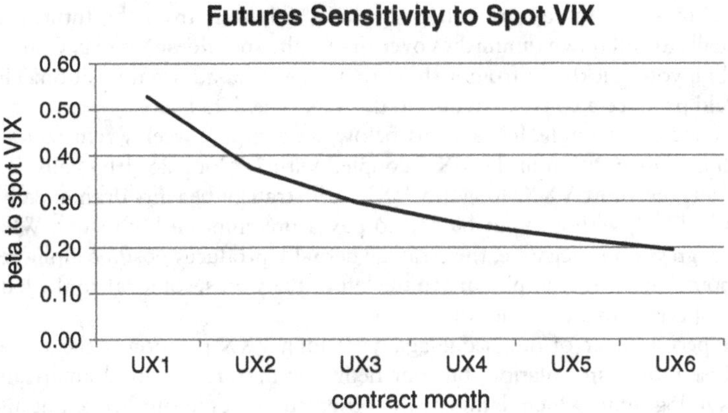

Futures Sensitivity to Spot VIX

FIGURE 4.34 Front month VIX futures are relatively responsive to changes in the spot VIX

VIX futures open interest. If the majority of speculators were short OTM VIX calls, there would not be enough inventory to delta hedge them during a risk event. When we also consider the intrinsic jumpiness of the VIX, replicating a short call seems extremely dangerous. If a large enough number of investors tried to hedge a short call with futures, there might be enough buying pressure to drive very high strike short-dated calls into the money.

A nice feature of VIX calls is that they become more potent close to expiration. In this way, they resemble the put and call butterflies we discussed earlier. We know that any futures contract has to converge to the spot at expiration and VIX futures are no different. The interesting thing here is that long-dated VIX futures are not nearly as volatile as the spot VIX. The market prices a certain amount of mean reversion into the futures. This suggests that the futures should become increasingly volatile as the time to maturity shrinks. We show this in the sparse Figure 4.34. We consider the front four VIX futures contracts in the graph. These have expirations that are one month apart. Next we calculate the rolling 30-day standard deviation of each contract as well as the VIX. We then graph the ratio of each standard deviation to the standard deviation of the VIX. The futures roll is transacted one week before maturity.

The front month futures are highly responsive, with a beta over 0.5 to the spot VIX. They jump around more actively than the other ones. This implies that an OTM VIX call should be nice and lively close to expiration. High strikes are more reachable late in the cycle. So long as VIX implied volatility is not egregiously priced close to expiration, weekly options can again offer tremendous potential payouts.

Before we get carried away with the idea of buying boat loads of low delta VIX calls, we need to keep one thing in mind. We don't derive the same benefit from the VIX call skew as from the S&P put skew. We have seen how the S&P put skew can steepen during a crisis. This gives an extra price kicker to an OTM put on the S&P. While ATM volatility does tend to spike at these moments, the call skew may flatten or even decline at the wing. The market may price some mean reversion at the far reaches of the VIX call skew. This strategy creates a convex payout on the VIX. It is well known that VIX futures generally trade in severe contango, which implies that a rolling long position has overwhelming negative carry. Front-month VIX futures have traded at an average discount of roughly 6% to the back (second) month. This compounds aggressively over time. The VXX (a US ETF that implements a rolling position in front month VIX futures) has lost −99.72% since its January 2009 launch and has required several 4:1 reverse splits to trade at a reasonable level!

Let's combine this information: front-month VIX futures usually trade at an unacceptable premium to the spot, and roll down affects a VIX call at a declining rate as the futures roll toward the spot. Can we build a strategy from these observations? One solution is to sell VIX futures while overbuying

VIX calls. This allows you to capture roll down on a 1:1 basis from the futures. Meanwhile, the exposure of the calls to roll down diminishes over time if the spot doesn't move. Conversely, if the VIX goes heroically bid, you quickly go from a short to a long delta-adjusted position. This suggests that the strategy should produce a convex payout on the VIX. The data bears this out.

Let's take a concrete example. In the chart below, we compare weekly returns for a long position in the VXX with a short position in the VXX coupled with 1.5 long 25 delta calls. If volatility either drops or rises a lot, the short VXX, long 1.5 VXX call strategy benefits dramatically. The payout is distinctly "straddle-like", without your having to pay a premium on both sides. While the intercept of the quadratic regression is negative, the strategy actually produces *positive* alpha relative to a long position. Most points in the scatter plot are to the left of the y-axis, some far to the left, which ensures that the VXX compounds in a horrible way.

The relative performance of our hedge against a long VXX position is shown below. Note that both strategies lose money in isolation, but our hedge outperforms quite dramatically. Also observe that the y-axis is in log units, which dampens the observed moves in our hedge but allows us to compare the relative roll down in the two approaches.

For every VIX futures contract that we short, we need to buy 15 50 delta calls to construct a position that is initially delta-neutral. The ratio is 15:1. Note that we buy 15 rather than 1.5 VIX calls as the futures contract multiplier is 1,000, whereas the options multiplier is 100. A short futures/long call strategy is conceptually similar to the short 1×2 put ratio on the S&P 500 that we discussed earlier. If volatility spikes, delta becomes strongly positive and the structure offers significant protection. Conversely, as volatility declines, the call deltas decrease. The structure then has net negative delta, i.e. is locally short volatility. This implies that your delta-adjusted exposure to roll yield is positive. You benefit from a term structure in contango at an ever-increasing rate. Relative to a rolling long position in VIX futures, the variable delta of the structure generates alpha. Figure 4.35 relies upon weekly data from 2006 to 2015 and suggests that the short futures/long call strategy is generally superior to a rolling futures benchmark.

The weekly alpha in the trade is 35 basis points, corresponding to roughly +20% annualised outperformance! While the strategy still loses money in the absence of market timing, it is not consistently hampered by negative roll yield.

The scatter plot suggests that the payout function is mildly convex relative to a rolling VIX futures strategy. This can be appealing if the VIX has recently spiked. You reason that risk aversion levels are *not* going to stay put. The market is at an unstable equilibrium, similar to a pendulum that is hanging upside down from its centre of rotation. The S&P probably will either collapse, forcing another spike

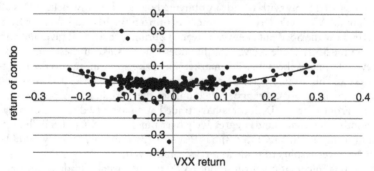

FIGURE 4.35   Convex payout of strategy where VXX calls are overbought

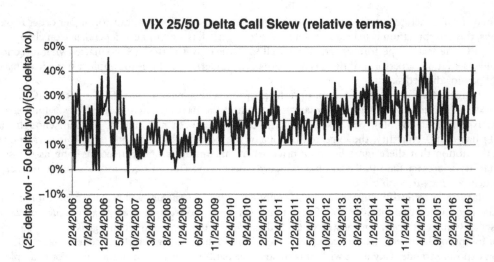

FIGURE 4.36 VIX 25 delta calls have traditionally traded at a large premium to ATM calls

in volatility, or recover, causing volatility to drop sharply. In both cases, the short VIX futures/long VIX calls approach should do relatively well. There are other ways to capture roll down while providing extreme event protection, e.g. using VIX put spreads instead of futures. However, these are conceptually similar to the short futures, long calls trade and so we do not include them here.

The reader might wonder why we have focused on buying ATM VIX calls rather than moving further along the skew. One difficulty with moderately OTM VIX calls is that the call skew tends to be very steep, probably too steep. Historically, the 25/50 delta implied volatility spread has been relatively large, though volatile. We can see in Figure 4.36 that implied volatility for the 1-month 25 delta call has typically been 10% to 40% higher than for the 50 delta one. If ATM volatility is 100, 25 delta volatility will typically range from 110 to 140. We suspect that there is large institutional demand for OTM VIX protection, causing these calls to be persistently expensive.

One drawback of the short futures/long call strategy has to do with margining. Since VIX futures trade at a different exchange from VIX options, offsetting legs need to be margined separately. This increases the amount of equity needed to finance the hedge. A reasonable alternative is to sell VXX ETF shares short, while buying VXX calls. However, we have to accept that the ETF will have a variable borrow cost and the calls may be less liquid than their VIX counterparts.

REFLECTIONS ON FIGURE 4.36

Figure 4.36 demonstrates that our strategy has a strong convex payout based on changes in the VIX. It particularly benefits from large moves in the futures. The quadratic regression shows the convex properties of the strategy. The regression has the form $= ax^2 - bx - c$, with an R^2 of roughly 0.25. Here, a, b and c are greater than 0. You shouldn't be fooled into thinking that, since the intercept is negative, our strategy has negative alpha. The "true" alpha of the strategy is probably close to 0 and materially positive in terms of its impact on a portfolio. The standard alpha interpretation only applies to linear regressions. A one factor linear regression takes the form $y = \beta x + \alpha$. We can think of x as the returns for a benchmark and y as the returns of an active manager who tracks the benchmark. α is the y-intercept of the regression, the place where the regression line crosses the y-axis. In the language of factor models, it also measures a manager's skill. If α is bigger than 0, the implication is that the manager can generate positive returns without market exposure. For quadratic or higher-order regressions, this interpretation is inadequate. Our strategy clearly has a non-linear dependence on changes in the VIX. The strategy performs particularly well for large moves in the VIX, no matter what direction. Conversely, it underperforms if there is no move in the underlying. This is the implicit statistical charge you pay for the hedge.

Imagine that we constructed an options position whose payout was $(S(T) - S(t))^2 - C$, where $C >= 0$. The intercept is negative by construction and the payout function resembles a long straddle. If $S(T)$ lands at $S(t)$, you lose $-C$ on the trade. However, assuming C is small enough and $S(T)$ has non-0 volatility, the expected payout of the position must be positive. This corresponds to the notion that there must be *some* price where an option is underpriced, as long as the spot volatility is greater than 0. Based on a standard linear regression, we generate a positive intercept, namely $y = \beta x + \alpha$, with $\alpha > 0$.

It remains to justify why we can be so confident that this structure will provide protection during a severe drawdown in the S&P 500. Recall that we have cautioned against relying too much on cross-asset class correlations when constructing a hedge. In some cases, the indirect hedge is relatively safe, if not foolproof. In others, the banked-upon correlation can disappear when you need it the most. Offsetting exposure to one risky asset with puts on another tends to work most of the time. For example, it seems reasonable to buy S&P 500 puts to hedge European equity and credit risk, on the assumption that US implied volatility is relatively cheap. In this way, you can minimise the cost of hedging against a systemic risk event. However, buying calls on a random asset that has historically been negatively correlated to your core portfolio is potentially dangerous. Treasury bonds are the canonical example. Treasuries have rallied during equity sell-offs over the past 30 years, implying persistent negative correlation. However, in a highly inflationary environment, there is no guarantee that they should do so. We refer to Illmanen (2003) for a detailed discussion of this subtlety. Given our reservations, do VIX calls offer a rock solid hedge against equity risk? After all, they are playing the role of the negatively correlated asset. We would argue that they do, as the VIX and S&P 500 are *structurally* linked (see Figure 4.37). VIX calls don't directly protect against adverse moves in the S&P. However, the VIX directly measures the price of insurance on the index. This implies that VIX calls will protect against an

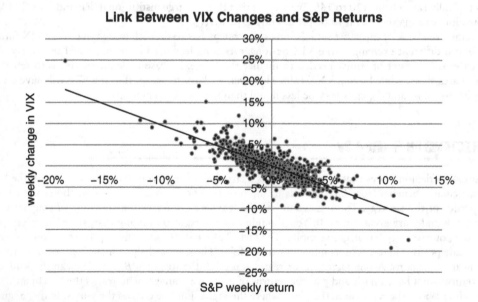

Link Between VIX Changes and S&P Returns

FIGURE 4.37   Strong structural linkage between VIX changes and S&P returns

increase in the price of S&P 500 puts, should you decide to buy protection later. The linkage between the performance of VIX calls and the magnitude of S&P sell-offs is strong. The mechanical connection between the VIX and S&P implies that there is likely to be a large negative correlation between the VIX and the S&P over the longterm, as there has been in the past.

MIGRATING TO DIFFERENT MARKETS: THE V2X

We have shown how to construct VIX options structures that provide significant protection against a risk event, while minimising negative carry. Can we apply the same technique to other volatility indices, such as the V2X? In theory, we could diversify our hedging overlays by venturing into other markets. Note that the V2X is the analogue of the VIX for the Euro Stoxx 50 index. As of this writing, the V2X doesn't trade nearly as efficiently as the VIX. This makes hedging difficult. Front month V2X futures provide reasonably accurate protection against severe drops in the Euro Stoxx 50 index. However, neither the options nor the futures market is very developed or liquid. This restricts the range of possible hedges. For example, there has been a December dip or kink in the V2X futures term structure for the past several years, as in the Figure 4.38.

The December dip in the term structure is terribly annoying. It feels like an itch that you can't scratch. The temptation is to try to trade away the Santa dip. An obvious idea would be to buy the Nov/Dec/Jan butterfly, buying 2 December futures while selling one each of November and January. This trade would be profitable as soon as the dip disappeared. You would disproportionately profit from the Santa V2X contract. Yield curves generally do not have seasonal dips in them. You can only argue in favour of a dip if realised volatility in December is expected to be dramatically below volatility in the surrounding months. The VIX term structure has no such irregularities, as you can see in Figure 4.39.

This implies that if you need to hedge a long portfolio of European stocks, you might be better off using VIX options. While the VIX hedge is clearly less specific, it should behave more predictably during a major risk event. Different strikes and maturities are likely to behave in a coordinated way. You need to find a balance between specificity, predictability and cost in any hedging mandate. As of this writing, the V2X is too unpredictable to strike this balance correctly.

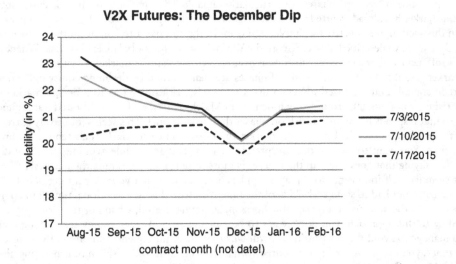

FIGURE 4.38 Santa sells V2X futures while attempting to buy global equities

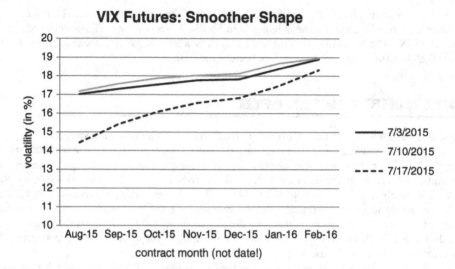

FIGURE 4.38   By comparison, the December dip in VIX futures is modest

RISK-REGIME ANALYSIS

We have harped on about the "every dog has its day" theme several times in this book. Every option structure has its moment to shine. Even a silly looking combination of options will pay out admirably in the right scenario. Some hedges outperform in quiet markets, while others offer relatively good value once volatility picks up. How can we quantify the conditional performance of various options strategies? We first need a regime indicator, which specifies the state of the market at any given time. We might not have any idea where we are going, but at least we know where we are on the map now. Then, we can tabulate the performance of each hedging structure based on the prevailing regime. This approach allows us to select reasonable hedges no matter what is going on in the market. From our perspective, hedges that offer decent value in "risk off" phases are particularly valuable. These might be the best defensive strategies after the market has already started to sell off. In short, they satisfy our "second leg down" imperative.

In this section, we construct a simple regime indicator and use it to condition the performance of the hedges we have described above. We use the VIX as a proxy for global asset class risk. Whenever the VIX is sufficiently above its 3-year historical average, we say that the market is "risk off". Otherwise, the market is said to be "risk on". Risk off phases are characterised by declining equity indices, widening credit spreads and increased FX volatility. Conversely, "risk on" refers to a benign market that is either rising or not moving around very much. As in Malek (2009), we have calibrated our regime indicator so that it spends more time in risk on phases than risk off ones. This seems intuitively correct. You want to spend more time invested in the market than sitting in cash. Markets *do* tend to go up, most of the time. You want to harvest the risk premia that are available, while avoiding potential disaster. There is a saying that goes "time in the market is more important than timing the market". While this might seem like self-indulgent word play, it applies here. Imagine that you were a long-only US equity fund manager, but had to sit in cash 75% of the time. You would need exceptional timing to come anywhere close to the index over a reasonable horizon, assuming the index had positive drift. By contrast, according to this approach, you don't want to be hanging around when things are looking ominous. If you manage to avoid the devastating drawdowns that occur infrequently but are in the market most other times, you may have a recipe for outperformance. This turns the problem of generating alpha on its head. Market beta is now your source of passive return, while risk management produces alpha. The idea is to make your money while the going is good and get out when things deteriorate.

This is a reasonable approach, on the assumption that risky assets go up most of the time. However, every now and again their progress is halted by sharp sell-offs or protracted bear markets. Malek (2009) uses a broader risk indicator than the VIX to tabulate the regime-based performance of various hedge fund strategies. This indicator was more comprehensive, in an attempt to deal with situations where volatility moves asynchronously across interest rates, currencies and equity indices. But is such complexity necessary? It is worth checking whether the VIX is sufficient as a risk indicator, for two reasons. When we classify the performance of various hedging strategies according to regime, we want to verify that our conclusions are not too sensitive to the choice of indicator. The last thing we want is a highly complicated risk index that optimises over a large number of indices, as it is less likely to be reliable. But there is another, more important, reason for advocating simplicity. We want to convince ourselves that, during a severe crisis, it doesn't really matter *where* you hedge. We have already argued that consultants tend to be overly focused on precise hedges, when something cheap that does the job in a crisis might be preferable. However, we haven't offered much evidence for this assertion. Our thesis is that you can buy puts on risky currencies, equities or high yielding bonds. All are fair game. In extreme market conditions, implied volatility across risky asset classes will be intertwined. If true, you can focus on finding inexpensive hedges across asset classes, without excessive concern for the most precise hedge. Figure 4.40 demonstrates that weekly changes in benchmark equity and currency implied volatility have a strong statistical correlation.

In Figure 4.41, we verify that the VIX is indeed a sufficient risk indicator. It might not capture all of the subtleties of market sell-offs, but it adequately flags the worst ones. We start with three implied volatility indices: the VIX, the CVIX and the MOVE index, one for equities, one for currencies and one for bonds. The VIX is a measure of US equity index risk. The CVIX is the currency analogue of the VIX, for currencies. It measures 3-month implied volatility for an aggregate of 9 major currency pairs, with a relatively large allocation to the EUR/USD, USD/JPY and GBP/USD crosses. The MOVE index is a weighted average of 1-month implied volatility for constant maturity 2-, 5-, 10- and 30-year US Treasury bonds. Recall that a constant maturity "bond" doesn't correspond to a specific bond, but is constructed from a weighted average of bond yields near the maturity target. We then calculate the 3-year trailing Z score of each index. The Z score simply measures how many standard deviations the index is away from its average. If an index has a Z score of 2, it is 2 standard deviations higher than normal. This is a significant difference, indicating that the index is severely elevated.

Having calculated the Z score of the VIX, CVIX and MOVE, we can check whether each index triggers a "risk off" signal at the same time. In particular, we choose a threshold, then ask the following

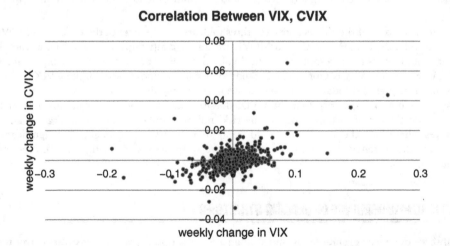

FIGURE 4.40 Weekly changes in currency and equity index implied volatility are inter-linked

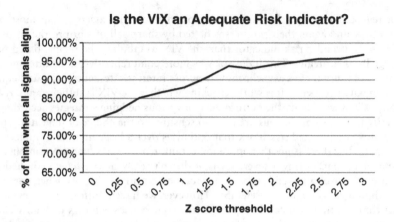

FIGURE 4.41   The CVIX, MOVE and VIX indices become increasingly correlated as the VIX rises

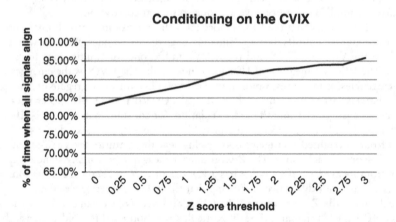

FIGURE 4.42   When the CVIX is high, the MOVE and VIX indices tend to be switched on as well

question. If the Z score of the VIX is above the threshold, are the Z scores of the CVIX and MOVE also above the threshold? If so, the CVIX and MOVE are simply confirming what the VIX already has to say. It turns out that, as the threshold rises, the 3 volatility indices are nearly always in agreement. For example, whenever the VIX is more than 2 standard deviations above normal, the CVIX and MOVE will also be more than 2 standard deviations above normal roughly 95% of the time.

It's also important to verify that the CVIX doesn't spike without confirmation from the VIX. We don't want the set of instances where one risk indicator spikes to be much larger than the set of instances where the others do. This would imply that the VIX (say) might miss significant "risk off" events in the currency markets. In Figure 4.42, we swap the CVIX for the VIX and re-apply the threshold test.

CONDITIONAL PERFORMANCE OF HEDGING STRATEGIES

In the absence of a mega event, buying and selling fixed delta options is a losing strategy over the long term. With this in mind, we want to identify strikes that are best suited to particular market regimes. In Figure 4.44, we graph our binary VIX-derived risk index. "Risk on" and "risk off" phases are denoted

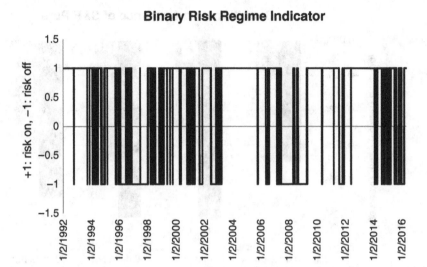

FIGURE 4.43   Our international bar code risk indicator

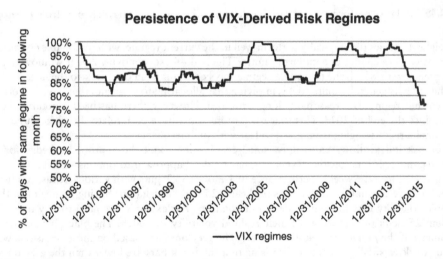

FIGURE 4.44   Decline in risk regime persistence since 2013

by +1 and –1, respectively. When the market is risk on, investors are driven more by greed than fear. They want to buy equities and credit, while selling volatility. Conversely, risk off phases span the range of emotions from cautiousness to abject fear.

Note that we have calculated the 2-year trailing Z score of the VIX and mapped it to +1 whenever the Z score was below 0.5 and –1 otherwise. This creates a binary signal that is biased toward "risk on" phases. We want risk on phases to be more frequent than risk off ones, based on the observation that quiet (bull) markets typically last longer than turbulent (bear) ones. Assuming that the Z-score series is reasonably normally distributed with 0 mean, the 0.5 threshold implies that the market will be risk "on" about 70% of the time.

A regime-based approach to strategy selection should intuitively work best when there is not too much switching from +1 to –1. More succinctly, we want persistence in the index. This allows us to

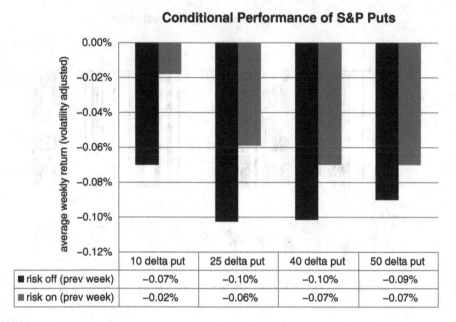

Conditional Performance of S&P Puts

	10 delta put	25 delta put	40 delta put	50 delta put
■ risk off (prev week)	−0.07%	−0.10%	−0.10%	−0.09%
■ risk on (prev week)	−0.02%	−0.06%	−0.07%	−0.07%

FIGURE 4.45 Relative performance of variable delta puts, conditioned on risk regime from previous week

overweight strategies that typically perform well in the current regime, with reasonable confidence that the regime will not change at a moment's notice. Figure 4.44 uses a moving 2-year window to calculate the frequency with which the prevailing regime stays constant from one week to the next.

The index is generally quite sticky, implying that allocating to strategies that have performed well in the current regime is a reasonable long-term idea. However, there has been a notable dip in persistence since the end of 2013. This suggests that investors have been relatively schizophrenic in their desire to take risk, swinging from greed to fear with high frequency.

Our risk index allows us to draw some conclusions about the appropriate hedge for a given market regime. It formalises the "every dog has its day" approach to options strategies. Figure 4.45 summarises the average weekly performance of 1-month S&P puts with various deltas, conditional on regime. We have normalised the returns of the 10, 25 and 40 delta put buying strategies so that their in-sample volatility matches the 50 delta put volatility. For example, we need to buy more 10 delta puts than 25 delta puts if we want their realised volatility to match. The black bars show average performance if the *previous* week was risk off. The grey ones are based on those occasions where the previous week was risk on. It's not surprising that the black bars are lower than the grey ones, as the cost of hedging increases after volatility jumps.

We want to know whether the current regime gives us a clue as to what to do next.

The 10 delta S&P put has outperformed in both regimes over the past 10 years. Even on a volatility adjusted basis, it has declined at a shallower pace than a rolling strategy with higher delta puts. The difference is especially large during risk on periods. Another observation is that the 10 delta puts (volatility adjusted) are superior to the 25 delta puts in both regimes. This suggests that a short 1×2 put ratio spread, with 25 and 10 delta strikes is a reasonable "all weather" strategy, as we have previously discussed. The square root payout has merit from an unconditional statistical standpoint. However, the 1×2 is particularly compelling when the market is risk on. This may be an issue of cost. 10 delta puts seem to offer good relative value in quiet markets as the put skew tends to be relatively flat when investors are feeling buoyant.

We can conduct the same analysis for VXX calls as shown in Figure 4.46. The VXX is an exchange-traded fund, or "ETF", that tries to replicate the performance of a rolling strategy in short-term VIX

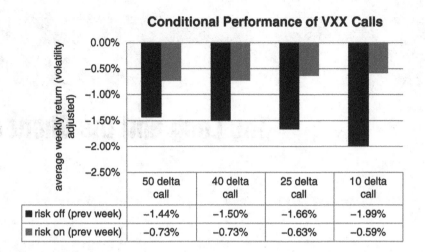

FIGURE 4.46 Conditional performance of VXX calls with variable deltas

	50 delta call	40 delta call	25 delta call	10 delta call
■ risk off (prev week)	−1.44%	−1.50%	−1.66%	−1.99%
■ risk on (prev week)	−0.73%	−0.73%	−0.63%	−0.59%

futures. Options data for the VXX only goes back to 2010, so we have to content ourselves with a fairly short study. Alternatively, we could try to analyse VIX options with various deltas allowing us to go back a bit further in time. However, testing a VIX options strategy can be treacherous. We would need to calculate the VIX forward price that precisely matches the time to maturity of a given call or else our Black–Scholes implied volatilities would be mis-specified.

As in Figure 4.45, we have matched the volatility of each call buying strategy. Here, the results are less overwhelmingly in favour of a single delta. The 50 delta put seems to function best in risk off environments, while the 10 delta call is best suited for risk on ones. Investors have a tendency to overprice the OTM call skew when VIX implied volatility spikes.

SUMMARY

Several important conclusions can be drawn from this chapter.

- Deep out-of-the-money puts on equity indices generally offer superior value to the mildly OTM puts that institutions favour.
- You can take advantage of institutional bias by selling put ratio spreads, i.e. selling a small number of overpriced OTM puts to finance the purchase of a large number of deep OTM puts.
- The short ratio spread can give you levered long exposure to the implied volatility skew in advance of a crisis, at low cost.
- While the VIX is theoretically attractive as a portfolio hedge, implementation is a major hurdle. You either face severe roll down or mean reversion when buying VIX futures. VIX call options face the added obstacle of time decay. It is extremely difficult to recreate the spot VIX in practice.
- A reasonable alternative involves simultaneously selling VIX futures and overbuying ATM VIX calls. This dramatically reduces exposure to roll down while providing a convex payout on implied volatility. In other words, the structure benefits from large changes in volatility in either direction.
- The VIX futures/call strategy can be useful in risk off regimes, after volatility has risen. It is a useful second leg down strategy if you believe that volatility is likely to slingshot away from its current level.

CHAPTER 5

The Long and the Short of It

Our analysis in Chapter 4 suggested that the implied volatility skew tends to be mispriced in the sense that there is excess demand for moderately out-of-the-money options. But what of the term structure? We want to say something about the value embedded in near-term options compared with longer-dated ones. Here, it is more difficult to be precise. Judging from broker flows, it seems as though institutional managers favour hedges with a few months to maturity. It is uncommon to see strategies that rely upon rolling weekly options and strategies that incorporate multi-year options (outside of the interest rate markets) seem equally rare. We can start with the hypothesis that, if there is any value to be found along the term structure, it probably resides with options that have a very long or very short time to maturity. We want to avoid medium-term options. If everyone wants to buy something, it's going to be expensive.

SHORT-DATED OPTIONS

Some traders argue that you don't want to hold options that are close to expiration. The standard argument is that short-dated options have the highest time decay. Figure 5.1 calculates the time decay of ATM options on the S&P 500 as a function of time to maturity. So if you buy a fixed dollar amount of options with different maturities and nothing happens on a given day, the short-dated ones will lose the most. This is true for any delta, e.g. a fixed dollar amount of short-dated 25 delta puts decay more rapidly than a fixed amount of longer-dated 25 delta puts. However, when you buy short-dated protection after a volatility spike, a number of things work in your favour. We explore these in the next section.

One way to study options is to analyse the extreme cases in time (maturity) and space (strike). For example, you can gain insights by comparing very short-dated options with very long-dated ones. Very short-dated options are characterised by a pitched battle between gamma and theta. Every day that passes quietly will destroy a large percentage of premium. This is bad for the holder of an option. However, large moves can provide a tremendous bang for the buck. It is not unusual to make 10 or more times premium paid on a weekly option. The old venture capital "four bagger", where you make four times your original investment, pales in comparison to what can be made here. IPO-style returns are possible, without the attendant risk.

Let's start by looking at theta, which can be misinterpreted for very short-dated options. Figure 5.1 shows the relationship between theta and time to maturity for an at-the-money option.

We have represented the data along an x-axis which is decreasing in time to maturity. This makes the severe decline in theta easier to visualise, as it occurs away from the x-axis. Since theta approaches

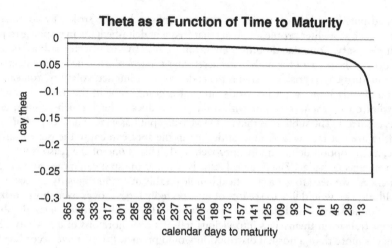

FIGURE 5.1 Time decay for a fixed delta option accelerates as maturity is approached

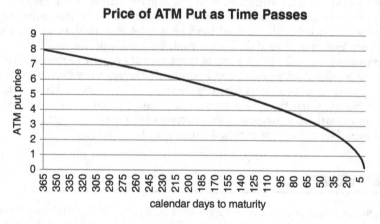

FIGURE 5.2 At-the-money protection rapidly cheapens near maturity

$-\infty$ as $T - t$ goes to 0, it's tempting to conclude that short-dated options decay too quickly to be useful. If the underlying asset doesn't move *pronto*, a short-dated put will burn off. In this context, it seems as though you need to time the entry point perfectly. However, the problem can be considered from another angle. While short-dated options do have severe time decay, we would argue that they have *already* decayed, based on the cumulative impact of many moderately negative theta days. Their absolute prices are low, relative to the amount of coverage they can provide. Given a fixed dollar budget, you can buy a relatively large number of short-dated options. Your protection might not last too long, but in a highly volatile market can make the difference between survival and oblivion. The ability to buy large quantities of options dramatically increases your profit potential if your view is immediately validated by the market. In Figure 5.2, we follow the price decline of an ATM put as time passes, assuming no change in the spot price or volatility. The cost of putting a 1-week floor on your portfolio is roughly 1/8 that of a 1-year floor.

OTM puts whose strike is a fixed percentage below the spot decay even more rapidly as a percentage of premium paid. The "Batman" trade in Figure 3.27 relies upon this phenomenon. You are a net payer of premium when you buy an ATM straddle and sell 2 OTM strangles. However, your theta is still positive until close to maturity, as time decay hits the wings harder than the centre.

Short-dated puts have lots of gamma as the spot approaches the strike. By contrast, long-dated options have a much straighter profile, implying that frequent delta-hedging in response to price changes is not all that necessary. Long-dated options are far more sensitive to investor risk aversion levels than to actual changes in the price of the underlying asset. This is particularly true for low-delta options with a long time to maturity. Here, risk aversion is the code word for implied volatility. You can't hedge vega risk unless you already know what investor sentiment is going to be in the future. It might be argued that a somewhat out-of-the-money put with a day to go doesn't have much gamma, either. Strictly speaking, this is correct. The subtlety is that an OTM 1-day put has a great deal of *potential* gamma. Big changes in delta are not far away. A modest decline in the spot can cause the put to slingshot up the payout curve, as the option delta rapidly approaches −1. This is one of the reasons we favour weekly options as an emergency hedge. The practical issue is whether the spot can move far enough to capture the slingshot effect? We need to get a statistical handle on this question to justify a weekly options buying strategy. Ideally, we would like to see lots of unexpectedly large moves over short horizons.

For equity indices, at least, things seem to work in our favour. A relatively large number of moderate initial drops transform themselves into vicious sell-offs over horizons of a few days. Significantly, their frequency is more than a normal distribution would predict. Prices move according to a positive feedback loop, where investors are forced into the market after an initial move. Day traders and other thinly capitalised investors have to push the escape button if they are severely caught on the wrong side of a trade. Whether explicit stop orders have been placed in the market or not, one large sell order can trigger another, in sequence. Standard econometric techniques are not necessarily the right way to analyse these moves, especially if the feedback function is non-linear. Markets can move almost discontinuously from one level to another if the level of panic becomes high enough.

In the next section, we will discuss some of the statistical evidence suggesting that markets have particularly fat-tailed distributions over short horizons. For now, suppose this empirical statement is true. It follows that you can buy gamma relatively cheaply in the form of weekly options, hedging your portfolio over a horizon where the most damage can potentially be done. If you buy and hold medium maturity options, you will have effectively paid premium over a horizon where market returns tend to be relatively benign. This reduces the expected return of an OTM hedge.

THE PHYSICISTS WEIGH IN

Numerous physicists and applied mathematicians have tried their hand at analysing financial data over the years. These were the early "big data" scientists, as financial markets had an abundance of data and few solid theoretical underpinnings. Over 50 years ago, Mandelbrot (1963) theorised that fluctuations in financial market prices might have infinite variance. Here was a man well ahead of his time, at least in this respect. The true volatility of a stock might be infinite.

Digest that for a moment. A distribution with infinite volatility (or variance) is a far cry from a normal distribution, whose every moment is finite. Moves in excess of 5 or 6 standard deviations essentially never occur for a normal distribution. The tails decay rapidly enough that the expectation of returns, returns squared, returns cubed and so on are all well-defined. Mandelbrot observed explosion in the second moment when analysing historical cotton prices. If correct, the main consequence of the random walk hypothesis would be invalidated. Asset price returns would not be remotely normal. Over time, the weaker notion that asset returns are non-normal has become widely accepted. The question is to what degree extreme events are underpriced by the random walk hypothesis. Conventional academics have a tendency to "stretch" standard models in an attempt to explain outlying data. They might add intermittent jumps to a Gaussian distribution, but are reluctant to develop entirely new models to account for outsized moves.

Are normal distributions accurate, first-order approximations of financial reality, or are they wildly inaccurate in times of crisis? Infinite variance suggests wild inaccuracy, but there are situations where returns look at least relatively normal. As we will soon see, one answer to this question depends on the investment time horizon. Many years later, Taleb (2007) managed to shoehorn Mandelbrot's ideas into a barbell approach to asset allocation. On the assumption that extreme events are statistically underpriced (both in terms of frequency and impact), he advocated a portfolio of safe short-term government bonds combined with a sprinkling of high risk speculative bets where you could lose no more than your initial investment. This is a radical departure from traditional portfolio theory, on the assumption that long-term returns may have greater dependence on the tails than the centre of the distribution.

We tip our hat to Taleb, but have more modest objectives. Our goal is to summarise some of the research suggesting that stock indices have fat-tailed distributions over short horizons. This research has practical application to weekly options. To our knowledge, the relevance of results from econophysics to weekly options has never received much attention and we believe that the discussion below is novel. The application of techniques from statistical physics and dynamical systems to large quantities of financial data is sometimes called "econophysics". This melding of disciplines gained traction about 20 years ago. Previously, financial economists had never been particularly focused on high-frequency data in their ongoing search for risk premia, which can only be extracted over long horizons. Yet masses of intraday data had been available for many years and by the 1990s, computers were powerful enough to process the data. Here, we restrict ourselves to a summary of a paper written by Stanley's group at Boston University in the late 1990s, namely Gopikrishnan (1999). Incidentally, it appears as though it was Stanley himself who coined the term "econophysics" (as in Gangopadhyay, 2013), so we are certainly going to the source. Our overriding goal is to demonstrate that low delta weekly options may be statistically cheap. The paper tracks the quantities $P(\xi > X)$ and $P(\xi < - X)$, as X gets large. These define the "asymptotics" or extremes of a distribution. Note that $P(\xi > X)$ is the probability that a random draw ξ from the underlying distribution is greater than the threshold X. $P(\xi > X)$ says something about the right tail of the distribution and $P(\xi < -X)$ about the left tail. We focus on the left tail here, as it refers to downside risk for stock indices and other risky assets. These are the sorts of things we typically need to hedge. If returns were normally distributed, $P(\xi < - X)$ would decay faster than $1/X^{(\alpha)}$ for any α, as X goes to infinity. But this does *not* turn out to be the case over short-term horizons. Over 1-minute intervals, the authors find that the left-tail alpha is roughly equal to 3. In other words, the tail decays at a rate proportional to $1/X^3$. This suggests that the distribution is not normal, but may satisfy a power law at the extremes. The variance of large moves is probably finite, but skewness and higher moments are likely to be infinite. We can't say with certainty that the variance of 1-minute returns is finite because of the "Mexican peso problem": the mega standard deviation event may simply not have been observed yet.

As the partition window extends beyond a day, we revert to daily data over a 35-year horizon. Alpha slowly increases as a function of window size, suggesting gradual convergence to a normal distribution. Extrapolating from the data, 1-day 10 standard deviation returns are expected to occur once every 10,000 trading days or so. By contrast, a 1 in 10,000 downside move is expected to be roughly 4 standard deviations in magnitude with a partition width of 16 days. This pales in magnitude to what we see in the data.

Gopikrishnan (1999) argues that the mechanism for fat tails over short horizons is serial correlation. Big moves have a tendency to pile up in the same direction. For the S&P 500, we observe that the autocorrelation of returns increases as the partition width contracts toward 0. Persistence is the mechanism that creates fat tails in the distribution over short horizons. Selling can beget more selling, as short-term traders chase the move and others are forced into the market in an attempt to manage their risk. This implies that we can use weekly options *reactively*. If there is a significant down move, we can bet on continuation using a short-dated put, with the statistical evidence in our favour. We don't need to roll our weekly options mechanically every week, as that would be prohibitively expensive. Rather, we can wait for the market to tumble, on the assumption that the probability of an extreme left-tail event over the next few days has increased. If history is a guide, you will usually get some warning before the market breaks through. A weekly options strategy can be implemented more cheaply and sparingly using a reactive approach. We conclude with a few words of caution. While many futures contracts trade overnight, weekly options contracts generally do not. This implies that you can't protect against weekend or overnight events using a weekly options strategy. You need to wait until the cash open to activate a hedge. This suggests that weekly options need to be supplemented with a less timing-dependent hedging strategy. The other obstacle is liquidity. While S&P 500, Euro Stoxx 50 and selected individual stock and ETF weeklies are relatively liquid, the range of tradable weekly options is still quite small. If you need to hedge an idiosyncratic or esoteric risk falling outside of this domain, you may be out of luck.

The following lines from the abstract are particularly significant:

> *We find that the distributions for t ≤ 4 days (1560 mins) are consistent with a power-law asymptotic behaviour (sic), characterized by an exponent α ≈ 3 . . . . For time scales longer than 4 days, our results are consistent with slow convergence to Gaussian behaviour (sic).*

We can see that there is a fairly sharp transition from heavy-tailed to nearly Gaussian behaviour at the 4-day mark. This implies that we would be well-served to focus on options with 4 days or less to go, namely weekly options after the weekend has passed. Intra-week options give us exposure over time horizons where the underlying distribution has the heaviest tails. It's a happy coincidence that the tails are fattest over horizons where vega is lowest. If the market attempts to adjust for increased forward risk by bidding up implied volatility, we can simply move to a further OTM strike to reduce our vega exposure.

While weekly options are an appealing way to react to short-term drops, they are not foolproof. Naturally, this is true of every options strategy. If markets sell off into a Friday close, there is not much we can do. We lose our theoretical edge if we buy a put expiring on the next Friday, as the option has 7 days to go. The underlying distribution is likely to be relatively Gaussian over this horizon. If we adhere strictly to the results of the paper, maintaining continuous coverage through a rolling weekly options strategy is going to be expensive.

A rolling strategy with weekly puts of a given delta generally requires greater premium outlay than one using monthly puts. If we fix the delta at 25, say, the weekly put strikes will start much closer to the spot than the monthly ones. This is a nice feature, but refreshing the strike each week comes at a cost. In Figure 5.3, we make the rough assumption that a month is exactly 4 weeks long. We then compare the price of 41-week 25 delta puts to 11-month 25 delta put for the Euro Stoxx 50 index. We have departed from the S&P 500 in this example purely for the sake of variety.

Buying and re-loading weekly options usually requires between 2 and 2.5 times as much premium as the equivalent monthly put strategy. Viewed from the standpoint of rolling costs, weekly options are egregiously expensive. This serves as an admonition that you should only buy weekly options when you need them. You can only go to the well so many times before the cost of hedging becomes prohibitive. The market is declaring that the "refresh" option for weekly puts has significant value. Weeklies will wind up in the money far more frequently than monthlies.

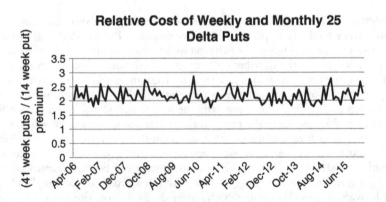

FIGURE 5.3 Mechanically refreshing weekly puts can be expensive

The reader may have observed that our analysis is heavily dependent on research that is nearly 20 years old. What if things have changed since then? Without replicating the study completely, we now give circumstantial evidence that scaling laws for price fluctuations haven't changed materially over time. We start our analysis with S&P 500 index futures. First, we calculate the standard deviation σ (21) of 21-day returns, using data from 1995 to 2015. This period roughly picks up where the Stanley group study left off. Note that there are roughly 21 trading days in a calendar month, so this is a reasonable convention. We then convert σ to a standard deviation for each series of n day returns. $\sigma(n) = sqrt\left(\dfrac{n}{21}\right) * \sigma(21)$ would be the correct transformation for all n, assuming that prices evolved according to a random walk. In our example, n ranges from 1 to 25 days. What is the meaning of this transformation? In the world of Brownian motion, where the standard deviation of returns fans out at a rate equal to $\sqrt{T}$, we would expect the percentage of returns greater than $2*\sigma(n)$ to be independent of n. In particular, the frequency of "2 sigma" events should be roughly 4.55% for any partition n. Recall that, when you sample from a normal distribution, 95.45% of all samples are expected to lie within 2 standard deviations of the mean. Equivalently, 4.55% of all samples are expected to be 2+ standard deviation events. The random walk construction does *not* turn out to be correct, as Figure 5.4 suggests.

For 1-day returns, the incidence of 2+ standard deviation returns is nearly twice what σ (21) would predict. There are lots of outliers over horizons less than a week. As the partition width grows, the extremes of our distribution look increasingly normal. The curve settles down to the 4.5% target level as we move to the right of Figure 5.4. This suggests that, after a large short-term drop, the index has a tendency to mean revert. At the very least, it doesn't tend to follow through. Note that we haven't considered long partition widths (i.e. where n is large), as we would then have to take the average return of the series into account. We would then be calculating deviations from an average historical return that may be quite different in the future.

We now branch out into other equity indices, as in the Stanley group paper. In Figure 5.5, we can see that the FTSE 100 and DAX indices follow roughly the same descending path. Figure 5.5 takes a simple average of the FTSE and DAX curves, for each partition width. In technical terms, we have calculated a rough version of the Hurst exponent, as in Beran (1994). This measures the range over which a stochastic process has "memory".

We can move even further afield, without much difficulty. Figure 5.6 tabulates the frequency of 2+ standard deviation moves for a concentrated global portfolio of bond futures. In particular, we have taken an equally weighted combination of US 10 year, Bund and JGB (Japanese Government Bond) futures. As above, we have averaged the frequencies across the 3 contracts, using data from 1995 to 2015.

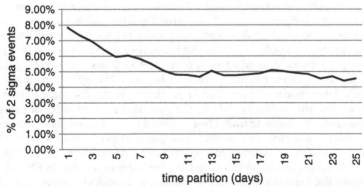

S&P 500: Frequency of Out-Sized Moves

FIGURE 5.4 Frequency of 2+ standard deviation returns in S&P 500, based on partition width

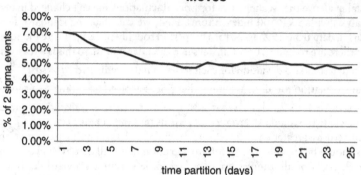

FIGURE 5.5 Frequency of 2+ standard deviation returns, DAX/FTSE blend

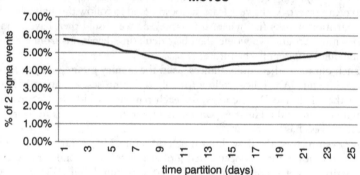

FIGURE 5.6 Frequency of 2+ standard deviation returns in global bond futures markets

Now we are faced with a more complicated situation. We observe the usual decay from 1- to roughly 10-day partitions. However, the curve now turns *up* for wider partition widths. This gives us the impression of an asset class where there are big intra-week returns that stall a bit and then follow through. This may be a momentum effect. Bonds have a greater tendency to trend over medium- to long-horizons, exaggerating an initial sharp short-term move. In Chapter 6, we will describe how bond futures have been very "trend worthy" since the 1980s. For now, we observe one other stylised fact. The bond futures curve never seems to wander too far from the 4.55% theoretical level. In this sense, bonds are more well-behaved than equity indices over short horizons. Having said that, it may be that the infrequent 2 standard deviation moves are much larger than a normal distribution would predict.

We end this section with an ideological point. If you use options to hedge or express a view, you may be picking relatively low hanging fruit. Most empirical research attempts to characterise the price dynamics of "primitive" securities, such as stocks and bonds, rather than derivatives, such as options. By contrast, options research has typically focused on pricing relative to an underlying asset. Derman (2016) has succinctly compared this to calculating the fair value of a fruit salad based on the price of the constituent fruits. But there is another alternative. As an investor in options, you can study the literature on underlying asset returns and see if it has application to the options structures you trade. We have tried to follow this prescription here.

BUYING TIME

When markets are volatile and profits are draining away, many discretionary traders find their eyes glued to the screen. They start to watch every tiny move, every tick, in the markets they trade. This is an affliction without any logical basis. What can you gain from watching the ticks? If you don't know how you will react to a given market move *before* it occurs, tracking the market offers no advantage. In a thought-provoking article, Gray (2014) argues that algorithms can outperform human judgment in many fields where it is tacitly assumed that experts should have superior insight. You might make bad decisions in the heat of battle if you haven't planned ahead. Systematic funds might argue that model-based trading eliminates the need for screen watching. Systems are not robots who think for themselves. Rather, they rely upon rules developed and tested by humans, far from the market frenzy. When a grandmaster is defeated by a computer, the implication that the computer is "smarter" than the player is false. The computer is simply a composite of a calculator, a database and the collaborative effort of other masters and developers in a research setting. These allow the computer to assess a given position in relatively broad terms.

In the same way, discretionary traders need time to react appropriately to market dynamics. Yet the market affords no such luxury. It keeps moving without regard for *your* position. So how can you buy yourself time in a market that waits for no one? Even if you are model-based, market conditions can change beyond the confines of the data over which your system was developed. Weekly options can help. They allow you to formulate an exit strategy, at low cost. Weeklies are currently available on major equity indices, stocks and ETFs in the US. Some exchanges even support "flex" options, where you can specify the strike and time to maturity that you wish to trade. So in many instances, it should be possible to construct a hedge that tides you over for a few days.

The following example highlights the potential utility of weekly options. Let's assume that a trader has bought a 1×2 put ratio spread on the S&P 500 at the worst possible time. Specifically, 100 1-year ATM puts have been bought and 200 1-year 25 delta puts sold. As soon as the combo went through the market, there was a flash −5% move in the index. 1-year volatility spiked by 5 points across all strikes (note that this simplifying assumption understates the skew effects in the trade). The structure is instantly in trouble. A range of catastrophic scenarios is now in play, as Figure 5.7 suggests.

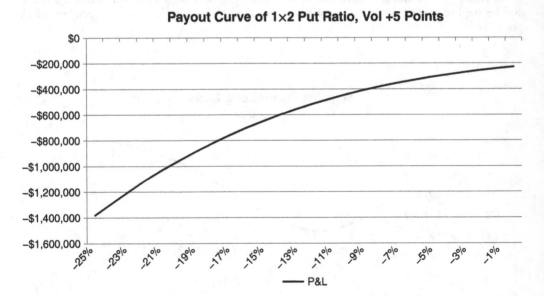

FIGURE 5.7   Impact of volatility expansion on a long-dated 1×2 put ratio

In all likelihood, things will calm down eventually. For the moment, however, holding on seems like a game of Russian roulette. What is the appropriate course of action now? You could just throw in the towel and liquidate the position at the close of what has been a devastating day. However, you are likely to get out at a horrible price as long-dated options are not going to be trading much. Other investors will also be scrambling to cover their short volatility positions. This will cause implied volatility to jump across all strikes and maturities. The deformable surface will rise and become more contorted. Market makers will extract their pound of flesh, given your desperation.

Another alternative is simply to *pray* that the markets recover overnight. This may sound absurd, but it is surprisingly common. All you need is a quick return to "rationality" from the market. When prices move against some traders, they do nothing, expecting the market to come back. No contingency is in place. Usually their positions do recover, which has a damaging psychological effect in the long-term. It reinforces reckless behaviour. Anyone who has teetered on the edge of the abyss, taken no action and been rewarded for it is likely to do the same again. Eventually, the market *doesn't* recover and their accounts are wiped out. After a spike in volatility, the 1×2 ratio from Figure 5.7 looks even more attractive to someone who trades mean reversion in volatility and the skew. The static "edge" in the structure has increased. The trouble is that you need the spread to converge *now* or else you may be forced out at an even worse level. Inexperienced traders often take aggressive short volatility positions with open-ended risk. As Ed Seykota notably said in Schwager (2012) "there are old traders and there are bold traders, but there are no old bold traders".

The vega profile of a 1×2 put ratio illustrates how quickly you can land into trouble. We can see from Figure 5.8 that vega sharply increases in magnitude, leveling off only when the index has plunged over −15%.

As the S&P drops, you are faced with the double whammy of increasing delta and vega. If you feel that volatility is over-priced, but need to block out the risk of an extreme downside price move, short-dated gamma hedging is appropriate. Weekly options can gear into a move faster than *any* algorithm, as their price responds continuously to changes in the spot. They are your ultimate defense against runaway algorithms, allowing you to focus on your core areas of expertise. The overriding conclusion is that specific options strategies can allow "old school" managers to keep investing the way they always have, while defending against runaway markets.

In Figure 5.9, we plot the payout curve for a put with 1 day to go against a put with 1 year to go. The implied volatility for both options is assumed to be constant and independent of the spot price.

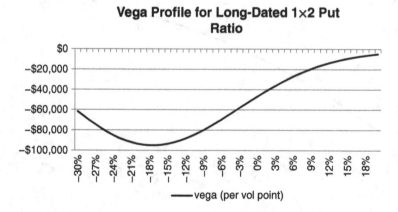

Vega Profile for Long-Dated 1×2 Put Ratio

——vega (per vol point)

FIGURE 5.8   Short vega exposure for a 1×2 put ratio, as a function of moneyness

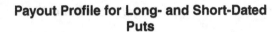

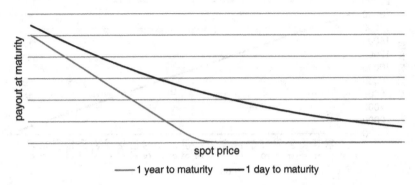

FIGURE 5.9 Long-dated puts have relatively high premium and vega, but relatively low gamma near the strike

We can see that OTM puts without much time to maturity trade at a low absolute price. This implies that we could buy 100 short-term puts against our 1×2 ratio spread to cap extreme event risk, while buying ourselves some time. Either the trade will recover or we can unwind some of the 1×2 while monetising some profits on the short-dated hedge.

For the 1×2 put ratio in 100 lots, your maximum exposure is roughly $20 million. If the index drops enough, you are effectively short 100 puts with delta 100. Assuming an index value of 2000 in this scenario and a multiplier of 100, your exposure is 2000*100*100 = 20,000,000. Suppose you want to eliminate gamma risk over a 2-day horizon, using 10 delta puts. If implied volatility is 15%, these puts will cost a bit more than $1, with strike less than 2% below the spot. This implies that your 100 lot hedge will cost roughly $100*1*100 = $10,000, or 0.05% of notional exposure. This can be a reasonable one-off cost for a few days of sanity!

In 2015 and 2016, there have been a few high-profile fund closures where managers argued that algorithmic trading had interfered with their core investment strategy. High-frequency mega moves were periodically occurring that seemed unrelated to what the managers considered to be market fundamentals. Anecdotally, we know that high-frequency systems typically rely on price and volume data when deciding whether to buy or sell. They're looking at information in the order book, as it evolves over time. Most systems fall into one of two categories, momentum and mean reversion. The impact of a well-capitalised mean reversion strategy is usually not much of a concern, as these strategies tend to push prices back into a range. It's momentum that we need to worry about, leading to blisteringly fast moves in one direction or another. Hammering the point home again, this is where weekly options can come in handy. Weekly options can gear into a move faster than any algorithm, as their price responds continuously to changes in the spot. You needn't worry so much about premium expansion, given the short time to maturity. They are your ultimate defence against runaway algorithms, allowing you to focus on your core areas of expertise.

LONG-DATED OPTIONS

Options with a long time to maturity, i.e. where T-t is large, have very different characteristics from short-dated ones. Gamma is relatively unimportant, as the payout curve is not very convex. At the other end of the spectrum, options with more than a year to maturity (i.e. long-dated options) can offer interesting and alternative hedging opportunities. As usual, we are trying to avoid those 2% OTM 3 month

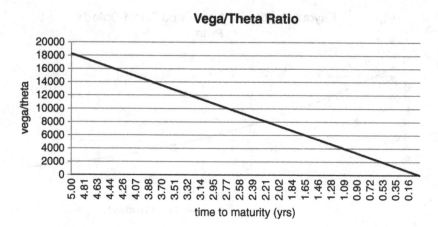

FIGURE 5.10 Vega/theta as a metric for selecting options

to maturity puts that many institutions seem to favour. While short-dated options tend to be gamma plays, vega plays a relatively important role when you buy a 5 year to maturity put on the S&P 500. One way to think about this is to compare the vega/theta ratio for fixed-delta options with different times to maturity.

Figure 5.10 shows the near-linear dependence of vega/theta on time to maturity. To be precise, we have calculated vega and theta for an ATM put trading at 20% implied volatility for a range of maturities. The discount rate has been assumed to be 0. In reality, theta is negative for a long call or put. We have taken its absolute value before calculating vega/theta – in reality, vega/abs(theta) – for ease of exposition.

When implied volatility is low, it's logical to buy long-dated options in an effort to maximise the ratio. You can then sit back and wait for volatility to rise without worrying too much about time decay. One nice thing about long-dated implied volatility is that it isn't particularly responsive to small moves in the underlying. An uptick in the S&P 500 won't affect the value of your 2-year put in the absence of a volatility decline. Sometimes, it takes a while for a move in the underlying to propagate to the long end of the volatility term structure. The situation is a bit like a giant dinosaur that has been bitten on the tail: it might take a while before the dinosaur realises what has happened. In the early stages of a sell-off, you can sometimes buy long-dated options at implied volatility levels that have hardly moved at all. This can be very beneficial if you want to hedge without paying up for implied volatility.

There are also times when long-dated options can offer exceptional value. Structured products desks at banks occasionally create supply and demand imbalances that are not absorbed by market makers or funds that specialise in liquid exchange-traded markets. For example, when interest rates are persistently low, some banks offer yield enhancement products that rely on selling options at the long end of the curve. Japan has been in a deflationary spiral since the 1990s, with rates hovering close to 0. We mentioned how the FX carry trade has been used as a yield surrogate for Japanese investors. Option writing has also been used as an income-generating technique in Japan. At times, this has caused extreme selling pressure on long-dated puts and calls. The long end of the volatility term structure has episodically become very cheap, creating buying opportunities for value buyers of volatility.

The academic literature also provides some evidence that long-dated options might be underpriced. Pastor and Stambaugh (2012) argue against the deeply entrenched belief that annualised stock volatility is lower over longer time horizons. If the expected return of an asset is not adequately estimated by historical data, annualised volatility can actually go *up* as the horizon increases. This can create a rich opportunity set for buyers of long-dated options.

FAR FROM THE MADDING CROWD

Sometimes, there are isolated sell-offs in an asset class, with no immediate impact on other asset classes. For example, energies might go into a bear market, while stocks and bonds continue to rise. These episodes can offer good opportunities for long-term hedging. Ultimately, markets are linked, especially when multi-asset class investors are forced to liquidate their portfolios. If you see bad things happening in one corner of the market, a clever strategy can involve buying options elsewhere, before volatility picks up universally.

Pring (2006) has proposed the idea of an investment clock, on the assumption that asset classes move in a fairly orderly sequence. Price trends in one asset class inexorably lead to trends in the others. We start at 12 o'clock in risk off mode. Investors are piling into the safe haven of government bonds, while reducing exposure to equities and real assets. As the clock approaches 3, volatility begins to stabilise and investors start to believe that bonds have low prospective returns relative to equities. While bonds continue to rally, equities eventually enter into an upward trend. It is now 6 o'clock. Corporations are finally feeling confident enough to engage in longer-term projects. Investment capital migrates from bonds and to a lesser extent stocks into the real economy, stoking the demand for real assets. Industrial commodities such as copper and oil rally and emerging markets are starting to outperform. By 9 o'clock, inflation is ticking up to the extent that central banks want to apply the brakes. Rates begin to rise and more importantly, central banks begin to withdraw credit from the system. Bonds sell off, then equities and finally commodities. The cycle is now ready to renew itself.

We can think of sequential moves across asset classes in a less structured way. Bond investors sometimes view stock pickers with disdain, as company specialists can be the last to realise something has fundamentally changed in the economy. While they myopically scour the balance sheets of a small set of companies, the entire economy might be tumbling into recession. The bond market gives important signals that are simply ignored by the fraternity of equity analysts. Bond prices are not affected by the idiosyncratic risk in the same way that stock prices are. This implies that, in many cases, increased volatility in the bond market can be a leading indicator of equity index volatility. Assuming that the investment clock idea is correct, it has direct application to a long-dated options strategy. In the same way that broad market trends can be asynchronous, long-dated volatility does not necessary move in tandem across asset classes. There may be times where stocks are volatile but commodities are still rising, as in 2007 and early 2008. Here, you would have been well-served to buy commodity volatility as a hedge against a systemic risk event. Long-dated commodity implied volatility was still low at the end of 2007, while there had been a repricing of risk in other asset classes.

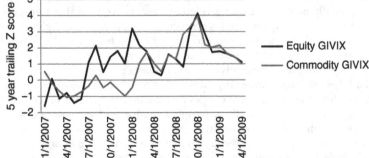

FIGURE 5.11   Commodity implied volatility lagged during the global financial crisis

The investment management company, 36 South, has constructed a series of global implied volatility, or "GIVIX" indices, that track long-dated implied volatility across equities, FX, interest rates and commodities. The indices can be used to identify value buying opportunities in various options markets. In Figure 5.11, we can see that commodity implied volatility was slow to respond to rising equity volatility in 2007. The figure is based on the 5-year trailing Z score of the equity and commodity GIVIX indices, in an effort to normalise the two data sets.

We conclude that you can sometimes find value in long-dated options even when aggregate asset class volatility is high.

R MINUS D

Suppose we have a stock index whose price is S. The risk-free rate is r and the dividend yield of the index is d. Then, a forward with time T-t to maturity will have price $F = Se^{(r-d)(T-t)}$. The sensitivity of F to changes in $(r-d)$ is then $(T-t)Se^{(r-d)(T-t)}$. This is the partial derivative of F in $(r-d)$, but we need not think in such technical terms. The key point is that, as $(T-t)$ grows, F becomes more sensitive to $(r-d)$ at an exponentially increasing rate. This has major implications for options of varying maturities, as we now see.

We recall that rho (ρ) is an option's sensitivity to small changes in interest rates. For short-dated options, rho generally isn't very important. The forward price will be quite close to the spot, regardless of rates. However, as we extend an option's time to maturity, rho plays an ever-increasing role. A small change in rates can have a relatively large impact on the price of the forward, which in turn impacts the option price. For equity indices, we need to measure sensitivity relative to $r-d$, where r is the risk-free rate and d is the dividend yield of the index. If $r-d > 0$, the forward curve will be upward sloping, i.e. "in contango". This implies that a 50 delta call with 1 year to maturity, say, will have a higher strike than the spot price S. In this scenario, the spot price may actually have to rally for an ATM call to wind up in the money. Suppose that we now fix r and isolate dependence on the dividend yield d.

The forward curve for d has some interesting properties. Let's use the Euro Stoxx 50 dividend futures term structure as a guide, as dividend-based contracts have been relatively popular in France and Germany for quite some time. We observe that a futures contract is nothing more than a forward that trades on an exchange. Dividend futures trade in yearly vintages, with December expiration. For example, on 1 February, 2016, contracts ranging from December 2016 to December 2025 in annual increments were listed. The value at maturity for a given vintage is the total realised cash dividend payout for that year. Investors who rely on fundamental analysis find this feature appealing, as the terminal payout is based on genuine cash flows from companies, rather than the market's perception of what a collection of companies is worth. The futures are vectoring toward something tangible. The front-year futures are generally not that interesting, especially in the second half of the year, as most of the dividends have already been paid out. This implies that there is not much uncertainty in the payout. The front-year contract usually plods along with a volatility that converges to 0 as time goes by. However, comparing the contracts for subsequent years is instructive. In Figure 5.12, we calculate the rolling beta of the first 7 vintages to the 2nd one. Our historical data set ranges from May 2009 to January 2016.

The 1st contract has substantially less beta than the longer-dated vintages. This is to be expected, as on average roughly 6 months of dividends have already been paid out. The uncertainty in the terminal payout is relatively low. What's more surprising is that the 2nd contract has a smaller beta than the 3rd to 7th contracts. Here, the smaller beta implies that the deferred contracts have materially *higher* volatility than the 2nd one. This is markedly different from what we have observed for the term structure of interest rates, volatility or commodity prices. For those markets, most of the action is in the spot and front contracts. Changes propagate through the term structure at a decaying rate. For dividend futures, conversely, a decline in corporate prospects has a disproportionate effect further down the curve. What is going on here? While dividend policy tends to be relatively fixed in the short-term, economic shocks can have a large impact on dividend policy further out into the future. A mature company

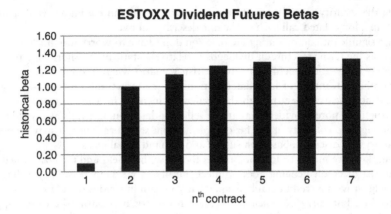

FIGURE 5.12   Historical beta of Euro Stoxx 50 dividend futures to 2nd contract

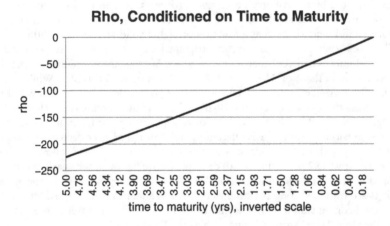

FIGURE 5.13   Rho has relatively large magnitude for long-dated options

will usually only cut its dividend if forced to, i.e. if it's severely strapped for cash. It's in the interest of the company to "amortise" the impact of a disastrous earnings season by gradually introducing the idea of a reduced dividend to the market. Bad news increases the probability of a slashed dividend in the somewhat distant future, after a company has prepared the market for it.

Both a call and a put are priced off the forward $F = e^{(r-d)T}$. If the dividend gets cut, $r - d$ goes up given the decline in d. This increases the value of the forward, pushing it toward the strike. An OTM call gets closer to ATM. So if you own a call on a high dividend-paying index, your existing position may actually *benefit* from a risk event. This may seem surprising at first, as calls are innately bullish plays. However, delta-related losses can be more than offset by rising volatility and a cut in prospective dividends. You benefit more than you might think when the dividend forward curve drops, as longer-dated options have relatively large rho (ρ). In Figure 5.13, we have calculated rho for a series of ATM puts, over a range of decreasing maturities. We have assumed that $r - d$ is equal to 2% for all values of $T - t$. We observe that the magnitude of rho decays to 0 as $T - t$ approaches 0, at a roughly linear rate. Viewed differently, rho is relatively large for long-dated options.

Taking advantage of forward drift in a 0 interest rate environment does have some subtleties, though. The "r" in $r - d$ is nettlesome. While bank deposit rates might be 0 or even negative, the cost of borrowing the security underlying a futures contract can be quite a bit above 0. This reduces the effective drift in a long-dated call such as the one described above.

There are significant compensating factors. You don't have to worry too much about drift on the futures hedge, as the term structure of dividends is relatively static at the short end. Yet you are delta-neutral, long volatility and benefit from the bearish scenario where corporations start cutting their dividends. Another advantage of long-dated options can be structural. Opportunities arise now and again, as yield hogs search for a trough that generates income. In a low interest rate environment, annuity or structured note providers may try to sell long-dated puts or calls as a yield enhancer. This can artificially depress volatility at the far end of the term structure. Then, it may be possible to buy implied volatility at a discount, based on supply and demand imbalances.

Credit markets are more straightforward, in the sense that yield and the cost of hedging move in tandem. The cost of credit hedging goes up mechanically as yields increase. If you buy a high yield bond, then hedge it with a credit default swap, what you gain in yield is offset by the increased cost of default protection. For carry currencies, however, this is not necessarily the case. Suppose that an emerging market country is in a rapid growth phase. The Central Bank might raise rates in an effort to prevent the economy from overheating, i.e. to prevent inflationary bubbles. This would increase carry if you bought a forward on that country's currency. At the same time, foreign investors might be pouring money in, attracted by the country's economic prospects. So you might wind up with a situation where the spot currency was stable or rising as forward carry increased. Then, your risk-adjusted expected return would increase *both* as a function of higher yield and lower volatility.

If volatility goes down as carry goes up, an intriguing idea is to "spend away" a bit of excess forward yield, buying OTM puts as a direct hedge on the currency. After all, the premium on a put should be relatively low after a rally in the spot. However, there is a difficulty with this idea. While roll down pushes the forward in your favour, it reduces the effectiveness of your hedge. The forward will drift away from your put strike unless the spot currency drops sharply. The situation resembles the short VIX futures, long VIX calls hedge we analysed in Chapter 4. Roll down helps our forward, but hurts our hedge. However, as we mentioned previously, our hedge is affected by roll down at an ever-decreasing rate. Delta declines as a function of forward drift. The reader can see that many of our strategies follow the short put spread or square root (i.e. short 1×2 put ratio spread) concept. We are happy to sell nearby insurance, so long as the wings are covered or even over-hedges. The idea rhymes if not repeats. We can engage in any number of statistically based trades, so long as extreme event risk is adequately accounted for.

From a pure hedging standpoint, it would be fantastic to find a currency that had the following properties relative to a "safe" store of value such as the US dollar.

- The currency was risky, with negatively skewed returns.
- It was likely to perform poorly during a systemic risk event.
- It had a put skew that would steepen after a risk event.
- Implied volatility was currently low.
- Finally, it had a *lower* short rate than the equivalent maturity US T bill rate.

All the stars would be aligned. We could buy a large quantity of puts on the currency in quiet times and then wait. Our theta decay would be partially offset by downward drift in the underlying forward rate. This suggests that it would not cost much to maintain the position. In the event of a spike in global market volatility, we would benefit from increasing implied volatility and skew as well as a drop in the currency. What a nice combination! Historically, risky currencies have had relatively high interest rates, violating the final condition above. They would typically be based in emerging market or commodity producing countries, where inflation was also a concern. It is only relatively recently that currencies such as the Euro have become riskier, while engaging in competitive devaluation. As of this writing, German yields with less than 5 years to maturity are *negative*, offering investors cheap hedging opportunities via puts on the Euro. While it is true that the Euro put skew is already steep (loosely violating one of the conditions above), new FX hedging opportunities have emerged at a time where the 0 bound for interest rates has been breached.

THE LUMBERJACK PLOT

There is another way to visualise returns in excess of 2 standard deviations. This requires a rescaling of the axes of the cumulative distribution function. "Log log" plots are commonly used in the sciences to characterise the extremes of a distribution. The motivation is as follows. When you plot the histogram of returns for an asset, it's hard to tell how fat the tails are. The probability of an extreme event always looks very close to 0. What is needed is a technique for magnifying the tails. "Log log" graphs allow us to take an expanded view of low probability events. We can examine the left and right tails of the distribution independently, as follows. Let's start with the left tail of a standard normal distribution, i.e. a normal distribution with mean 0 and variance 1. How likely is a return smaller than $-1 = -10^0$, than $-10 = -10^1$ and so on? We can ask a sequence of questions like this and plot the result. Obviously, the sequence of probabilities decays rapidly for virtually any distribution, so we need to use a scale that accounts for very low probabilities as well. In particular, we graph the move sizes according to the sequence $\{-10^1, -10^2, -10^3, \ldots\}$ and the probabilities according to $\{-10^{-1}, -10^{-2}, -10^{-3}, \ldots\}$. For normal distributions, the curve decays so rapidly that you will essentially *never* see a move below -10^6, even on a scale that decays exponentially in p. Other distributions go to $-\infty$ more slowly when plotted this way. Distributions that have fat tails may follow a "power law", where the rate of decay is a straight line. The probability of finding a negative number that is a huge power of 10 increases proportionately as you sample 10 times as many random numbers.

We should mention that there is a region even *beyond* the power law. Observe that the log log graph ultimately *does* rely upon curve fitting. You collect lots of data, plot the probability of extreme moves on stretched axes and then fit a line through them. It may be that the regression line is so flat that the distribution appears to have infinite variance. That's already quite a statement. But what if new data points arrive that are even more extreme than the power law predicts? After all, the analysis above still relies upon extrapolation at some level. Sornette (2003) calls these outliers "dragon kings". They are far larger than even a fitted power law distribution would predict. Assuming that we are long the tails and the dragon kings do not prevent the markets from functioning, this distinction should not concern us. When we buy enough OTM options to cover our existing positions, our potential losses are strictly bounded over the life of the options. Equivalently, we have truncated the tails of the underlying distribution. There are no tails in our composite position, so all moments in our profit and loss distribution are strictly bounded.

Vega Grows in T – t

Short-dated options have relatively little vega. Their price is not very sensitive to changes in volatility. This implies that you do not have to pay up for an OTM option after a risk event, in volatility terms. In Figure 5.14, we assume that we have taken a long position of 100 ATM puts on the S&P 500, with maturities ranging from 1 to 15 months. The term structure of volatility has been assumed constant, at 17%, across maturities. We then "shock" the term structure by +5 volatility points across all maturities and calculate the impact on the value of our puts. The long-dated options near the y-axis have considerably higher vega than the short-dated ones further to the right.

We acknowledge that the high vega in long-dated options is partially offset by the fact that long-dated volatility has a relatively low beta to short-dated volatility. It doesn't move all that much in the early phases of a sell-off. However, if there is a sustained down move, long-dated implied volatility should move enough to give you a relatively large bang for the buck.

When volatility jumps, many options become prohibitively expensive. Portfolio managers may need to hedge against disaster for a few days while they rebalance their portfolios. In this context, very short-dated options can be useful, as they are not very sensitive to changes in volatility. In this chapter, we review the literature on fat tailed distributions over short horizons. We also describe how weekly options can deliver very high payout ratios at low cost. We focus on how implied volatility can be persistent over horizons less than a week. We also discuss profit-taking strategies when delta-hedging is impossible.

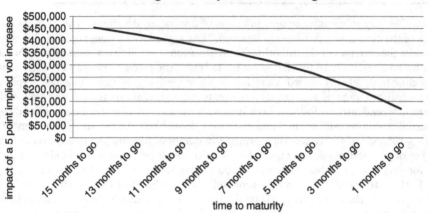

FIGURE 5.14   Long-dated options have relatively high sensitivity to changes in volatility

SELECTIVE APPLICATION OF THE WEEKLY OPTIONS STRATEGY

In the context of crisis hedging, it's worth revisiting weekly options. We already know that the frequency of extreme moves is relatively high over intra-week horizons, but perpetually buying and rolling weeklies comes at a severe cost. However, we can selectively apply a weekly options strategy, based on the following observation. When equity markets go into a down trend, heightened risk may be in the offing. Leveraged long investors are under pressure to slash risk. It turns out that we can use a straightforward trend indicator as a buy signal for the weekly strategy. The following analysis is based on a 10-year trailing data set for the S&P 500. We have calculated the average return of a 25 delta weekly put buying strategy during up and down trends for the index. Our trend indicator simply compares the closing index value in the previous week to its trailing 52 week average. If the index is higher than the trailing average, the market is said to be in an uptrend. Otherwise, it's in a downtrend. Specifically, when the S&P was in an uptrend, the average gross return of the puts was −0.02% per week. During downtrends, which occurred less than 1/3 of the time over the sample period, the average strategy return was higher, at +0.01% per week.

Our analysis suggests that you can usually wait until the market officially goes into a downtrend before unleashing your weekly put buying strategy. Even then, you might only want to buy those puts if you really need them, in an effort to be as judicious as possible. We accept that our weekly study (i.e., using Friday close to close data) does not precisely apply to an intra-week put buying strategy. Given the results we quoted from econophysics, this may be sub-optimal. However, a fixed 1-week holding period allows us to test the relative performance of our timing strategy easily and directly.

Our trend indicator allows us to cut hedging costs by reducing the number of times we buy the weekly. In particular, we only buy after the market has given us some confirmation. This suggests that we will typically be loading the strategy after sell-off, when volatility is relatively high. It's worth confirming that the relative cost of the weekly put strategy is not too sensitive to the level of volatility. Otherwise, our timing edge would be offset by the increased cost of buying weekly puts. Reassuringly, the relative cost of a weekly put strategy is almost completely uncorrelated with implied volatility for the 1-month 25 delta put. Once again, we use the Euro Stoxx 50 as a trial horse.

At very high implied volatility levels, the term structure is likely to invert. In other words, short-dated implied volatility will typically trade at a premium to longer-dated volatility. According to Figure 5.15, however, weekly 25 delta puts do not seem unduly expensive relative to their monthly counterparts in the extreme. This reinforces the idea of weekly puts as a last ditch hedge.

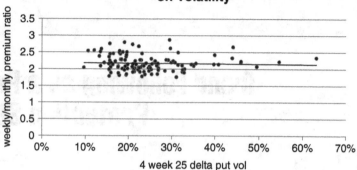

FIGURE 5.15   The relative cost of weekly puts is inelastic to the level of volatility

SUMMARY

It's a curious thing, but short- and long-dated options on the same asset have radically different characteristics. Short-dated OTM options are all about gamma. They're relatively cheap and insensitive to volatility, but offer tremendous potential when there are large realised moves. Weekly options benefit from contagion effects that tend to have the largest impact over short horizons. Conversely, long-dated OTM options reprice based on sentiment and do not have large direct dependence on price action.

The prescription, then, is to buy long-dated protection when investors are overconfident and short-dated options when you need an emergency hedge after an initial spike in volatility. From a hedging standpoint, medium-term options are the worst of both worlds and should generally be avoided.

CHAPTER 6

Trend Following as a Portfolio Protection Strategy

"If you want to make a million you don't have to understand money, what you have to understand is people's fears about money."

-William Gaddis, JR

In this chapter, we discuss how trend following can be used as a risk mitigation device after a market drop. It offers a potential alternative to long options strategies, particularly when the cost of insurance (i.e. implied volatility) is already high. We describe what the catch-all phrase "trend following" means, both in practical and philosophical terms. We study momentum from a variety of perspectives, calculating correlations with volatility indices and pushing the analogy with insurance as far as we can. Our conclusions will not be definitive, but will give some insight into the complex relationship between momentum and portfolio protection. Ultimately, we argue that trend following is a moderately reliable form of statistical insurance. There is no guarantee that your trend following system will be up during a rapid sell-off. However, trend following is structurally diversifying, with a high probability of strong performance during sustained bear markets.

Trend following benefits from price volatility when the signal to noise ratio is high. A market that shoots off in one direction or another, without too much choppiness *en route*, is ideal. Conversely, volatile range-bound markets are just about the worst environment for a trend follower. A system is likely to get "topped and tailed", repeatedly having to exit positions at a loss as the market keeps changing direction. Since high volatility typically corresponds to market liquidations, there are more likely to be large-scale directional moves in risk off regimes. An investor who wants to use trend following as insurance is relying upon this stylised fact.

WHAT IS TREND FOLLOWING?

Imagine you were given some money to invest, but didn't have any idea about what to do with it. Value investing, i.e. attempting to buy underpriced securities over time, was not in your wheel house. Graham (1999) had never found its way onto your desk. Broadly, you had no conception of how much a given asset might be worth. What could you reasonably do other than stick your finger in the air? Following price trends might be a start. You could always follow the herd, with an exit strategy if the trend reversed. If an asset went up enough, you would buy it. If it sold off enough, you would sell it. You would simply invest in the direction that was being confirmed by the market.

Many seasoned investors have started with such an approach, drifted into other areas as they "learned" more about how markets operate and finally returned when they found that following trends was just about the most effective thing they could do. One advantage of trend following is that it purely relies upon market prices and to a lesser extent, volumes. The system is self-contained, as you make the limiting assumption that all relevant information is contained in the price action of a given market. Once you start to incorporate economic releases, news and so on, the problem of investing becomes open-ended. You never know whether you have missed something vital. To be fair, trend following is not the only strategy that restricts itself to price inputs. Other technical trading strategies fall into the somewhat amorphous category called "statistical arbitrage". They might trade mean reversion in spreads or identify more complicated exploitable patterns in price data.

However, trend following does offer one advantage over other pattern recognition techniques. The trend following signal indirectly helps to manage risk. In particular, the signal forces you to reduce if not eliminate exposure as a trend breaks. In the absence of an outsized intra-day price jump, cumulative losses from a losing position are unlikely to get too large. While pure trend following might not offer very high risk-adjusted returns, it allows you to stay in the game while you wait for a large-scale directional move in one of the markets you trade. It is widely known that longer-term trend followers usually make the bulk of their returns in 4 or 5 markets each year. Another advantage of trend following is capacity. Some of the strategies presented earlier in this book are not scalable enough for large institutional investors. Weekly options are particularly constrained in terms of maximum trading volumes. Long-term trend following has no such limitations. The largest trend followers comfortably manage more than $100 billion total of gross notional exposure. Note that the notional exposure of a fund can dramatically exceed the amount of equity in the fund. It's only necessary to post a small amount of cash into a margin account to finance a relatively large position. For funds of this size, there may be some price impact at execution time. However, the impact can be minimised under "normal" market conditions by clever trade execution.

A pure trend follower is committed to following a sell-off *all* the way down. There is no question of taking some profits on a short position (say) and finding a higher re-entry point at a later time. This mentality is colourfully captured by Edwin Lefèvre in *Reminiscences of a Stock Operator*[1] (1923). The book was written nearly a century ago, but continues to be relevant today. In the book, Mr. Partridge, also known as "Old Turkey" for the way he would stick his chest out while pacing the office, was a successful trader and a dyed-in-the-wool trend follower. As the story goes, he would never fade the prevailing trend. Rather, he would hold on to winning trades indefinitely, so long as they were broadly moving in the right direction. One day, a colleague offered a humble suggestion: Perhaps Old Turkey should consider trading around a trending long position, selling strength every now and then, with the hope of buying back the position at a lower price later. If the trend followed a rough path, with frequent reversals, the total profit in the trade would increase.

> "Slip them that stock of yours and buy it back on the reaction. You might as well reduce the cost to yourself."
>
> "My dear boy," said old Partridge, in great distress "my dear boy, if I sold that stock now I'd lose my position; and then where would I be?"

Several well-known macro hedge funds follow this principle today. They meticulously develop investment ideas, but make a point of waiting for market confirmation before entering a trade. Once in, they are willing to maintain a position well beyond what might be considered "fair value", relying on glacial repositioning within a market. In mid-2014, who would have imagined that oil would trade below $40 a barrel? There was a near universal belief that producers would stop pumping oil below $60 or so. If oil plunged any further, oil production and delivery would be a loss-making enterprise. Yet, here is the spot price chart for WTI (West Texas Intermediate) oil. We refer to Figure 6.1 below.

In Schwager (1992), Stanley Druckenmiller was asked about George Soros's style of trading. He claimed that Soros had the psychological ability to stick with and even increase winning positions, concluding with the comment that "it takes courage to be a pig". Trend following systems automatically behave in this way. Rather than taking profits quickly and letting their losses run (which arbitrarily transforms losing trades into long-term positions), they chase winning directional moves. The pig-headedness encoded in a trend following system can be very reassuring to a client who needs portfolio protection. So long as risk assets decline in a steady enough fashion, the client knows that the trend follower will stay short. A downside hedge will always be in place. In this way, trend following

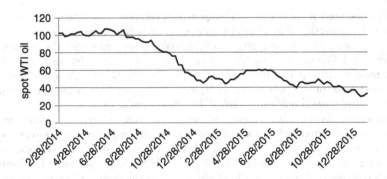

FIGURE 6.1 Trends can persist longer than one might expect

complements some of the options strategies we presented in Chapters 4 and 5. Recall that we rotate from puts, to put spreads, to broken flies as implied volatility increases and the put skew steepens. While these hedges are well-adapted to the prevailing market regime, they become progressively less potent as risk conditions deteriorate. Put spreads and butterflies do not protect you all the way down. To a large extent, we have addressed this issue by incorporating VIX and weekly options into our overall hedging strategy. Trend following provides another mechanism for protecting against vicious sell-offs when volatility is already high.

TREND FOLLOWING DOGMA

Strict trend followers can sometimes be a belligerent lot. In the late 1990s, the technical support staff of a well-known trend following website would get irate if you asked them a question about their data.

You might send a seemingly innocuous question such as, "How do you adjust for the roll in commodity futures contracts?" They would send this sort of response, "It doesn't matter, markets trend. Stop asking us irrelevant questions." An answer in the spirit of Mark Twain (1883) would have been preferable. "I was gratified to be able to answer promptly. I said, 'I don't know'."

And so it goes. There's no room for debate with certain hardliners. However, if we are to take a pragmatic approach to investing, we need to investigate further. In the example above, it's vital to choose the correct scheme for interpolating across contracts. You need the interpolation scheme to match the trading strategy you actually plan to use. By "interpolating", we mean constructing a continuous price series from a string of futures contracts with different maturities. Suppose you naively take the raw prices of the front month contract, making no adjustment for roll. Then, your trend follower will not be taking into account the total return of a rolling futures strategy and your long-term systems may point in the wrong direction. For natural gas (which has historically traded in severe contango), you would lose the natural short bias that arises from the persistently negative roll yield arising from the futures term structure.

Strategies that have relatively low win/loss ratios with high payouts tend to be associated with dogmatic managers. They have a tendency to be pamphleteers, publishing long articles about the virtues of their strategy when things are not working out. This is understandable, given that a trend following strategy can become mired in a long drawdown every now and then. It's to be expected that a long term trend follower running at 15% volatility will have a 30% drawdown if it survives 10 years. Trend followers steel themselves for the task with their articles. It may be that this is psychologically necessary, as the average investor in hedge funds tends to crave steady returns.

One idea that often gets bandied about is that trend following provides a form of portfolio insurance. Some studies, notably Fung and Hsieh (2001), suggest that the returns of a momentum strategy have "option-like" characteristics. This is an intriguing concept, implying that trend following may provide a floor on losses in a client's core portfolio. However, as we shall soon see, the analogy between trend following and a long options position is a very loose one.

THE CRISIS ALPHA DEBATE

Many institutions allocate to trend following strategies, on the assumption that they perform well in adverse market conditions. Trend followers had a banner year in 2008, with strong performance in the eye of the storm. The Barclay CTA index, which has a reasonably large weight in trend following strategies, posted a +3.45% return in October 2008. Pure trend followers generally returned closer to + 10% for the month. More generally, trend followers have performed relatively well at times when equities and other hedge funds have fared the worst. In Figure 6.2, we have tabulated the performance of CTAs during the worst 10 months for the S&P 500, from January 1980 to April 2016.

In 7 of the 10 months, the CTA index recorded a positive return. Moreover, the positive returns were generally much larger than the negative ones. This suggests that CTA returns have typically been positively skewed whenever equities sold off severely.

Recently, several academics and practitioners have introduced the term "crisis alpha" to describe trend following strategies. Fancy phrases abound in finance (don't get the author started about the marketing industry) and it's best to be wary of them before investigating further. Even Old Turkey was acutely aware of the connection between trend following and risk management. To some extent, this is simply the rebranding of a strategy that has been around for a long time. However, crisis alpha does turn out to be a succinct description for a strategy that has a larger than usual expected return during extreme market conditions.

Based on the historical evidence, trend followers have been an excellent diversifier in the past. The graph below demonstrates the impact of adding trend following to a long equity portfolio. We have used the S&P 500 and Barclay CTA indices as proxies for equities and a trend following futures strategy, respectively. Our data set reaches back to 1999. While CTA indices include strategies other than trend following, managers who have been around for a while (and are thus eligible to appear in the index) tend to focus on trends. Hence, broad CTA indices are reasonable proxies for trend following. The volatility of each index and the correlation between them has been calculated using historical returns, at monthly intervals. Since alternative indices suffer from a variety of biases, we have made an optimistic

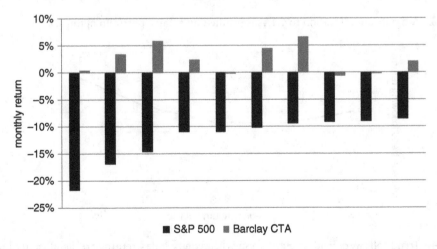

FIGURE 6.2 Historically, CTAs have performed admirably during S&P 500 draw downs

assumption about the return potential of equities and a punitive one about the expected return of trend following. This is intended to level the playing field a bit. In particular, equities are assumed to have an expected return that is 5% above the risk-free rate, while trend followers offer 0 excess return. Under these assumptions, an allocation of roughly 22% to CTAs maximises the Sharpe ratio of an equity/CTA portfolio. We have sketched the Sharpe ratio for a range of CTA weights in Figure 6.3.

In principle, crisis alpha strategies offer a modestly positive return in quiet markets and a punchy positive return during market downturns. Greyserman (2014) has characterised trend following return patterns in terms of a "CTA smile". The idea is to collate monthly returns for a generic trend following system and a benchmark equity index over different time periods. The equity returns are sorted in quintiles and the average trend following return in each quintile is taken. We have used the Barclay CTA index to create our own homespun CTA smile in Figure 6.4.

We can see that the single lowest and highest two quintiles deliver particularly strong historical performance. The logical conclusion is that trend followers tend to outperform when equities are either rising or falling strongly. The "payout" of CTAs has historically been convex (i.e. resembled a smile), with relative underperformance when equity returns are flat. Their approach may have been inspired by Fung and Hsieh (2001), who suggested that trend following returns are qualitatively similar to the returns generated by a lookback straddle. Note that a lookback straddle pays the difference between the highest and lowest values reached by the spot during the life of the option. It is a path dependent variation of the plain vanilla straddle we described in Chapter 3. Fung and Hsieh's paper has been widely cited by the managed futures community. While the analogy is intuitively appealing, we will see later in the chapter that it should *not* be interpreted too literally.

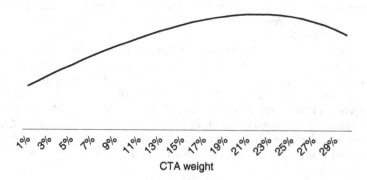

CTA weight

FIGURE 6.3 A significant allocation to CTAs is justified by a naive portfolio optimiser

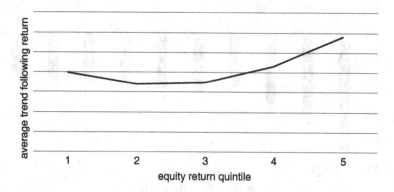

FIGURE 6.4 Trend followers tend to outperform when equity index returns are significantly higher or lower than normal

In an asset allocation context, a true crisis alpha strategy can have an enormous impact on performance. If it does what it says on the tin, crisis alpha can reduce marginal risk with virtually no drag on portfolio returns. Cole (2013) has played an important role in broadening the concept of crisis alpha to long volatility strategies.[2] His intricate and entertaining papers and presentations are well worth reading. In this section, however, we restrict ourselves to the issue of trend following as a crisis alpha strategy.

Trend following is clearly a market timing strategy, in contrast to traditional value strategies such as distressed bond investing. You don't need to "buy low" (i.e. below some notion of fundamental value) and "sell high". It's sufficient to wait for a trend, buy high and sell higher. The success of a trend following strategy is directly dependent on entry and exit points. This makes it difficult to measure alpha as a static quantity. Trend following doesn't make money by investing in the right securities, but rather by moving in and out of markets at the right *times*.

Measuring the alpha of market timing strategies has been explored in the literature by Henriksson (1984) and others. The Henriksson–Merton model focuses on measuring the market timing skill of a long-only manager relative to a benchmark, so the application is slightly different. However, the idea is to run a 2-factor regression of a fund's returns against the returns of its benchmark and the returns of a 0 premium put on the benchmark. If there is a positive loading to the put (i.e. if the regression coefficient is positive), the manager might be adding value through market timing, as he or she knows when to reduce exposure. The crisis alpha approach, however, takes things a step further. It doesn't run a regression against all returns, but rather focuses on the quality of returns *when they are needed the most*. In this sense, it rewards investors who take a regime-based approach to asset allocation. We are on the lookout for strategies that can perform well during "risk off" phases of the market. When the rest of your portfolio is collapsing, you are grateful for any source of positive return.

We can also think about crisis alpha in terms of regime-specific performance. Malek (2009) has created a risk index that allows them to see how various hedge fund strategies perform in different market regimes. It's closely related to our "international bar code" index in Figure 4.43. Contrary to popular claims, hedge funds don't really hedge all that much, at least in terms of exposure to systematic risk. Many hedge funds, especially those in the arbitrage or relative value category, advertise themselves as "market neutral". They go long and short related assets, in an attempt to reduce directional risk. Many claim that they can generate a positive return in all regimes, given that they are initially delta-neutral.

Judging from past returns, this claim is an optimistic one. Malek observed that most strategies performed dramatically worse in risk off regimes. The "risk off" underperformers included relative value hedge funds and convertible arbitrage, which had been advertised as a long volatility strategy. Market neutral equities that focused on buying "value" stocks also had a negative loading to volatility. The trouble is that value stocks can experience very long periods of underperformance during economic slowdowns. They become "unloved" as investors scramble for stocks that exhibit some form of price stability. Other than dedicated short-selling, which accounts for a tiny percentage of total hedge fund assets, trend following CTAs were the only category that outperformed when the market was "risk off".

Let's up the ante a bit. If trend following was guaranteed to provide significant protection after a market sell-off, most of the chapters in this book would be irrelevant. You would be able to hedge *without* paying an option premium after volatility had spiked. The reality is that trend following is a genuine diversifier, but does not hedge exposure to individual markets or systemic risk. Correlations across asset classes change over time and it may well turn out that stocks and bonds move down together in the next crisis. In this scenario, trend followers will not take a stubborn long position in sovereign bonds and should be well positioned relative to risk budgeting strategies. Eventually, they will be on the right side of a sustained move in equities, bonds or currencies. These results also point to the "crisis alpha" effect described above. When you allocate to a trend following fund, however, you are *not* long extreme event risk. The classic references comparing trend following to a long options strategy should not be interpreted too literally. Even if volatility increases, performance is very path-dependent. If a market makes a large move but is very choppy along the way, there is no guarantee that a trend follower will make money. The signal to noise ratio might be too low for a manager to stay in the trend. To some extent, it may even be accidental that trend followers have done so well in recent flight to quality environments. We review the recent literature and conduct experiments using a simplified trend following strategy. Our results are not conclusive, but imply that short-term trend following systems may provide more protection against a volatility spike in the future. During risk aversion periods, they are a valuable adjunct to options hedging strategies.

AN ASIDE: DIVERSIFYING ACROSS TIME

Trend followers have made an important contribution to asset allocation practice that rarely appears in the literature. They have focused on the idea of diversifying across *time*, something that Markowitz theory would not even consider. While this is not a central issue in our attempt to decide whether trend following acts as insurance, it is worthy of discussion. One of the goals in this book is to introduce the reader to alternative yet important ways of thinking about risk.

Standard risk models focus on diversifying across assets. At any given time, you take a snapshot of your portfolio. All risk calculations are based on the snapshot. It doesn't matter how or when the assets got into your portfolio. How your portfolio is likely to look in the future is a trivial detail, as you can dynamically recalculate portfolio risk over time. Risk is encoded in the covariance structure of the assets in your portfolio at that instant. However, this approach breaks down when one thinks of allocating to *strategies*, rather than assets. Many strategies will reallocate predictably as market conditions change. The beleaguered fund of hedge funds industry has had to deal with this issue for many years. Time diversification is a difficult problem that has traditionally been beyond the capability of a run-of-the-mill fund of funds. Yet, it is vital. If you can't rebalance your allocation very often, instantaneous risk measurements don't do you much good. You are better off knowing the qualitative properties of each strategy you invest in.

Managed futures and multi-strategy hedge funds have been far ahead of the curve in dealing with this issue. The problem is cleaner when you allocate to various sub-strategies that you have designed yourself. You might, for example, have several different models that trade US Treasury futures. Each system can go long and short and generates a series of returns over time. The individual series will differ, even though each system is only trading the Bund. To an outside observer, who has no idea what each strategy is up to, it might seem as though each return series corresponds to a static position in a different asset. The various systems will have a covariance structure and we can apply Markowitz theory to them as though they were individual assets. In Figure 6.5, we show that the pairwise correlations between different moving average crossover (MAC) systems decline as the lengths of the lookback windows move further apart. This creates a diversification effect.

Each MAC system above has the form $(1,n)$, where n ranges from 5 to 100 trading days, and is always in the market. If today's price (i.e. the 1-day trailing average price) is higher than the average price over the previous n days, the system will be long going into the next day. Otherwise, the system is short. By construction, each system is always in the market.

We have applied the MAC signal to 3 markets: US 10-year futures, S&P 500 futures and the spot US dollar index, using daily data from 1996 to early 2016. In each market, we have measured the correlation of a short-term (1,5), medium-term (1,50) and long-term (1,100) system to all of the other systems. We then averaged the correlation graphs across the 3 contracts. It can be seen from the graph that each system has 100% correlation to itself. This obviously should be the case. More interestingly, as the lookback windows move further apart, the correlation between any two systems decreases. Finally, we observe that the (1,50) MAC system bears a closer relationship to the (1,100) system than the (1,5) one. This implies that more diversification can be achieved by lumping together nearby short-term systems than nearby long-term ones.

It is worth noting that the average holding period increases with the length of the lookback window. The probability of flipping from long to short or *vice versa* ranges from roughly 25% for MAC (1,5) to about 5% for (1,100), with a decay rate proportional to 1/sqrt(n). This suggests that snapshot

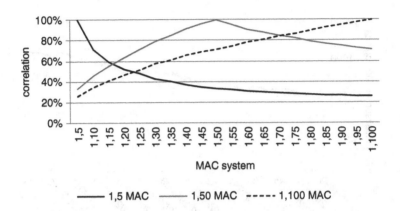

FIGURE 6.5 Systems with different lookback windows and expected holding periods are diversifying

risk estimates are reasonable for long-term trend following systems, but may be wildly inaccurate for shorter-term MACs. The conclusion is that we need to understand the dynamics of a trading strategy before we can estimate its marginal contribution to the risk in a portfolio.

TAKING ADVANTAGE OF A CORRECTION

Institutional money managers are forced to put money to work most of the time. Hedge funds can't just sit on their hands when T bills have 0 yield, as costs will significantly eat into performance every month where nothing is done. If you stay un-invested, investors will question your commitment. However, having cash in hand can be enormously beneficial during a fire sale. You can find bargains among the rubbish. This is an important area where less sophisticated investors may have an advantage over their institutional counterparts. In Chapter 7, we give several examples of trading strategies that can take advantage of high volatility. While these are not without risk, an investor who has plenty of dry powder can take advantage of the opportunities available. We also survey some of the intriguing and possibly controversial academic research that relates the price of variance swaps to the equity risk premium. Our more humble examples focus on the idea that market valuation ratios, such as price to earnings, are far more sensitive to price than anything else. This automatically creates value-buying plays after a sell-off.

THE NIEDERHOFFER ARGUMENT

Recently, Niederhoffer (2014)[3] has argued that trend following might not provide adequate protection during future crises. The paper starts with a historical observation. Since the 1980s, interest rates have been in a secular bear market. Bond prices, which move inversely to rates, have persistently trended up. On a risk-adjusted basis, bonds have outperformed stocks by a very wide margin. It's a one horse race, as illustrated in Figure 6.6. We have tracked the performance of a rolling position in S&P 500 and US 10-year note futures. The 10-year note returns are geared so that their 1-year trailing volatility matches that of the S&P. The performance differential is so large that we need to represent it on a logarithmic scale. Even if we use the cash S&P 500 index rather than S&P futures, the gulf is enormous.

Note that our bond proxy is a rolling long position in 10-year note futures. The fact that we have generated bond exposure through a rolling futures strategy is significant, as we will soon find out. The extended bull market in bonds has created a fertile environment for trend followers. They typically

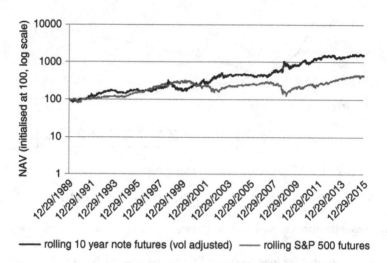

FIGURE 6.8 Bond futures have delivered relatively high absolute returns as well as protection during a crisis

have taken long positions in US 10 year, Bund, Japanese Government Bond and other interest rate futures markets in an effort to capture a move that has transcended market cycles. We argue that a large proportion of returns has come from bonds and other interest rate futures. Since these markets tend to be very liquid, large CTAs have been able to deploy significant amounts of capital to rates. Their allocation to interest rates has been proportionately high. In turn, the bias toward bond futures over other classes has boosted returns. Trend followers have benefitted not only from declining spot rates but also from the roll yield embedded in interest rate futures. As we mentioned previously, the US yield curve has usually been upward sloping since the 1980s. When yields started to come down following the Fed's attempt to control inflation with tight policy, short-term rates declined more rapidly than long-term ones. This generated an upward sloping yield curve or, equivalently, a downward sloping futures term structure.

Figures 6.7 and 6.8 emphasise the importance of futures roll down. These graphs encapsulate the results of Monte Carlo simulations. First, we calculated the average level of backwardation for US 10-year futures over the past 20 years. As it turns out, the back month has historically traded at a 75 basis point discount to the front month. We then simulated multiple interest rate paths over 1000 day horizons, making the crude assumption that constant maturity Treasury yield returns evolved according to a random walk. The volatility of our random number generator was calibrated to match the historical volatility of the relevant constant maturity rate. The zero coupon yield curve was initialised at 2%, for all maturities. This is a reasonable synopsis of where longer-dated yields are trading as of this writing. Next, we priced 10-year note futures off this curve, assuming that the cheapest-to-deliver bond was always the one with the shortest duration. Burghardt (2005) and Choudhry (2006) are useful references for readers who want to become familiar with the intricacies of pricing and hedging sovereign bond futures. Finally, we calculated the cumulative return of the futures on a simulation-by-simulation basis. This incorporated the roll yield that we have calculated above.

The previous paragraph was a mouthful. Let's just say that we simulated some bond prices using the historical futures term structure, assuming no trend in rates. The simulation was reasonably realistic, given the current market environment. Figure 6.7 summarises our results.

Nearly all of the futures price paths compound to a positive 1,000 day return. With backwardation at this level, the shape of the term structure dominates random fluctuations in rates. We only start to reach break-even levels if we aggressively reset the drift in our simulation. More precisely, we need

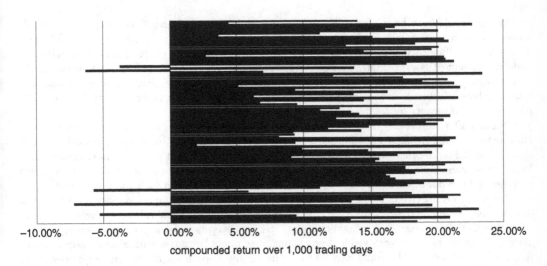

FIGURE 6.7 Roll down overcomes randomness in interest rate paths when the term structure is in significant backwardation

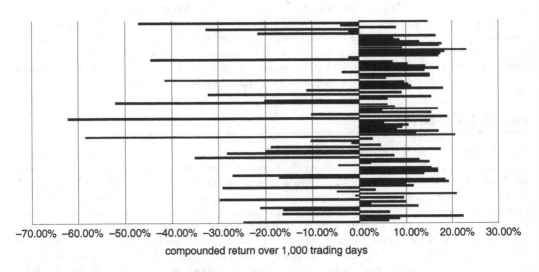

FIGURE 6.8 Even if rates are ratcheting up, bond futures can have positive expected return

to assume that rates have roughly +20% annualised drift before the futures have a greater likelihood of going down than going up! (See Figure 6.8.)

We note that the average down moves appear to be bigger than the average up moves because our simulation has effectively constrained longer-term rates to be above 0. The distribution of interest rates is effectively assumed to be log normal. As rates approach 0 in a given simulation, the magnitude of subsequent rate moves becomes smaller.

Now we come to the crux of the Niederhoffer argument. Bonds have generated remarkably strong returns since the 1980s, with recent performance dominated by capital appreciation rather than yield. The trend has been almost unilaterally positive. At the same time, they have acted as the *de facto* flight to quality security, providing statistical insurance during spikes in global market volatility. Over this period, you would have been *paid* to hold insurance in the form of bonds. How nice is that? While sell-side economists were busy rattling on about how bonds were overpriced, dedicated trend followers were happily rolling their long positions. As we observed earlier in the chapter, pure trend followers make no attempt to assess the fair value of bonds or any other asset. Their decision-making during the "great moderation" was price-based, as ever. Given that the typical CTA allocation to bonds has been relatively high and bonds have consistently performed well during risk events, it may be that CTAs have provided insurance *by accident*.

Niederhoffer emphasises this point, in an effort to place doubts in the minds of investors who allocate to trend following as a portfolio anchor. He argues that trend followers might not offer protection should the term structure of interest rates change, i.e. if short-term rates rise more quickly than longer-term ones. Most US investors haven't seen an environment where stocks and bonds go down together and it is not obvious that trend followers would perform well in such an environment.

Broadly, there are two important scenarios where trend followers might not provide any protection against rising volatility. If yields started to rise for a sustained period, trend followers might find themselves short, on the wrong side of a flight to quality spike in government bond prices. Conversely, if there were an inflationary shock with yields skyrocketing, they might be caught with a long position. As of mid-2016, short-term yields would have to rise quite rapidly to push the futures curve into contango. Otherwise, bond *futures* and yields might rise simultaneously, forcing trend followers to maintain a long position in bond futures. They would be ill-equipped to handle a shallow rise in yields followed by a violent inflationary spike. This is yet another case (e.g. recall the VIX discussion in Chapter 4) where a portfolio manager is handicapped by an inability to access spot market moves in an efficient way.

We have started this discussion by outlining a number of reasons why trend following *might not* function as a portfolio hedge in the future. However, there are other factors at play, that may increase an allocator's comfort in the strategy. To illustrate this point, we refresh a study on the properties of momentum models that operate in different markets over different horizons. We first check whether short term momentum tends to work well within a given market when volatility picks up.

CHASING 1-DAY MOVES

If we don't resort to intra-day data, the shortest lookback window for trading breakouts is one day. So let's start with that. We want to test the hypothesis that short-term breakout system returns are correlated with changes in volatility. This was shown in several specific cases by Kremer (2007). In Figure 6.9, we compare the performance of a one day breakout model on the S&P 500 with changes in the VIX. Our trading rule is very simple and is simply used to illustrate a point. We are by no means recommending it as an absolute return strategy. Contrarian trading over 1-day horizons may in fact be a better strategy across markets. For the moment, suppose we have a trading rule that buys the S&P 500 whenever the trailing 1-day return is positive and sells the S&P 500 whenever the return is negative. We are simply chasing 1-day trailing performance. In the scatter plot below, we can see that the returns of this strategy have a mild positive correlation to changes in the VIX.

This at least is suggestive. If you chase every 1-day move, you are looking a bit like a long volatility strategy in the markets you trade.

An interesting variation of this trade involves trading 1-day moves in the US 10-year note. We can regress the performance of the 10-year chaser against 10-year implied volatility. Taking into account the high conditional correlation between the TVIX and VIX, however, it may be more instructive to regress performance against changes in the VIX. By "conditional correlation", we mean the correlation given (i.e. conditional on) a large spike in one index or the other. This is consistent with an idea we presented earlier in the book. Usually, "flash crashes" are preceded by a sequence of down days. The down days put pressure on leveraged investors. At some point, these investors reach their pain threshold and liquidate large chunks of their portfolio. This has the potential to cause a dramatic sell-off. However, there is no guarantee that the next flash crash will develop in such a predictable way. If there

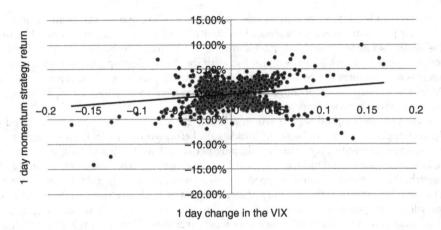

FIGURE 6.9 1-day momentum returns have a moderately positive correlation to changes in the VIX

is an entirely unexpected credit or geopolitical event, the one day "chaser" might not be on the right side of the move.

As we lengthen the breakout horizon, the correlation between signal returns and volatility in a given market typically decreases. This means that we have to content ourselves with the following rather conservative conclusion. Trend following strategies with well-defined stops generally provide diversification (though not pure insurance) when there are sustained outsized market moves. Meanwhile, shorter-term systems have a greater chance of being on the right side of the market when there is a spike in volatility. Unlike many other hedge fund styles, they do not rely upon selling an explicit risk premium. Usually, you are *taking* liquidity while trading in the direction of the prevailing trend.

PUSHING THE ANALOGY TOO FAR

The analogy between trend following and long options strategies originates from the days when many managers used hard stop losses. If crude oil futures were trending and your system generated a buy signal at 80, you might have an exit at 70. If prices continued to rise, you would gradually move the stop loss higher to lock in a profit. At the point of entry, your payout profile would look a bit like a long call option at expiration.

This simple observation probably motivated Fung (2001) to compare trend following to a static long options position (i.e. a lookback straddle). Since a straddle benefits from rising volatility, it's tempting to conclude that trend following is also structurally long volatility. However, we caution against interpreting the analogy too literally. Trend following is somewhat similar but *not equivalent* to a long options strategy. You do not directly profit from increases in volatility. We illustrate this using a simple example. Even the hard stop loss assumption is a stretch. Most trend followers scale in and out of positions as their signal changes. When a trend breaks, the short-term indicators exit the position first. Over time, longer-term indicators follow suit, so that the entire position is not liquidated or flipped in a single go. For large trend followers, "bang bang" controls on positions cause unnecessary slippage. You don't want to enter or exit a large position in one go. It is preferable to vary your sizing fairly continuously through time. In this way, your returns are not overly sensitive to split-second timing. You can also trade more when there is more liquidity in the market. For concreteness, though, let's assume your trend following strategy *does* use explicit stop losses. This is a conservative assumption if we are trying to disprove the hypothesis that trend following is equivalent to a static options position. However, for simplicity, assume that your strategy does have specific exit points for trades. Assuming that you can execute at the stop level, your payout profile looks like a call or put at any point in time. For long positions, your potential gains are theoretically unlimited, while your losses are bounded by the stop.

This all seems fantastic. You now have a strategy that equates to buying an option, with no premium outlay. Or so it seems. There is a problem with the downside-stop-as-insurance argument. First of all, there is no guarantee that you will be filled at the stop if there is a very sharp move in the underlying. More importantly, in our example, you are only *instantaneously* long a call. There is no telling what your position might be tomorrow.

Let's say you are long oil with a sell stop below the current price today. If the trend reverses strongly, you might be selling oil with an upside stop before you know it. Even if the instantaneous payout resembles an option, you wind up flipping between a long call and long put over time. It is worth adding that many trend followers use a risk-budgeting approach when sizing positions. Roughly, this means that the notional amount assigned to each contract is inversely proportional to the volatility of the contract. In addition, if the volatility of an asset goes up with no change to the trading signal, the position will automatically scale down over time. Volatile contracts, such as natural gas, get smaller allocations than contracts that don't move very much over time. How does this affect the qualitative properties of a trend following strategy?

Let's return to our old faithful, the S&P futures contract. We can construct a simple example demonstrating that risk-budgeting can offset the implied "gamma" in a trend following system. Suppose that a client wants to hedge long exposure using a dedicated short trend follower on the S&P. The hedge is outsourced to an overlay manager. The trend following algorithm progressively builds into a down move by moving from cash into an ever-increasing short futures position. This certainly has the characteristics of a long put on the index. However, a meaningful sell-off in the S&P is usually accompanied by an increase in realised volatility. Bear markets are characterised by ferocious down moves and equally vicious relief rallies. If the overlay manager has a risk threshold and volatility spikes, it may be necessary to cut a fully loaded position to stay under the threshold. Increased signal strength is offset by a risk constraint. This reduces the return potential of the hedge if there is another leg down. The owner of a put has no such concerns, as the put will *automatically* gear into a sell-off, with an added kicker from any increase in implied volatility.

Is a strategy that flips between calls and a put long volatility? We can test this directly. Suppose we alternate between buying a 1-month ATM call and put on the S&P 500 based on the flip of a coin. We repeat the coin flip at the end of each week, unwinding our old position and initiating a new one. We calculate a weekly return by repricing the option, based on the change in the underlying price. Note that we keep the time to maturity and volatility of the option *fixed*, as trend following strategies do not have any theta or vega. Finally, we calculate the correlation between our strategy returns and changes in the VIX. Figure 6.10 is based on 1000 simulations of weekly returns from 2005 to 2015.

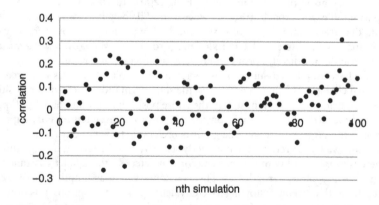

FIGURE 8.10 Random switching between puts and calls is not analogous to a long volatility position

It turns out that the average correlation between strategy returns and changes in the VIX is close to 0. This suggests that there is no obvious relationship between trend following on a single market and volatility in that market, even if the strategy uses stop losses at point of entry. We emphasise that this is not a conclusive study. It merely suggests that a strategy with stop losses is quite different from an options buying strategy.

The analogy becomes even weaker when we reflect that trend followers don't use explicit stop losses any more. The largest and most established funds tend to scale in and out of positions almost continuously, based on signal strength and changes in volatility. Position sizes tend to be inversely proportional to volatility in a given market. This implies that if a manager is fully short the S&P and volatility increases, the position will be reduced, to ensure that the S&P risk contribution is not too large. So the "long gamma" effect of scaling into a winning position is partially offset by a risk constraint that sets an upper bound on position size, based on volatility.

Malek and Dobrovolsky (2009) convincingly argue that long gamma strategies are not automatically long volatility. On a statistical basis, trend strategies may appear to be short volatility over modest horizons. This is particularly true for managers who rely upon long-term trends, when the trend is breaking violently. The converse is also true: short gamma strategies can outperform in high volatility regimes. As we will see in Chapter 7, contrarian strategies that buy dips in equity indices can have a high correlation to the level of volatility in the market. Similarly, asset allocation schemes that re-balance to a set of strategic weights may also outperform when volatility is high.

Most fund managers tend to distinguish between "good" and "bad" volatility, relative to their trading style. When the market aimlessly wanders around like a drunken sailor, that's good for contrarians and bad for trend followers. Conversely, when a given asset crashes through its historical range and keeps going, trend followers rejoice. The conclusion is simple. Since you are not paying an options premium when you follow a trend, you should not expect to benefit from every expansion in realised volatility.

ANALYSING THE DATA DIRECTLY

The reader may have noticed a strange pattern in this chapter. We initially asked whether trend following is a long volatility strategy. Since then, we have waffled back and forth, without giving a definitive answer. This pattern will continue here. Hopefully, we are not starting to resemble one of those banks that have a habit of presenting two opposing views, in order to have something to sell. The truth is that trend following is a highly diversifying strategy with some option-like characteristics. In our opinion, it is a vital component of a diversified, multi-asset class portfolio. However, the options analogy is not a precise one. We can't say how a bog standard trend follower will perform during the next crisis. The random switching strategy from Figure 6.10 is suggestive but not definitive. When there is a strong move in one direction or another, trend following might be analogous to holding a call or put for quite some time, without switching. By contrast, random flipping between a call and a put shows no persistence. So let's try another approach. The most direct way to see how trend following performs as a function of volatility changes is to build a momentum strategy explicitly. So long as our version is representative, we can then regress the returns of the strategy against changes in the VIX and just see what we get. We have used the VIX as a risk indicator since it is widely quoted, has a reasonably long history and is sensitive to large changes in risk aversion across markets.

Our trend following signal is very basic, but representative. We focus on breakouts over six different time horizons, 1, 5, 10, 20, 50 and 100 days. Note that a "breakout" occurs when the price of a contract moves out of its historical range. For example, let's consider the 5-day breakout signal. If the closing price today is higher than the maximum over the previous 5 days, we go long. If it's lower than the minimum over the previous 5 days, we go short. Otherwise, we maintain our position. After an initial breakout, the signal is always in the market.

Our composite return is simply the average of the individual breakout system returns. We use multiple breakout horizons in an attempt to capture trends over a variety of time horizons. Note that we have not said anything about how to combine our multi-frequency signals across markets. We are simply checking whether there might be some connection between trend following returns and volatility changes within a specific market.

Next, let's take our composite signal and apply it to a representative market. In Figure 6.11, we have applied our homespun trend follower to the S&P 500.

The results are actually quite promising. The R-squared of the regression is close to 0.2 over a 20-year horizon, using daily returns. There does seem to be some connection between volatility and the performance of a momentum strategy on the same underlying equity index. Why should this be so? We can only speculate. The sharpest spikes in the VIX have usually occurred after an equity bear trend has already formed. They do not appear completely out of the blue, but represent liquidations from long-biased managers who have come under increasing pressure to exit their trades. This implies that our trend follower has a tendency to be short *in advance of* the largest jumps in the VIX and will frequently provide protection when markets go into crisis mode. Broadly speaking, the same results apply to US 10-year futures, i.e. returns from our basic trend following system are positively correlated to changes in bond implied volatility.

If equities and credit move into an extended bear market, trend following is likely to come to the rescue. Almost any reasonable system will eventually accept that risky assets are in a down trend and will short the market thereafter. However, choppy markets with intermittent flash crashes do not play into the hands of momentum-based strategies. The only way to cover rapid wholesale liquidations within the larger context of a bull market is with options. Ideally, we should be able to identify conditions where rapid sell-offs or protracted bear markets are likely. This is the topic of Chapter 8.

LEGO TREND FOLLOWING

We can increase the probability that a trend following system will provide protection against adverse moves by customising it. This involves reassembling the building blocks of a full trend following system, "LEGO" style. Suppose that we want to hedge the future liability stream of a pension fund against a decline in yields. If the discount rate drops, the fund will become less solvent unless the asset pool

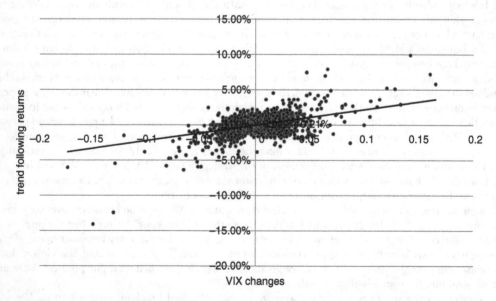

FIGURE 6.11 Moderate historical correlation between trend following returns on the S&P 500 and changes in the VIX

goes up by an equal amount. The present value of liabilities (i.e. the amount required to fulfil future obligations given current interest rates) will have increased. While a system that goes long and short in major markets will have some correlation to rising market volatility, we can be more precise than that. We can increase the expected duration of our system by overweighting long signals in global sovereign bonds. In particular, we don't want to get caught with a short position in bonds if rates drop. It's true that if rates go into a sustained down trend, the trend follower will eventually take a long position in bond futures. However, actuarial losses may have been compounded by a short futures position along the way.

A reasonable solution is to customise the trend following system by focusing on a subset of available trades. This may degrade the stand alone alpha of a trading system, but is likely to increase its marginal utility relative to an existing portfolio. In particular, you could constrain a full system in the following ways to extend the duration of an existing portfolio:

- only trade bond and interest rate futures (note that equity indices and commodities have unreliable duration from a statistical standpoint)
- avoid shorting these futures, to ensure that the aggregate duration of the overlay is never negative
- overweight short-term trend signals, to increase the expected correlation of the overlay to volatility.

A wide range of static portfolios can be hedged using the same line of reasoning. For example, we might hedge an equity portfolio by restricting ourselves to short signals in equity index futures. If our full trend following system generated a long signal in S&P E-mini futures, we would simply ignore it and stay in cash. From the standpoint of hedging, we would never want to be positioned in the wrong direction in advance of a move.

Institutions that are unable to trade futures directly can outsource a bespoke trend following strategy to an external manager. This might take the form of a managed account, which is easily customised and requires a relatively low cash outlay.

SUMMARY

Once volatility picks up, outright options buying becomes expensive. We've explored range-based hedges as a way to maintain some level of protection while keeping costs low. Another alternative is to follow trends in major markets. This approach has offered statistical protection during historical risk events and does not force you to pay up for volatility once it has become expensive. We caution that trend following may have provided historical protection for structural reasons that may not persist into the future. A reasonable hybrid approach combines options with trend following algorithms, with an emphasis on short-term systems that have been particularly responsive to volatility spikes in the past. Trend following enhances the expected return of a hedging overlay, while providing statistical protection against large-scale directional moves in a given asset. It also defends against fundamental high conviction views that are not currently being validated by the market.

NOTES

1 Lefèvre, Edwin. *Reminiscences of a Stock Operator.* New Jersey: Wiley, 1923.
2 Cole, Christopher. "Volatility Paradigm and Paradox." CBOE Risk Management Conference, March 3, 2013. http://www.cboe.com/rmc/2013/Day1-Session3-Cole.pdf
3 Niederhoffer, Roy, and Coen Weddepohl. "CTAs and Rising Interest Rates: Is the Party Over?" White Paper, April 2014. http://www.dailyspeculations.com/CTAsAndRisingInterestRates_040714.pdf

CHAPTER 7

Strategies for Taking Advantage of a Market Drop

For investors who still have some dry powder, market drops can create opportunity. While overextended investors are scrambling to constrain losses or meet margin calls, others can selectively buy assets that have become oversold. Although mechanical value-buying can be susceptible to long periods of underperformance, other strategies can add value when markets appear "oversold". In particular, we examine short-term contrarian strategies for equity indices and volatility-selling strategies with bounded risk. One theme of the chapter is that, when volatility gets sufficiently high, it may be profitable to swap long equity exposure with short volatility exposure.

THE ELASTIC BAND

It has been said that the most powerful force in financial markets is mean reversion. Mean reversion is the poor cousin of Maxwell's equations connecting electricity and magnetism or Newton's laws of motion, as there are no "laws" to speak of in finance. The rough idea is that an asset can't move far away from "fair value" or "equilibrium" indefinitely. Fundamental reality has to set in at some point. As the theory goes, the price of a stock can only overshoot for so long before value investors start to sell, based on unsustainable valuations. We can put this more precisely by looking at multiples, rather than raw prices.

Campbell and Shiller (1988) have created a financial ratio that continues to be followed closely. It is suitable for our current purposes. In Figure 7.1, we track the cyclicality of their CAPE index over long horizons. CAPE stands for the "cyclically adjusted price to earnings ratio". Earnings are first adjusted for inflation over a trailing 10-year period. This ensures that older earnings have a similar impact as recent ones. Short-term fluctuations are then averaged out, to ensure that the "E" in CAPE is relatively stable. We can think of CAPE as a relatively stable and noise-free price to earnings ratio.

Whenever the CAPE ratio exceeds 25, the market may be in a state of "irrational exuberance". In other words, prices are probably higher than justified by fundamentals. Drops in excess of 10 points (corresponding to severe corrections in price) have only occurred in this zone of frivolity and folly.

However cleverly "E" might be defined, "P" is the real driver of short-term changes in CAPE. Earnings are updated roughly 150 days per year and are not very volatile in the absence of a 2008-type recession. So if prices move more rapidly than fundamentals, ratios such as CAPE will typically become depressed after a major sell-off. It stands to reason that buying into large-scale equity drawdowns should work over the long term.

More formally, we can say that long-term prospective returns are inversely proportional to the CAPE ratio. As prices rise, forward expected returns decline. However, it may take a while to realise

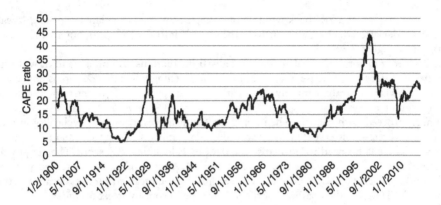

FIGURE 7.1 Shiller's CAPE ratio as a precursor to equity market crises

any gain. While equity bull markets are relatively durable, bear markets can also persist for longer than one might expect.

Are there other asset classes where mean reversion kicks in a bit more quickly? On the surface, currencies seem to be good candidates for a mean reversion strategy. They *should* be constrained by purchasing power parity (PPP). However, PPP tends to be a very weak attractor. An orange in Brazil can get cheaper and cheaper than an orange in the USA, without investors selling their dollars to buy oranges in Reals. Currency rates can drift for many years without interruption, based on carry differentials, relative growth rates and other factors.

Bond term premia, which measure excess demand for safe long duration assets, can also take years to converge to long-term average levels. You may have to wait quite some time before making money on a valuation-based model.

One thing to be wary of when measuring the degree of mean reversion in a series is the widely used Z score. Recall that a Z score measures the distance between a quantity and its moving average, in units of standard deviations. We cheekily relied upon it ourselves when constructing our risk indicator in Chapter 4, but accept that it needs to be applied with caution. Z scores can *create* cycles in an index that has a dominant trend, especially as the lookback window shrinks.

Figure 7.2 tracks US M2 money supply over time. This quantity includes cash, current, savings and money market accounts. It unambiguously trends from the lower left to the upper right of the graph. In nominal terms, this is *not* a quantity that cycles around an average level.

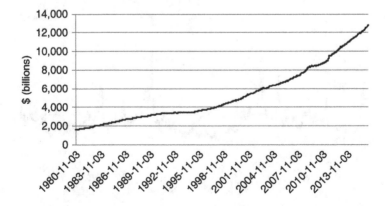

FIGURE 7.2 M2 money stock has a powerful trend

However, if we select a lookback window of 1 year, say, we can calculate the rolling 1 year return μ and standard deviation σ. Once we transform the series X into $Z = (X - μ)/σ$, our series looks strongly oscillatory, as in Figure 7.3.

The Z score transformation calculates normalised fluctuations around a trend. It will find cycles in any series that does not increase at a super-linear rate. Selling when the Z score is above average is unlikely to be a winning strategy for any series with a strong upward drift, as the trend dominates small deviations around it.

We must proceed with caution when searching for mean reversion and cyclicality in a financial data series. However, we observe that credit spreads and volatility *do* seem to mean revert quite quickly after a spike. There is no need to normalise the data by calculating a Z score. The choppy and ultimately directionless VSTOXX index appears in Figure 7.4. After a spike, it tends to decay rapidly back to the 20 to 30 range. We do not have to keep readjusting the mean to force cyclicality in the series. Note that the VSTOXX is the analogue of the VIX for the European Stoxx 50 index.

When something oscillates as much as the VSTOXX, with no discernible trend, we can at least take a stab at measuring its long-term average level. (We hesitate to use the phrase "equilibrium level", as the oscillations around any fixed level are so severe.)

Having accepted that volatility mean reverts more strongly than equity prices, we can still try and identify situations where equity reversals are likely. In the next section, we examine one such scenario.

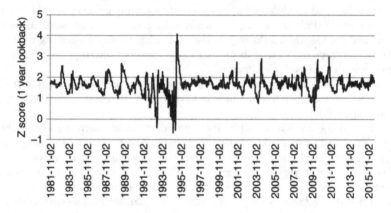

FIGURE 7.3 1 year deviations from trend for M2 money stock

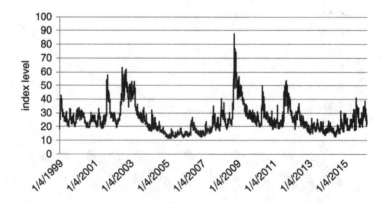

FIGURE 7.4 The V2X as a barometer of risk aversion for European large cap stocks

While there are many other potential configurations leading to predictable price moves, these remain in the "secret sauce" category for a fund manager. This is not to say that the fancy strategies work all the time, only that they are outside the scope of this book.

TRADING REVERSALS

It has often been said that volatile markets create opportunity. What exactly does that mean? If the volatility of an asset in your portfolio jumps from 10% to 20% then yes, your profit potential goes up per contract held. For a given level of gearing, there is more total movement to take advantage of. The trouble is that your potential for losses goes up proportionately. We need to investigate a bit deeper than that. The increased opportunity set is in fact created by rising dispersion and widening of spreads. Dispersion measures the degree to which a collection of securities moves apart over time. During liquidations, similar stocks might diverge, based on the holdings of large institutions who might be selling. This can create spread trading opportunities. As volatility rises, credit spreads tend to widen, creating bond buying opportunities. While you can't "eat volatility", as some old-fashioned investors say, there *are* strategies that offer the prospect of converting volatility into return. During severe "risk off" regimes, individual securities can move far away from fair value. At the extreme, a company's market capitalisation may even drop below its liquidation value, as investors furiously sell the stock. These are the sorts of buying opportunities sought out by Graham (1949). Such obvious buying opportunities are probably less common today, as investors have access to better and more timely information. However, it is worth repeating that the market was pricing pair-wise correlations above 100% in 2008, so extreme mispricings still occur episodically. This is a theoretical absurdity caused by multiple investors having multiple panic attacks at the same time. Crises can breed opportunity in a variety of ways.

Before rushing in to buy every mispriced security, you need to keep a few things in mind. How much firepower do you have left? If you have already absorbed heavy losses, it might be too late to add more risk onto your book. Indeed, you might be going in the other direction, slashing positions in an effort to stay afloat. Even if you are still in the game, you need to allocate with appropriate caution. Suppose you displayed admirable patience early in a crisis. If you pile in thereafter and conditions worsen, your patience might not be rewarded. Another leg down could make you one of the casualties in the end. Piling into opportunistic trades might seem reasonable if you hedge your portfolio aggressively at the macro level. However, this almost defeats the purpose, as hedging costs will erode the premium you were trying to collect in the first place. Our humble advice is to stay small and nimble after a sell-off. Markets are unlikely to stabilise instantaneously and you will have numerous opportunities to extract alpha in the future.

We start with a simple mechanism that can force markets to be overstretched over short-term horizons. In bear markets, equity indices frequently sell off hard into the close. A trader who can't bear too much overnight or weekend risk (e.g. a day trader or market maker) may be a forced seller at the end of the day. This may trigger a sequence of events. When the market drops, leveraged ETFs have to reduce exposure mechanically, to ensure that their total exposure is a fixed multiple of equity. The following example, for a leveraged long ETF, might clarify things.

- Suppose that there is a 2× leveraged ETF on an index and ETF has $100 of equity.
- In order to generate 2× leverage, the provider needs to borrow $100 and invest a total of $200 in the index. In this way, the ETF will generate 2× the index return from today to tomorrow, gross of fees.
- If the index drops –10% the next day, the ETF has lost –$20. Equity has gone down to $80.
- The ETF then *has to sell* $20 of index exposure to reset leverage at 2, i.e. to match the amount of borrow with the amount of equity.

In the meantime, leveraged short ETFs need to scale into the move, increasing their short exposure. Trend following CTAs might be forced into the move if the move is extended enough. Things can get ugly in the last hour of trading, with cascading sell orders pushing the market down.

You might try and take advantage of the move, on the assumption that a given equity index is oversold, at least in the short term. Historically, buying bad closes and holding for one day has been a reasonable strategy. In the charts below, we examine the S&P 500 and Nikkei indices, using a trading strategy from 1995 to the present. The strategy makes a bold assumption, namely that you can execute at the close on each day. Here, we introduce a simple strategy that takes advantage of exaggerated sell-offs into the close for major equity indices. While the strategy has historically worked in a variety of volatility regimes, the opportunity set tends to increase when volatility is high. You get more trading signals when investors are seized by panic. We emphasise that the contrarian strategy below has open-ended risk, hence should not be traded too aggressively. The strategy also assumes that you are able to transact at the market close and that there are no transaction costs. Transacting at a level close to the cash market close should not be too difficult, as you can always trade the futures immediately thereafter. Our digression into levered ETFs was intended to show that market forces can drive prices well beyond fair value going into the close. Leverage, risk limits and restrictions on holding large overnight positions can all contribute to ugly end of day sell-offs. So how can you take advantage of the overreaction? One strategy is to buy into the sell-offs. Figure 7.5 focuses on Nikkei 225 futures. We classify hard sell-offs into the close as days with a larger than average range, where the distance between the close and the low is more than 0.5 standard deviations below average (using a 2-year lookback window). Assuming that we can transact at market close, with negligible costs, historical performance is surprisingly strong over a trailing 20-year period.

Buying dips, or short-term sell-offs, is related to another concept called "trading the coastline" as shown in Figure 7.6. While Richard Olsen popularised the concept (Dupuis and Olsen, 2012) we need to refer back to the work of Mandelbrot for the original inspiration. The "rough" idea is that, when an asset goes from A to B, the total distance travelled will generally be much greater than (B − A). As the time partition gets finer, the total distance travelled must increase, and it is the rate of increase that is important.

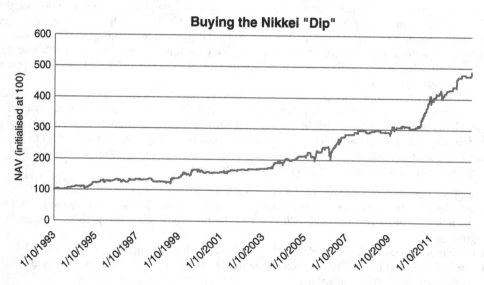

FIGURE 7.5 Buying the nasty 1-day dip, NIKKEI 225

FIGURE 7.6 Trading the coastline, when the signal to noise ratio is low

For fractal-type paths, the total distance travelled will diverge to infinity as the partition size shrinks to 0. Even when we deal with movements in discrete time, the length of the path can be surprisingly long. We want to take advantage of small meanderings away from the trend, so long as our transaction costs are not too high. While Old Turkey from Chapter 6 would vigorously disagree with this idea, modern market making algorithms try to convert "noise" into return by taking contrarian positions in small movements away from trend.

Whenever you decide to "fade" a major sell-off or spike in volatility, you are assuming that there is less information content in the move than the market thinks. In other words, the market doesn't know something that you are unaware of. This is the basis of contrarian trading.

MORE TEXAS-STYLE HEDGING

A Texas hedge is a trade that actually *adds* to the risk of your overall portfolio. It's not really a hedge at all, but a correlated alpha trade that appears particularly attractive after a sell-off. We would only recommend such a trade if you had been underinvested going into the initial down move.

The system in the previous section was short-term in nature. You waited for an ugly sell-off into the close, bought the index and then dumped the position at the close of the following day. The holding period of the trade was 24 hours. But consider another alternative. What if you want to buy into a sell-off and hold the position for a while? In this context, risk reversals can be useful. As we discussed in Chapter 3, a risk reversal involves selling a put and buying a call on the same asset. The call and put have the same maturity. Otherwise, we would classify the structure as some sort of diagonal spread. If you sell an OTM put and buy an OTM call, the put strike will be lower than the call strike. OTM risk reversals attempt to take advantage of distortions in the implied volatility skew for an asset.

They can be traded opportunistically. After a sell-off, the slope of the skew (for an equity index or other risky asset) becomes increasingly negative. Put implied volatility typically rises more than call implied volatility. Figure 7.7 shows how the differential between 25 delta put and 25 call implied volatility increases as a function of ATM volatility for the S&P 500 index. We assume that both options have 1 month to maturity.

Carry currencies, such as the Australian dollar, typically have the same property. The demand for downside hedges escalates after a drop. We can see this in Figure 7.8. Again, we have focused on 1-month implied volatility collected at weekly intervals. The data ranges from 2003 to early 2016.

The amount of premium collected from a fixed delta risk reversal increases when investors become fearful. OTM puts are in demand, increasing the steepness of the implied volatility skew. We can harvest premium from a "risky" without taking on too much directional risk by shorting futures against it. This allows us to isolate distortions in the skew, at least at the moment of trade entry. While shorting does not eliminate extreme event risk (and may in fact disguise it), it cushions against moderate declines in the spot.

In Figure 7.9, we have constructed a hedged risk reversal using reasonably long-dated (roughly 7 months to maturity) options on the S&P 500. The resulting structure was initially short 100 25 delta puts, long 100 25 delta calls and hedged with futures. We have sketched the payout curve for a range of spot prices, with 2 months to go and at maturity. Note that the short futures hedge is not rebalanced along the way.

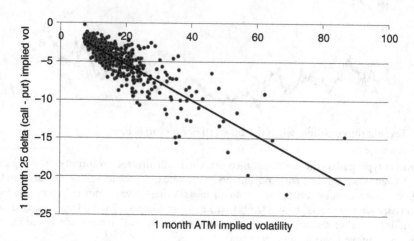

FIGURE 7.7   Selling the skew after a risk event can be attractive

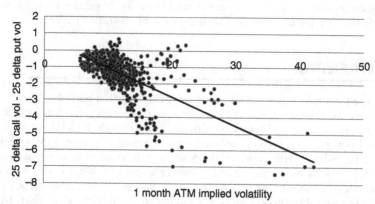

FIGURE 7.8   The AUD put skew also has positive sensitivity to changes in ATM volatility

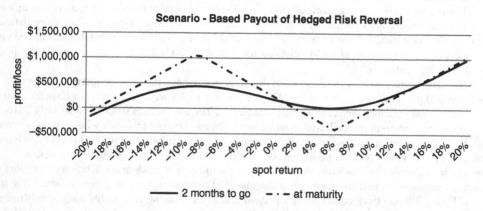

FIGURE 7.9   Elevated put skews can create intriguing risk reversal trading opportunities

The combined structure is a beauty if the index either drops moderately or rises sharply. Structurally, we are short downside gamma and long gamma to the upside. The implication is that a hedged risk reversal requires some maintenance if there is a shallow recovery or a severe fall. For large downside moves, the structure has unbounded risk, implying that it should be sized conservatively.

It is tempting to flatten the middle section of the payout curve by selling fewer futures against the risk reversal. This creates a more constant profit for a wide range of moderate scenarios. The problem is that you have "Batman-style" risk for large drops in the index. If you cut back on the hedge, the extreme downside risk of the structure is *larger* than for a long position in the futures. You should be careful not to do too much of an open-ended structure such as this, lest you violate the time-honoured principle of "being able to sleep at night".

SELLING INDEX PUT SPREADS

Selling put spreads on the S&P 500 after a drop in the index is another fine second leg down idea, assuming you are still in the game. The index doesn't need to recover for you to turn a profit. All that is required is stabilisation. Things need to stop going down so quickly. We test the put spread selling strategy below, using a simple rule. Whenever the weekly return for the S&P 500 is negative, we sell 2 put spreads at the close on Friday. Our returns are calculated as a fraction of the cash S&P index level. The short strike has a 40 delta and the long strike has a 25 delta at the point of entry. The maturity of the spread is always 4 weeks, i.e. we price it from the interpolated implied volatility surface using the Black–Scholes equation. This is similar in spirit to selling a put spread whenever the market goes "risk off". However, it is less restrictive as we wind up selling the spread roughly 50% of the time. We can gauge the benefit of the timing signal from Figure 7.10. The grey line tracks the performance of a strategy where you continuously roll the put spread. Conversely, the black line only enters the market following a negative week for the S&P.

It is clear that the conditional strategy outperforms strongly, even though it spends a large chunk of time out of the market. Note that we have made the conservative assumptions that the return on cash is 0% when there is no trade signal. As a result, the black line has some flat sections. The volatility of the conditional strategy is roughly 25% lower than the volatility of the strategy that's always in. This

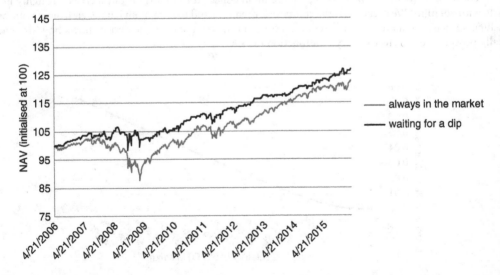

FIGURE 7.10 Selective selling of put spreads can generate interesting risk-adjusted returns

implies that waiting for a weekly drop before selling put spreads adds considerable value, especially on a risk-adjusted basis.

BREATHING SOME LIFE INTO THE EQUITY RISK PREMIUM

For many years, the equity risk premium was thought to be a relatively static thing. The long-term expected return of stock indices over bonds was assumed to be nearly constant. However, intuition suggests that the expected returns on a risky asset should go up quite strongly after a sell-off, assuming nothing has fundamentally changed. The lower the price of a stock index, the higher its future expected return should be. Legions of value investors in equity and corporate bond markets have operated on this premise. Over time, academics have loosened their assumptions and allowed the equity risk premium to move around a bit. In Campbell (2008), estimates of the global premium range from roughly 1% to 4% per year from the mid-1980s to 2007. These estimates are based on static return on equity and dividend payout ratio assumptions. Martin (2013) has developed a more flexible framework for estimating risk premia over shorter well-defined time horizons. He concludes that the equity risk premium might move considerably more radically than convention would dictate. The idea is that it is possible to establish a lower bound on the premium, using market prices for S&P 500 variance swaps. The premium is mathematically derived, using Black–Scholes–Merton type assumptions. Variance swaps go up even faster than implied volatility during risk off phases, suggesting that expected S&P returns can go from 2% annualised, say, to over 50% (!) annualised during a very nasty sell-off.

While the results are bound to be controversial in some circles, the idea that risk premia vary widely across time should resonate with anyone who has sold options over a market cycle. You want to buy risky assets after very severe sell-offs, assuming you can endure periodic bouts of short-term volatility. The amount of premium collected from selling fixed-maturity puts is highly variable. A liberal application of Martin's research involves selling OTM put spreads whenever implied volatility is high. In Figure 7.11, we demonstrate how the premium collected for selling a 5% OTM put on the S&P 500 varies as a function of implied volatility. In this case, we have assumed that the option has 3 months to maturity.

For implied volatility above 10%, the premium collected from a short put increases roughly linearly with volatility. We accept that the equity risk premium and the premium harvested from an options selling strategy are materially different quantities. However, the example above shows how dramatically prospective returns can vary as a function of risk.

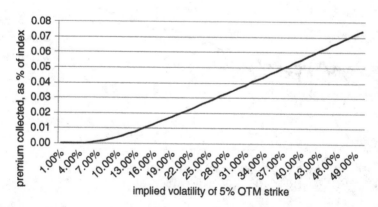

FIGURE 7.11 The premium from selling an OTM put varies roughly linearly as implied volatility increases

Selling volatility is based upon the same premise as buying credit. When you buy a high yield bond, you collect an excess return relative to the risk-free rate, so long as the bond doesn't default. Time is also on your side when you sell an OTM put. You would like nothing more than for the market to wander around aimlessly for a while. After a risk event, bond yields and cross-asset class implied volatility tend to be very high. If the future is not as bleak as the present, you can generate a return simply by sitting on your hands. Note that we are selling a put *spread*, rather than an outright put. We don't want to be exposed to a spiral down to 0. This is in keeping with our "second leg down" premise. There is always the possibility of a *third* leg down and there are no prizes for surviving the longest before getting wiped out.

BUYING VIX PUTS

Any number of premium capture strategies should work after a sell-off, assuming that you have deep enough pockets. What if you have nearly exhausted your risk budget, but want to participate in a recovery? Here is an alternative idea, with bounded risk. Buying VIX puts or put spreads seems to be a fairly consistently winning strategy, on a historical basis. This might seem surprising at first, as long options strategies are rarely associated with consistent profits. When you buy and roll an OTM option, the expectation is that you will burn premium most of the time, in exchange for the occasional large positive return.

But let's think about this problem in a bit more depth, with reference to futures options. Suppose you have options on two different futures contracts. The futures prices are the same and the market assigns the same volatility to both of them. The strikes and expiration dates are the same. Then, the Black 1976 pricing model assigns the same price to both options. The precise formula appears in the appendix. Black 76 is surprising for a piece of information that it *doesn't* include. The shape of the futures term structure never appears in Black 76. This is significant. It might be that the term structure of the first futures contract is in backwardation while the second is in severe contango. Still, Black 76 implies that their options prices should be identical. This is of no matter: their theoretical options prices must be identical. The absence of forward curve dependence is analogous to the dog who *didn't* bark in the night in Conan Doyle's *The Silver Blade*. The Black–Scholes–Merton approach relies upon instantaneous replication of an option, so roll down never appears. Recall that replication involves buying or selling an appropriate number of futures to match the option delta. If we continuously rebalance, we might not realise that the specific futures contract we use to hedge is changing form over time. The time to maturity is shrinking and the futures is rolling down the term structure.

If we choose not to hedge dynamically, Black 76 ignores a very important piece of information. The term structure is telling us where the market expects the futures to trade at a forward point in time. If the term structure is in contango and nothing much happens, the futures price will drift down over time. The steeper the curve, the greater the roll down. Hence, if we buy a put on a futures contract that has an upward sloping term structure, we're in business. Every day that goes by quietly, we lose a bit on time decay. However, this is offset by futures drift toward the strike. Roll down is an important source of return that is well known to experienced options traders. It might be argued that shorting the futures is a more direct way to play contango in the term structure. However, such a strategy does not play into a hedging mandate as it has unbounded risk. Buying VIX puts or put spreads is the safer way to go.

Figure 7.12 tracks the performance of a no frills put buying strategy on the VXX (short-term VIX futures ETF). We have bought a 4-week 50 delta call, held for a week and rolled. Each call has been priced from the VXX implied volatility surface.

Here is a rare bird, a long options strategy with positive drift! The strategy benefits from roll down whenever the VIX is in contango and mean reversion in the spot VIX after a volatility spike. These factors have been enough to overcome options time decay, at least historically. Based on the evidence,

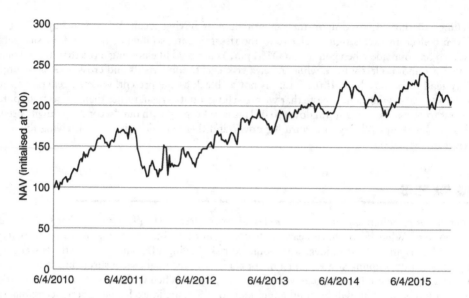

FIGURE 7.12 Historical performance of rolling long put strategy on the VXX

VXX puts are an intriguing addition to a hedging overlay. The offer positive gamma and expected return, with bounded risk. Your loss is restricted to the initial premium outlay. If you manage to call the bottom of an equity sell-off, you can also collect a windfall from mean reversion in volatility.

There is an extended form of the VXX put buying strategy. After a moderate sell-off, you can combine nearby puts with far out of the money call spreads to profit from either a severe continuation of the sell-off or a reversal. You might reason that volatility is unlikely to stay put at the current level. As of this writing, we have to admit that the "edge" in buying VIX puts after a volatility spike seems to have diminished. The market has cottoned on to the idea and appears to be pricing in a steeper VIX skew than before. However, the trade still offers the possibility of offsetting option theta with roll down and mean reversion.

SELLING VIX UPSIDE

Selling VIX call spreads can be an effective strategy after a sell-off. For example, if front month VIX futures have jumped from 15 to 25 in the past week, it might be reasonable to sell a 1-month VIX 25/30 call spread. Once markets stabilise, you have the potential for a solid return. We emphasise that you don't need the S&P to recover. The index just has to stop accelerating to the downside. There is another advantage to selling VIX calls after a spike in volatility, as we will see in the graph below. In particular, we observe that the level and implied volatility of the VIX are closely related. When the VIX spikes, it also becomes more volatile. The relationship is sub-linear, in the sense that the market starts to account for mean reversion if volatility becomes *really* high. Nonetheless, if you believe that the current crisis will not get appreciably worse, selling a call spread gives you two sources of return. Since you are short delta, you benefit from a decline in the level of the VIX. Additionally, your call spread will benefit from declining VIX implied volatility, as vega in the near strike will dominate vega in the far one.

We graph the porcupine-type relationship between VIX level and VIX implied volatility in Figure 7.13.

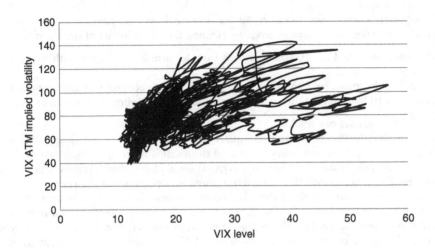

FIGURE 7.13 Porcupine exposure of VIX implied volatility relative to VIX level

The reader might wonder why we haven't recommended selling an outright call, rather than a call spread. We don't recommend selling naked calls on the assumption that it is inadvisable to take unbounded risk in a quantity that can jump as much as the VIX. Trades that can fly in your face in an instant are to be avoided. History is a powerful guide. The VIX approached 90 in October 2008 and probably would have exceeded 100 in October 1987 if it had been quoted then. A 1-day –20% move would annualise at nearly 300% volatility if it occurred every day (assuming that we do not subtract the mean return in our volatility calculation).

Notice that this trade is a variation on the put spread buying strategy we discussed earlier. In both cases, we are taking the view that forward volatility will decline. However, the put spread is a more subtle trade, as it is focused on roll down in the VIX futures term structure. If we buy a put spread after the curve has gone into backwardation, we potentially gain on delta but lose on vega. Declining implied volatility works against the put spread. In the meantime, selling a call spread is probably a cruder trade, as it is not overly concerned about term structure dynamics. However, it can be very effective after a sell-off. You needn't get too fancy once things are out of whack.

THE REMARKABLE SECOND MOMENT

We have observed that selling put spreads after a spike in implied volatility can be a very attractive strategy. The idea is to "fade" a large move, while betting that volatility will revert to more normal levels. This is a variation on the short VIX call spread idea above, as it also relies upon compression in implied volatility. Why is it that we want to trade volatility after a crisis? There are two reasons. First, as we will see, volatility is the easiest parameter of the forward return distribution to estimate. More specifically, volatility is strongly mean-reverting.

Let's examine why volatility can be estimated with at least some level of accuracy. Our argument is heuristic, but hopefully illustrative. The simplest realistic assumption is that asset returns can be modelled by a time-invariant, or "stationary" process. While stationarity is violated in practice, this assumption allows us to build our intuition. Also suppose that returns are normally distributed and each return is independent of all others. If we simulate a reasonable number of returns according to these assumptions, which moment is most reliably estimated? It turns out that the standard deviation (square root of the second moment) has the least variation across alternative realities. This implies that, if the "true" distribution is not too different for a normal one, we have some hope of estimating volatility. We can make this concept concrete by running the following set of simulations.

- Each simulation, we draw 100 daily returns from a normal distribution with mean 0 and volatility 10%.
- We calculate the mean, volatility, skewness and kurtosis of the returns in each simulation.
- We then run 10,000 simulations, so that we can build the sampling distribution for each moment.

Table 7.1 summarises our results.

We can see that the standard deviation (square root of the second moment) varies the least across simulations. To be fair, the sampling distribution of the mean is nearly as tight as that of the standard deviation. However, the standard deviation in a typical simulation is over 10 times larger in magnitude than the mean. This suggests that, in relative terms, standard deviation stays in a very tight range across simulations. It's somewhat surprising that the second moment is more well-behaved than the first, third or any higher central moment. As it turns out, volatility is not only the easiest moment to measure, but also the easiest to predict. This is true in relative terms, at least. Volatility has a tendency to mean-revert whenever it becomes particularly stretched. We can express this idea in rough but intuitive terms. Barring a collapse, it's unlikely that the S&P 500 will trade at its average level over the last 20 years (roughly 1270 as of February 2016) in the near future. However, most of us would expect the VIX to intersect its long-term average value on a fairly regular basis. In 2015 alone, the VIX crossed its 20-year trailing average 6 times (using daily data).

It's possible to be a bit more rigorous in our discussion. Our VIX call spread trade is dependent upon mean-reversion, so it is worth having an accurate picture of the underlying dynamics. An obvious point of reference is the GARCH model, as in Bollerslev (1986). GARCH is one of the most widely-quoted econometric models and serves two basic purposes. It is suitable for generating point estimates of volatility and can also forecast volatility forward in time. More precisely, GARCH models the evolution of an asset's variance, i.e. the square of its volatility.

We now give a very rough but intuitively correct description of the model. A point estimate of GARCH variance is dependent on yesterday's estimate, the long-term average variance and the square of the most recent return. Critically, the loading to the long-term average term is negative. This "pulls" volatility toward a long-term equilibrium and suggests that, at the extremes, changes in volatility are somewhat predictable. A direct consequence of the model is that volatility is persistent over short horizons and mean reverting over long ones.

A direct way to convince yourself that volatility is mean-reverting is simply to look at the data. Rather than using the spot volatility estimate from a calibrated GARCH model, we can focus on mean reversion in implied volatility. After all, implied volatility is a key driver of the performance of a short put or put spread strategy. In Figure 7.14, we have mapped the current level of the CVIX onto its

TABLE 7.1 Standard deviation has the tightest sampling distribution

Empirical Standard Deviation of Sampling Distribution	
Mean	6.26×10^{-4}
Standard deviation	4.50×10^{-4}
Skewness	2.41×10^{-1}
Kurtosis	4.78×10^{-1}

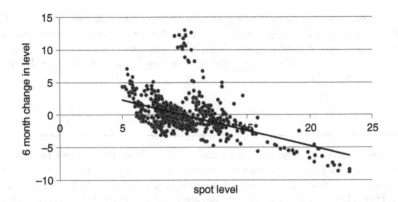

FIGURE 7.14　Currency implied volatility tends to be mean reverting over 6-month horizons

6-month forward change. The graph relies upon 20 years of weekly data. We can directly see that level and change have a significant negative correlation. When volatility is high, odds are that it will decline over the next 6 months. This suggests mean reversion in implied volatility.

Unsurprisingly, the VIX also exhibits strong mean reversion, as we observe in Figure 7.15.

The level of dispersion around the regression line for implied volatility above 30 is very low. In practical terms, this means that the VIX has a high probability of reverting whenever it crosses 30. The reversion may take a few months, but based on the evidence it is very likely. This point is worth investigating further. If we can control for extreme left-tail risk and carry costs, selling the VIX above 30 seems a very good trade. Assuming we have hedged or adequately accounted for the extreme left tail, the last thing we want to do is to buy outright VIX calls after a volatility spike. Volatility (and likely the volatility of volatility) is likely to decline if nothing dramatic happens in the near term. GARCH-like forces are pushing volatility down. It's also interesting to observe that a short volatility position seems to have the greatest relative risk when the VIX is around 20. The "fear index" hasn't tended to jump directly from 15 or so all that often in the past. A plausible explanation is that the VIX needs to get a bit hot before large scale sell-offs become imminent.

We can take advantage of high volatility levels by selling VIX futures calendar spreads. In particular, we might sell front month futures and buy the deferred month when the term structure becomes inverted. In this case, we are playing mean reversion in the spot rather than roll down. Our roll yield is

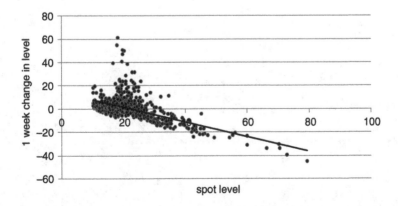

FIGURE 7.15　The VIX tends to revert over 6-month horizons, too

in fact negative, though we do not think it will stay that way for long. Rather, we are betting that spot volatility will decay. Buying the second month partially hedges against a further spike in volatility. Observe, however, that your potential loss is theoretically unlimited. You can lose your shirt on calendar spreads, as the saying goes. The second month futures will move far less than the front month if spot volatility continues to rise.

SUMMARY

Misery sometimes creates opportunity in financial markets. You do not need to be a "vulture" or "wolf" to turn a nice little profit during turbulent regimes. During liquidations, certain types of investors are forced out of the market, while others scramble for protection. Anyone who still has capital to deploy can take advantage of price dislocations in a volatile market. Buying dips in risky assets, selling volatility and selling the skew are all effective strategies when traded selectively and opportunistically. However, careful sizing and structuring of trades is vital, as there is no way to know when the worst is over.

CHAPTER 8

"Flash Crashes", Crises and the Limits of Prediction

We have spoken at length about hedging after a drop and even ventured into offensive strategies for a high volatility market. But is it possible to *anticipate* sharp sell-offs or longer-term crises? The words "predict" and "forecast" are a bit more loaded. These words bring to mind the admonition that the goal of economic forecasting is to lend credence to astrology (1984). Nevertheless, we will wade into the muck and see whether it is possible to say anything about the likelihood of a quick correction or longer-term bear market. We informally describe how a flash crash can develop, using an analogy from mathematical biology. There are attempts to predict crises in the recent literature. We discuss some of these approaches, ending with a cautionary note about the limits of forecasting in financial markets.

LORD OF THE FIREFLIES

Many investors (especially those influenced by Taleb, 2007) vigorously argue that market crises are inherently unpredictable. Portfolio managers sometimes feel that they are operating in a sea of randomness, with a low signal to noise ratio for even their best ideas and systems. Large-scale liquidations are particularly baffling. If conditions had been even slightly different, they may never have occurred. In this context, the claim in Sornette (2009) that extreme moves can be predicted and possibly controlled seems remarkable. It's like trying to solve the hardest problem in a scientific field without having a reasonable understanding of the simplest cases.

We need to be a bit more precise here. Sornette does not claim that *all* market movements can be predicted. In most market regimes, the degree of predictability is low. However, he would argue that there is a brief and reliable "window of predictability" for financial disasters. Sornette is not focused on high frequency liquidations, but rather the sort of longer-term market disasters captured in Reinhart and Rogoff (2009). In his paradigm, the fog of uncertainty lifts just before something really awful is about to happen.

A signal arrives in the form of unsustainable price action. Markets go parabolic, rising at an ever-increasing rate, before the inevitable correction. "Weak hands" enter the market near the end of the rally, in a last-ditch effort to participate. These investors are easily flushed out at the first signs of weakness and can create a strongly negative feedback loop. An ever-increasing number of investors are forced to sell as their downside stop levels are hit. Sornette has identified various boom/bust cycles in China and US technology stocks where in his view, a major sell-off was inevitable.

Sornette's analogy between phase transitions and market collapses is suggestive, though not entirely accurate. It is not necessarily the case that markets move from a state of order to disorder during a liquidation. Over long horizons, characterised by unpredictable waves of buying and selling, this may be the case. However, at the tipping point where panic selling begins, investors tend to be aligned in the same way. While it is true that there must be a buyer for every seller, buyers can aggressively drop their bids and still get filled when the market is cratering. The investors who are initiating large blocks of open interest are almost invariably sellers.

The notion that liquidations actually represent somewhat *orderly* behaviour (however hair-raising) requires a different analogy. The sum of investors can be thought of as a collection of agents whose activities become synchronised in advance of a fat-tailed event. Once the level of synchronisation crosses a threshold, a crisis becomes inevitable. Steven Strogatz's model of the synchronised bursting of fireflies is particularly appropriate and we briefly review it here. We highly recommend Strogatz (2004) for its fine exposition and interesting ideas. The story goes as follows. In the 1500s, European explorers started to relay stories about Asian fireflies back to their mother continent. As the cover of this book humbly suggests, large clouds of these flies were able to coordinate their activities to the extent that they could illuminate the river banks as night began to fall. This was the stuff of wonder and awe, as it would be several centuries before the electric light bulb was invented.

Given that fireflies are not renowned for their expertise in strategic planning, it seemed astonishing that they could organise themselves into swirls of light, synchronising their flashes. It took quite some time for scientists to understand how such an organised network could form spontaneously. It was eventually discovered that the movement and timing of flashes could be controlled by a light of variable intensity. This implied that fireflies could send each other simple messages by flashing in a specific way. Referring back to Sornette's argument, the important point was that if enough flies started behaving in a co-ordinated way, others would follow. Beyond a threshold, the short-term movement of every fly would follow a fairly deterministic process. This is the window of predictability we referred to earlier. You could almost tell when the fireflies were about to act collectively. While crises tend to build over horizons of months rather than minutes, the firefly example demonstrates that co-ordinated behaviour can arise from a collection of agents who act independently under normal circumstances.

CASCADING SALES

Intraday sell-offs do not fit precisely into the Sornette framework. They are not necessarily preceded by accelerating rallies that drive valuations to extreme levels. Over short horizons, valuation is relatively unimportant. Prices tend to be driven by technical considerations. Still, it seems as though investors exhibit the same sort of collective behaviour during a severe drop, independent of horizon. Negative feedback loops feature in sell-offs over all frequencies. Proceeding from the Strogatz analogy, we can think of each order as a single firefly. As their behaviour becomes more organised and directed, the probability of an outsized move becomes increasingly likely.

Whenever someone asks you *why* the market crashed today, there is always an easy answer: *positioning*. In this case, the easy answer isn't very helpful, but it's invariably correct over short time horizons. There's no need to scan your news feed or process large quantities of sentiment data. Whatever may have happened in the outside world only provided an initial impulse for the larger move. At some point, larger investors were forced into the market in an attempt to reduce margin requirements, meet redemptions or manage their losses. But how do large volumes of selling precipitate intraday crashes? In this section, we attempt to address this question using a simple model of price impact.

We start with another analogy. Suppose you're at a public auditorium and you see lots of people heading for the exits. If they all belong to the same group, you wouldn't be too worried. They might all be going somewhere else; collectively, they have a single mindset. However, if people are leaving from throughout the hall and the show isn't over, you might be inclined to leave too. Something must be up (assuming, of course, that it isn't the performance itself). The information content seems much higher when unconnected agents are all doing the same thing.

The same argument applies to price moves in the financial markets. A large number of small trades in the same direction will typically move the market more than a single trade of the same total size. The graph below is loosely based on Bouchaud (2009), which surveys various price impact models. Here, we assume that price impact is inversely related to the square root of volume, as in the BARRA model. Suppose that there are a series of buy orders in S&P 500 futures, accounting for 5% of average daily trading volume. What is the estimated price impact?

Under the following assumptions, we can sketch the price impact function. The third of these is based on conversations with execution brokers and should not be interpreted too rigidly.

- About 2 million S&P E-mini futures contracts trade each day.
- The futures have a volatility of 15%.
- If a 10,000 lot goes through the market, its price impact will be around 0.3% of the index level, i.e. 6 points if the futures are at 2000.
- The volatility of the contract is 15%.

The third assumption allows us to solve for C in the price impact function

$$\sigma \frac{\sqrt{S}}{2C}$$

where σ is the volatility of the index and the trade size S is set as a percentage of daily trading volume.

We can break up 5% of daily trading volume in a number of ways, 100 trades of 1,000 lots, 50 trades of 2,000 lots and so on. If the trades are all buys or sells, we end up with an impact curve as in Figure 8.1.

The curve is remarkable because it suggests that 100 trades in the same direction will have 5 times the impact of 4 trades that amount to the same total volume. This is insightful and ultimately troubling, given the current trend toward automated order routing systems. These systems tend to slice large orders into smaller blocks, leading to smaller average trading sizes. If the price impact curve remains the same in the new regime, the probability of fat-tailed moves in individual securities is likely to increase.

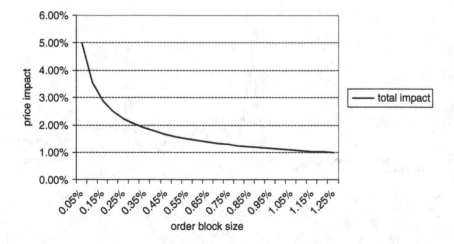

FIGURE 8.1 Small unidirectional trades collectively have larger impact than a single block

A CONCRETE EXAMPLE

At the risk of oversimplification, we can try to codify Sornette's collapse point theory into a small set of rules. Roughly speaking, Sornette is looking for two conditions that might precipitate a crisis. First, prices need to have gone up very rapidly in the recent past. More recently, the pool of potential new investors has been exhausted. This is reflected by an increase in realised volatility. The aggressive tug of war between buyers and sellers has intensified. So let's test these conditions on some real data. We consider an index that has experienced two bubbles and crashes over the past 10 years, namely the Shanghai composite index as shown in Figure 8.2. Our data set ranges from 1990 to 2015. We start by specifying the year on year (YoY) change in the index. Next, we calculate the 5 year trailing Z score of the YoY returns. We also calculate the 5 year trailing Z score of 1 month historical volatility for the index, using daily returns. Our crisis warning indicator flashes if both Z scores are above 2. In other words, recent price increases and current volatility need to be at least 2 standard deviations above normal.

It can be seen that this basic implementation is reasonably effective, accepting that the effective sample set is small. A false signal is given in mid-2006, but the signal is quickly washed away. The remaining signals occur fairly close to the point of collapse. The idea that elevated volatility is predictive of danger is not new and underpins many asset allocation schemes. However, Sornette deserves credit for moving away from a largely valuation-based approach to predicting crises to one that relies upon price action itself.

AN ASIDE

Sornette pushes things even further with his second assertion. Somewhat remarkably, he contends that a small policy control applied near the threshold should be able to subvert a bubble or crash. In the firefly example, this might correspond to drawing some fireflies away from the group as they start to co-ordinate their activities in some area.

Many of us have not even reached the point of deciding whether it is *possible* to predict a crisis, let alone come up with a model that claims to do exactly that. Sornette's two claims may strain the

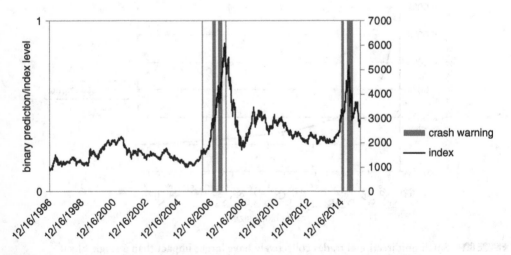

FIGURE 8.2   Nuts and bolts implementation of Sornette's crisis indicator, Shanghai Composite Index

imagination a bit. From a technical standpoint, it is hard to model singularities (i.e. extreme solutions to dynamical systems) in physics, let alone finance. Some equations in physics have solutions that "blow up" in finite time. But do these singularities really exist, or are they artefacts of the modelling process? There might be an equation that is nearby the original one, in some sense, yet does not have any singularities. One has to be very cautious. However, it does seem as though Sornette has made some progress in identifying price movements that are too fast to be sustainable. This naturally leads us to a discussion of more concrete models that can be used to say something about rapid sell-offs and longer-term crises.

PATHS, PRINTS

We have described above how a large succession of trades in one direction can have surprisingly large price impact. Some short-term traders are left scratching their heads, thinking that they have missed something. They eventually pile into the market, exaggerating what was perhaps an uninformed trade in the first place. Eventually, levered investors hit their pain thresholds and are forced into the market. If lots of selling is going on around them, they have to sell in an effort to cut risk. Is there any way we can model the interaction between random moves in the market, leverage providers and leveraged funds in a way that generates outsized moves?

Thurner (2012) has developed a model that might not predict fat-tailed market moves, but generates the right sort of qualitative dynamics. Chaos theory, which held such promise in the 1980s, is similar in spirit. You can generate a rich set of dynamics that "looks right" by perturbing a relatively simple equation. While you can simulate a wide range of outcomes, however, you can't predict real world outcomes with much accuracy. Farmer's group at Oxford has subsequently built more realistic representations of the economy. This is a promising area that may allow central bankers to simulate the impact of policy decisions on financial markets and the real economy. Interventions that are likely to destabilise the economy can be ruled out. The paper develops a "toy" model with 3 agents: a bank, a noise trader and a leveraged investor. The market is initialised to move randomly through time. For simplicity, it might be worth thinking of the "market" as a broad-based stock index. Noise traders respond to the random moves, buying short-term dips and selling rallies. They operate on the assumption that there is no information content behind these small irregular moves. Things are likely to revert quickly. Noise traders have a tendency to generate mean reversion in prices in "normal" regimes. The leveraged investor is called a "value investor" in the paper, but in general could take a long position based on value or momentum criteria. The point is that, as leverage increases, these value investors have a relatively small margin for error. They will be forced to sell out of their positions relatively quickly and aggressively if there is a material downside move. Otherwise the bank, providing leverage to the investor, will threaten to close out their positions. In this scenario, the noise traders (i.e. self-styled liquidity providers) are forced to pull out of the markets, as they do not have sufficient capital to hang on to losing positions for an extended period of time.

As leverage approaches a critical threshold, we can show that the market return distribution deforms into a fat-tailed one. The potential for large down moves increases. All it takes is a sharp enough drop in the index for long investors to be forced into the market. Selling can become desperate and indiscriminate when investors are in danger of having their credit lines pulled. In this context, leverage is the key variable driving large-scale moves in the broader market. If we follow this argument though to its natural conclusion, the central bank must have an impact on the formation of bubbles and crashes. When investors are trying to magnify returns with leverage and the central bank is simultaneously trying to withdraw credit from the system, the conditions for a crisis are in place. Commercial banks will eventually have to curtail their lending activities once they lose easy access to cheap revolving credit. The tightening ultimately gets passed on to corporations and investors, who now have a harder time maintaining a borrow. Under these circumstances, a –10% drop in the S&P index will have a disproportionately large effect. Banks will be quicker to enforce large margin calls at a time when investor gearing is at a cyclical high. If we are to understand the relationship between tail risk and credit, we need to understand the workings of the central bank in a bit more detail. This is the topic of the next few sections.

THE ROLE OF THE CENTRAL BANK

Rothbard (2008) is an entertaining, though agenda-fueled, romp through the history of banking. It argues that governments have always been incentivised to inflate the supply of money. A king might recall existing coins, melt them down, dilute the gold or silver content and stamp a larger quantity of new coins. The king could then keep the extra supply for himself. In this way, monetary expansion (i.e. increasing the quantity of coins) was an implicit tax on the people. Their coins would theoretically be worth less on the open market. In modern times, credit dwarfs the supply of physical money. Accordingly, governments have more sophisticated tools for encouraging growth and consumption in the system. These are typically deployed by the Central Bank.

Rothbard encourages us to take a critical look at the inner workings and motivations of central banks, notably the Federal Reserve Bank in the US. One of his main points is that, once the US moved away from the gold standard, bubbles became more likely. The government could quickly increase the domestic money supply without having to back it with gold. Major economies could now engage in competitive devaluation, as there was no need to withdraw money from the system after selling gold to another central bank or into the market. For asset owners, inflation has a "feel good" factor associated with it. People's houses are worth more, their stock portfolios rise and there is an urgency to buy things before the next price increase. The winners in the inflation game are the ones who buy first, before prices increase. Conversely, investors who favour safety and income pay an implicit tax in an inflationary environment. This can stimulate real growth in the short-term, but the growth is unsustainable. Hyper-inflation can create political instability, as in post-World War I Germany. If a central bank turns off the liquidity spigot too aggressively or at the wrong time, a bubble can rapidly turn into a crash.

Sornette and Woodard (2009) trace the roots of the 2007–8 financial crisis back to monetary policy from 2000 to 2004. This is the same Sornette as before, now giving a historical perspective on credit expansion before the crisis. Although stocks sold off quite dramatically from 2000 to 2002, economic growth remained relatively strong. Nevertheless, the Fed Funds rate was steadily cut from 6.5% to 1%. The Fed was presumably responding to market price action, rather than its stated dual mandate of employment and inflation. Recall that Fed Funds is the rate at which commercial banks borrow from the Federal Reserve Bank. A low Fed Funds rate encourages banks to finance long-term corporate projects using revolving short-term credit. This can stimulate the economy if there is adequate demand from the private sector. Otherwise, the excess credit may be misdirected to assets that are already overvalued.

Low interest rates encouraged leveraged speculation in real estate, equities and high yield bonds from 2003 to 2007. Giant bubbles formed in the credit derivatives markets. Once fundamental cracks appeared in the system, the genie couldn't be stuffed back into the bottle. Perversely, the Fed had to do *more* of the things that had caused excessive speculation in an attempt to prevent a collapse in the global banking system. Overly lax policy and bank lending are nearly always behind the speculative bubbles that ultimately collapse.

CREDIT CYCLES AT THE ZERO BOUND

It has been remarked that all assets are in some sense derivatives of the Fed Funds rate. While there are clearly other factors at work, variations in target rates can have a large impact on various asset classes, ranging from bonds to real estate. A drop in rates typically causes yield curves to steepen and may increase demand for risky assets such as real estate, equities and high yield bonds. The implied carry in these strategies becomes relatively attractive. A rise in short-term policy rates tends to have the opposite effect. Bank profits have a tendency to decrease, given that the spread between borrowing and lending rates has shrunk. (Note that a collapse in long term yields can have an even more pronounced negative effect on bank profits.) Once rates get really low, all sorts of distortions can occur. Risky assets such as stocks, corporate bonds and notably housing can rally. Investors and home buyers can now borrow at rock bottom rates. This increases the amount of money and credit chasing a fixed pool of assets and can cause speculative bubbles. Eventually, the market overheats, forcing the Fed to start hiking rates again.

But how can we apply this reasoning when short-term rates are stuck at 0? There is no value in measuring the sensitivity of an asset to a quantity which does not move. We can no longer extract information about central bank policy from month over month changes in rates. Consider the current situation. Even if most observers agree that rates should be higher, there never seems to be a good time to raise them. As Sornette and Woodard have remarked (2009), forward guidance seems to be increasingly dependent on what is going on in the market. This is an unfortunate legacy of the Greenspan era. Suggestions of a rate hike have been met with panic selling, pushing actual rate hikes further out into the future. Is there a viable way to track central bank policy in a 0 rate world? An idea emerges when we start to think of what the Fed and ECB have actually done over the past few years. Their ability to cut short-term rates has become severely restricted. Rather, they have engaged in various rounds of "quantitative easing", or QE. This has included printing money to buy long-dated bonds ("operation twist") and lending money against dubious collateral, such as mortgage-backed securities. These sorts of strategies have increased the balance sheet size of the major central banks. The goal has been to increase the quantity and movement of credit at times where commercial banks would have been otherwise reluctant to lend.

THE MONETARY POLICY PALETTE

Central banks can inject money and credit into the financial system in a variety of ways that are largely ignored by the mainstream financial media. In this section, we focus on the US Federal Reserve Bank, or "Fed", as it is usually called. Since the 2008 crisis, Fed watching has become a major commercial enterprise. The US Fed is unequivocally the most actively followed central bank worldwide. In terms of sheer balance sheet size, the People's Bank of China, or "PBoC", has surpassed the Fed. However, this is a relatively recent phenomenon.

There are some misconceptions as to how the major central banks operate. We hope to clarify some of them here. The financial industry seems obsessed with the Fed funds rate. A great deal of energy is spent trying to gauge where the rate is likely to go. Mathematical algorithms have been written, in an attempt to uncover subtle changes in the wording of monetary policy committee releases or speeches given by Fed governors. At some level, this is all quite ridiculous. The Fed Funds rate is actually a blunt policy instrument. It roughly measures the *cost* of credit. However, it doesn't say anything meaningful about its *availability*. Banks may be unable (e.g. for regulatory reasons) or unwilling to borrow at rock-bottom rates. This implies that the supply of credit available to the real economy need not increase as rates decline.

However, suppose that banks are unconstrained, greedy and able to access more credit at a reasonable rate. Then, there should be a multiplier effect on the private sector. Every dollar that enters a bank can contribute to 10 or more dollars of available credit. This can be viewed as a positive thing, on the assumption that working capital can be accessed more efficiently. The downside, as Rothbard (2008) suggested, is that reckless uncollateralised lending bears some of the hallmarks of a Ponzi scheme. If, in a crisis of confidence, all depositors withdrew their cash from a bank, the bank would go bankrupt immediately. The Fed can increase the quantity of credit available to primary dealers by expanding its balance sheet. There are a number of ways to increase credit supply and we list some of the most important ones below.

- **Direct lending.** Initially, direct lending was the only monetary policy tool used by the Fed. Since the Fed offered cheaper loans than the benchmark commercial paper rate, some banks abused the facility and borrowed excessively. The Fed divides its direct lending activities into primary and secondary credit. Primary credit is offered to banks that are deemed to be in good shape. The duration of primary loans ranges from overnight (possibly to cover settlement issues) up to 28 days. Conversely, secondary credit essentially consists of emergency loans. "Secondary" is a polite way of saying that the bank in question is in trouble. Borrowing through the "discount window" is life support for critically injured banks, on the assumption that they will be able to repair their balance sheets once financial conditions stabilise.

  Armantier (2015) has observed that, over time, banks became increasingly reluctant to borrow though the discount window. This was largely an issue of perception. Once the market discovered that a bank was asking for emergency loans, speculators would swoop in, shorting its stock and credit. In 2008, however, many banks were well past the point of worrying about perception during the next beauty pageant with shareholders. It was a simple matter of survival. Loans soared to unprecedented levels, triggering a huge jump in the size of the Fed's balance sheet. At the apex of the 2008 crisis, the Fed responded by offering a huge quantity of emergency loans, placing the US banking system on life support.

- **Buying Treasuries in the secondary market.** The New York Fed is responsible for cash transactions in Treasury bonds. These are called open market operations. When the NY Fed buys Treasuries, especially at an auction, a fresh supply of money enters the financial system, as they pay in cash. This is a fairly direct form of money printing. Conversely, selling Treasuries represents a withdrawal of cash from the system, as money is paid back to the Fed.

- **Repo activity.** Repurchase loans, or "repos", are short-term collateralised loans. In particular, you need to post an asset in exchange for a loan. Usually, the asset needs to be something backed by the government. However, this requirement was famously relaxed in 2008, when a variety of lower-grade credits were accepted by the Fed. Once the loan is repaid, you get the asset back. Primary dealers can repo securities such as Treasury bonds to the Fed. They nominally sell the bonds to the Fed and are contractually obliged to buy them back at a higher price at settlement. The prearranged price differential between selling and buying determines the repo rate. If a bank can continuously roll its repo agreements forward in time, it has a perpetual source of credit that can be applied elsewhere.

It remains to establish a link between central bank activity and the booms and busts that occur every so often. We proceed according to the hypothesis that most of the major crises in recent memory have been credit-related. We accept that there have been various "flash crashes" over the years that do not fit into this framework. Some have been triggered by geopolitical events and others by rapid liquidations. There was a relatively silent crash in the summer of 2007, when quantitative equity funds were forced to liquidate stocks with the same characteristics at the same time. As of early 2016, we have seen lots of algorithms trading intraday price momentum across various markets. This may have triggered large-scale directional moves in markets such as oil and China, followed by violent reversals. Algo-driven moves are not easily predictable by liquidity analysis, as they can occur over arbitrarily short horizons. These may occur with greater frequency in a marketplace increasingly dominated by machines. However, most of the sustained downturns in recent memory have been credit-related. The 1991 US Savings and Loan crisis, the various bankruptcies in 2002 and the banking failures in 2008 all had their roots in a liquidity crisis. Banks lost their access to revolving loans and the Fed eventually had to increase the size of its balance sheet to compensate.

CrossBorder Capital has developed a series of liquidity indices that track central bank and private sector lending activities over time. Their policy indices focus on global central banks, covering over 75 countries. The private sector indices move further down the chain and track the amount of bank and shadow bank lending to corporations and individuals. However, for simplicity, we will focus on

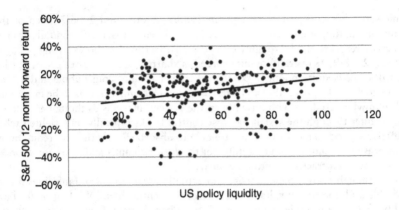

FIGURE 8.3 Liquidity is the tide that lifts all boats

the US and Global policy indices only. The indices are normalised and range from 0 to 100. When an index is close to 0, the supply of central bank credit is growing well below trend. When it's close to 100, credit expansion is significantly above trend. These indices allow us to condense loan, swap, repo and cash Treasury data into a single index for each Central Bank. In Figure 8.3, we explore the connection between US policy liquidity levels and 12 month forward returns on the S&P 500. The S&P 500 is used as a rough proxy for risky assets. The regression is based on monthly data from 2000 to 2015.

The historical correlation between the two time series is around 24%. This is more than respectable for a one-factor non-parameterised forecasting model. We observe that forward returns are especially strong after a period of aggressive easing. This can be seen in the upper right portion of the graph, where the data is almost exclusively above the x-axis. It suggests that aggressive credit expansion is very bullish for equity and credit markets.

It is also instructive to examine the global liquidity index on a stand-alone basis, as in Figure 8.4.

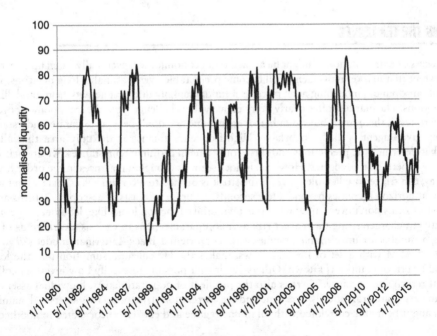

FIGURE 8.4 Time series of CrossBorder Total Liquidity Index, Global

The time series has conspicuous troughs in 1988/9, 2000/1 and 2006/7. Each of these troughs preceded a major banking or credit crisis (the savings and loan crisis, the Enron/fallen angels crisis and the Lehman crisis, respectively) by roughly two years. The series also shows strong policy responses in 1994, 1999 and 2008/9. As overall liquidity surged, a sharp increase in asset prices quickly followed. 1994 preceded an EM equity boom, 1999 helped trigger the dot-com bubble and 2008/9 caused a violent rally in credit and equity indices. The transmission mechanism seems to be faster when liquidity is increased than when credit is withdrawn from the system. It seems as though a decline in liquidity takes longer to filter through the system because central banks typically only tighten when the economy is in relatively good shape. Companies are able to absorb slightly tighter credit conditions. Conversely, an increase in liquidity can be rapidly put to work by banks and other investors who rely on leverage to generate an attractive return on equity.

It seems as though central bank activity can actually *create* financial fault lines for major crises. This is inevitable and does not invalidate the role of the central bank. While it might be argued that there would be an economic cycle in any case, a central bank's credit facilities can serve to amplify the cycle. After a bubble or an extended bull market, the liquidity spigot eventually gets turned off. Central Banks finally revert to their original remit, namely inflation control. Credit delivered from the central bank to primary dealers becomes more restrictive. At the same time, banks are ratcheting up their exposure. These bullish conditions can persist for quite some time, even if Central Banks are trying to put the brakes on. What we can say, however, is that crises usually occur for liquidity rather than solvency reasons. So long as a bank or sovereign nation has unlimited access to cheap revolving short-term credit, it is unlikely to default. It doesn't matter whether the entity is creditworthy or not.

Our Central Bank-derived approach to analysing crises does not quite fit into Sornette's blueprint. In particular, liquidity is an *exogenous* factor. It moves markets from the outside. Sornette would argue that crises do not require external shocks to appear: they are simply the byproducts of a complex network that can exhibit strong positive feedback over time. From our perspective, however, liquidity offers a near-universal mechanism for bubbles and crises. Crises might form spontaneously, but their likelihood is much higher when large investors are stretched and banks are unwilling or unable to lend. This idea is neatly encapsulated by the global liquidity index.

READING THE TEA LEAVES

By a process of extrapolation, it might be argued that economics will eventually catch up to astronomy, to the extent that market movements will become predictable over reasonably long horizons. We don't agree. In our opinion, modelling asset prices is a fundamentally different activity from modelling planetary motions. The markets offer nearly every conceivable challenge from the standpoint of prediction. At a micro level, there are a huge number of agents and we don't have an accurate understanding of how any given agent is likely to behave. High-frequency finance is the only area that allows for somewhat-deterministic predictions and this is only true in certain circumstances. We are neither high-frequency experts nor advocates. However, it does seem as though imbalances in the order book for a stock, say, can trigger predictable moves if the stock is pushed to a certain level. That's about it. As the investment horizon increases beyond a few seconds, accurate forecasts of asset price returns are out of reach. Most of us don't even know what our own utility function looks like, let alone someone else's. Alternatively, characterising the market risk aversion parameter, as in various incarnations of CAPM, requires a number of unverifiable assumptions. The original Black–Litterman model (1990), which combines CAPM with a set of investor views, makes the Herculean assumption that the long-term expected return of equities is known. Otherwise, it isn't possible to specify how investors collectively trade off return and variance. There is also the problem of non-stationarity. Individual asset distributions can vary quite dramatically over time and the correlation structure across assets is dynamic. Swiss equities might be highly correlated with oil in one regime and entirely uncorrelated in another.

We can follow a thread from astronomy to meteorology to finance. Planetary motions have been predictable with great accuracy over long timescales since the 1600s. Weather prediction allows for reasonably accurate predictions over horizons of about a week. While the forecasting horizon is not very long, it allows accurate warnings to be issued and precautions taken. In financial markets, however, things are not quite so simple over any discrete time horizon. Feedback is a near-intractable problem. Even if catastrophic sell-offs *could* be predicted over weekly horizons or longer, issuing a warning might have an unpredictable impact on investor behaviour. Some investors might start selling right away, leading to severe losses for others who decided to wait until the forecast date. Alternatively, Central Banks might take heed of the warning and act decisively, either averting or pushing the predicted crisis further into the future.

Specific market patterns and anomalies are unlikely to persist indefinitely in liquid markets. Eventually, other investors will cotton on to a scalable high Sharpe ratio strategy and trade the edge away. In the same way, if investors universally believed in a certain crisis prediction model, the timing and trajectory of crises would change as they acted upon the model. All that we can say is that when aggregate investor gearing is high and Central Banks are simultaneously applying the brakes, the probability of a sell-off is relatively high. In turn, it is well known that sell-offs can presage recessions. In summary, crisis prediction is a complicated brew of exogenous factors and positive feedback loops.

SUMMARY AND CONCLUSION

We have come to the end of our journey. Hopefully, it was an entertaining and instructive one. The narrative takes several twists and turns, which we review here. We first argued that sell-offs can come unannounced and that it is not clear whether any given one will follow through. Investors start to get panicky, margin calls are triggered and doomsday economists generate considerable air time. Cortisol levels are reaching unsustainable levels. The odds might be 4 out of 5 that everything will revert to normal and 1 out of 5 that things will get dramatically worse. In most cases, the initial sell-off in risk assets is met with strong buying. However, investors can't be certain what will happen next, so have to hedge or liquidate positions. Everyone is thinking that they need to hedge and this jacks up the price of insurance. At this point, what hedges can be placed that offer significant protection, yet are not egregiously priced? This is the vital question that we have tried to address. The central chapters of the book analysed specific strategies for hedging against a risk event. We delved into short 1×2 ratio spreads as a way to cover extreme event risk with low premium outlay. We also explored range-based hedges, such as spreads and non-centred butterflies, demonstrating how you could rotate from one to another as the market risk regime changed. We then focused on weekly options as the hedge of last resort. Our idea was that weeklies played a similar role to emergency loans provided by central banks, allowing you to stay in the game until market conditions stabilised. We also examined long-dated options as a value buying proposition, when the far end of the volatility term structure was relatively low. Later, we offered various perspectives on trend following as a protection strategy. Our tentative conclusion was that trend following offered less reliable protection than options, but was relatively cheap and likely to profit in a sustained bear market. We also tried to turn the problem on its head by investigating various contrarian strategies for making money after a sell-off. We ended with a wide-ranging though somewhat open-ended discussion as to whether crises can be predicted or even averted. In our opinion, that is a fitting end to the difficult and ever-changing problem of investing when the chips are down.

A secondary theme is that, philosophically, there is no universal solution to hedging or risk management. If everyone tries the same approach, it is almost guaranteed not to work over time. When using options as insurance, value is to be found in areas that the broader market finds uninteresting or in scenarios that are considered implausible. Trend following as a defensive strategy can be viewed as an adjunct to contrarian or "low-impact" (i.e. low vega) options strategies. Historically, at least, momentum-based systems seem to have worked particularly well during large-scale liquidations, without any direct volatility exposure. Investors have tended to forcibly push the market in a trend follower's favour as they unwind positions.

The level of demand for hedging strategies is highly time-sensitive. While there are legions of investors who are always "in" the equity market, hedging goes in and out of fashion through the market cycle. When equities and credit are quietly rising, many institutions frown upon the need for hedging. Knowing what to do when the need for insurance suddenly becomes apparent is a vital skill that can save large institutional portfolios from ruin. This all needs to be planned in advance. One has to be pragmatic. Mike Tyson has remarked that everyone has a plan until they get punched in the face and this seems relevant here. A reliable set of mechanical techniques, or "bag of tricks" is needed to respond appropriately in tough conditions. Imagination, technical skill and a decent amount of fun and amusement are necessary in the research phase. However, at the point where an emergency hedge needs to be placed, there should be minimal uncertainty about what needs to be done.

While we have written this book in an informal style, the reader should benefit from reviewing the specific options structures and trading strategies that have been presented. Investors who wind up outsourcing their hedging to an overlay manager will hopefully develop a feel for the range of exchange-traded strategies available. Back-testing extreme event hedging strategies will always be a challenge. Forecasting crises outright is at best an inexact science. However, by using a mixture of statistics, intuition and practical trading experience, it should be possible to justify the choice of a particular type of hedge for a particular situation. Ultimately, this book is based upon the realisation that most investors only want to hedge when they are already in trouble and responds accordingly. Relatively prudent investors might be faced with illiquid long positions that need to be hedged before they can be properly unwound. It focuses on ambulance-style strategies, designed to keep the patient going while doing minimal harm.

Glossary

Alpha (α) This refers to the return that can be delivered by a strategy, in excess of the relevant benchmark.

Alpha Alpha is the component of return produced by an active manager that is independent of the market or other systematic risk factors.

Backwardation A futures term structure is in backwardation if long-dated contracts trade at a discount to shorter-dated ones.

Beta (β) This is the sensitivity of an asset or strategy to changes in the relevant benchmark.

Bleed The bleed on an option is its time decay, or **theta**.

Contango A futures term structure is in contango if long-dated contracts trade at a premium to shorter-dated ones.

CTA CTAs are Commodity Trading Advisors. They are authorised to trade futures on behalf of clients and regulated by the CFTC in the US.

Delta Delta is the sensitivity of an option to small changes in the underlying price. In mathematical terms, it is the partial derivative of an option with respect to the underlying price.

Futures term structure The futures term structure consists of the prices of futures contracts on a single underlying asset, with different times to maturity.

Gamma Gamma is the sensitivity of an option's delta to small price changes. It measures how quickly the delta can change for small price moves. It is the partial derivative of an option's delta with respect to the underlying price or, equivalently, the second derivative of the option with respect to price.

Greeks Greeks measure the sensitivity of an option to small changes in the underlying price, volatility, time and other factors. Options traders use Greeks to estimate their instantaneous risk and to hedge their overall exposure.

Implied volatility skew The implied volatility skew for an asset is derived from options with different strikes but a constant maturity. It measures the change in Black–Scholes implied volatility across option strikes or deltas.

Plain vanilla option A plain vanilla option is one with a relatively uncomplicated payout structure, such as a call or put.

Rho Rho is the sensitivity of an option's price to changes in interest rates.

Roll yield This refers to the return you collect (or pay) when selling a nearby futures contract and buying a deferred one on the same underlying asset.

Sharpe ratio The Sharpe ratio of a strategy is its risk-adjusted return, i.e. its return over the risk-free rate divided by its volatility.

Vega The sensitivity of an option to small changes in implied volatility. Mathematically, it is the partial derivative of an option's price with respect to implied volatility.

References

Ane, T., and H. Geman. (2000). "Order Flow, Transaction Clock and Normality of Asset Returns." *The Journal of Finance* 55 (5) 2259–2284 (October).

Armantier, O., E. Ghysels, A. Sarkar and J. Shrader. (2015). Discount Window Stigma during the 2007–2008 Financial Crisis. Federal Reserve Bank of New York Staff Report 483 (August).

Bailey, D., and M. de Prado. (2014). "The Deflated Sharpe Ratio: Correcting for Selection Bias, Backtest Overfitting and Non-Normality." *The Journal of Portfolio Management* 40 (5) 94–107 (40th anniversary special issue).

Beran, J. (1994). "Statistics for Long-Term Memory Processes". Chapman&Hall/CRC Press Monographs on Statistics & Applied Probability 61, Boca Raton, Florida.

Black, F., and R. Litterman. (1990). Asset Allocation: Combining Investor Views with Market Equilibrium. Goldman Sachs and Co. Fixed Income Research Report (September).

Bollerslev, T. (1986). "Generalized Autoregressive Conditional Heteroskedasticity." *Journal of Econometrics* 31 307–327.

Bouchaud, J. (2009). Price Impact. Preprint. (arXiv:0903.2428v1)

Burghardt, G., and T. Belton. (2005). *The Treasury Bond Basis: An In-Depth Analysis for Hedgers, Speculators and Arbitrageurs (3rd edition)*. McGraw-Hill Education, New York.

Black, F., and M. Scholes. (1973). "The Pricing of Options and Corporate Liabilities." *The Journal of Political Economy* 81 (3) 637–654.

Campbell, J., and R. Shiller. (1988). "Stock Prices, Earnings, and Expected Dividends." *The Journal of Finance* 43 (3) 661–676 (July).

Carr, P., and D. Madan. (1998). "Towards a Theory of Volatility Trading." In *Volatility: New Estimation Techniques for Pricing Derivatives*. Jarrow, R., editor. RISK Books, a division of Incisive Financial Publishing Ltd., London (pp. 417–427).

Choudry, M. (2006). *The Futures Bond Basis*, 2nd edition. John Wiley and Sons, Ltd., Chichester, UK.

Derman, E. (1998). "Reflections on Fischer." *The Journal of Portfolio Management* 23 (5) 18–24 (special issue).

Derman, E. (2016). Models. Preprint.

Derman, E., and J. Zou. (1999). Strike-Adjusted Spread: A New Metric for Estimating the Value of Equity Options. Goldman Sachs Fixed Income Strategies (1999).

Dowd, K., J. Cotter, C. Humphrey and M. Woods. (2008). How Unlucky is 25-Sigma? Preprint.

Dupuis, A., and R. Olsen. (2012). "High Frequency Finance: Using Scaling Laws to Build Trading Models." In *Handbook of Exchange Rates*. James, J., I. Marsh and L. Sarno, editors. Wiley Handbooks in Financial Engineering and Economics. John Wiley and Sons, Inc., Hoboken, New Jersey.

Fung, W., and D. Hsieh. (2001). "The Risk in Hedge Fund Strategies: Theory and Evidence from Trend Followers." *The Review of Financial Studies* 14 (2) 313–341 (summer).

Gangopadhyay, K. (2013). "Interview with Eugene H. Stanley." *IIM Kozhikode Society & Management Review* 2 (2) 73–78.

Gatheral, J. (2006). *The Volatility Surface: A Practitioner's Guide*. John Wiley and Sons, Inc., Hoboken, New Jersey.

Gopikrishnan, P., V. Plerou, L. Nunes Amaral, M. Meyer and H. Stanley. (1999). "Scaling of the distribution of fluctuations of financial market indices." *Physical Review E* 60 (5) 5305–5316.

Graham, B. (1949). *The Intelligent Investor*. Harper&Brothers, New York.

Gray, W. (2014). Are You Trying Too Hard? Preprint.

Greyserman, A., and K. Kaminski. (2014). *Trend Following with Managed Futures: The Search for Crisis Alpha*. John Wiley and Sons, Inc., Hoboken, New Jersey.

Haug, E., and N. Taleb. (2007). Why We Have Never Used the Black-Scholes-Merton Option Pricing Formula. Preprint (3rd version).

Haug, E., and N. Taleb. (2011). "Option traders use (very) sophisticated heuristics, never the Black-Scholes-Merton formula." *Journal of Economic Behaviour and Organization* 77 97–106.

Henriksson, R. (1984). "Market Timing and Mutual Fund Performance: An Empirical Investigation." *The Journal of Business* 57 (1) 73–96 (January).

Hiatt, J., and I. Nelken. (2007). "Comments on the New VIX." *Swiss Derivatives Review* 34 42–44 (summer).

Hua, P., and P. Wilmott. (1997). "Crash courses." *RISK magazine* 10 (6) 64–67 (June).

Ilmanen, A. (2003). "Stock-Bond Correlations." *Journal of Fixed Income* 13 (2) 55–66 (September).

Kremer, P., H. Krishnan and M. Malek. (2007). *Trend Following as a Long Volatility Strategy. Volatility as an Asset Class*. Risk Books, a division of Incisive Financial Publishing Ltd., London.

Malek, M., and S. Dobrovolsky. (2009). "Volatility Exposure of CTA Programs and Other Hedge Fund Strategies." *The Journal of Alternative Investments* 11 (4) 68–89.

Martin, I. (2013). Simple Variance Swaps. Working Paper (January).

Mehrling, P. (2005). *Fischer Black and the Revolutionary Idea of Finance*. John Wiley and Sons, Inc., Hoboken, New Jersey.

Pastor, L., and R. Stambaugh. (2012). "Are Stocks Really Less Volatile in the Long Run?" *The Journal of Finance* 67 (2) 431–478 (April).

Pring, M. (2006). *The Investor's Guide to Active Asset Allocation: Using Technical Analysis and ETFs to Trade the Markets*. McGraw Hill, New York.

Reinhart, C., and K. Rogoff. (2009). *This Time is Different: Eight Centuries of Financial Folly*. Princeton University Press, Princeton, New Jersey.

Rothbard, M. (2008). *The Mystery of Banking*. Ludwig von Mises Institute, Auburn, Alabama.

Schwager, J. (1992). *The New Market Wizards: Conversations with America's Top Traders*. HarperCollins, New York.

Schwager, J. (2012). *Market Wizards: Interviews with Top Traders, Updated*. John Wiley and Sons, Inc., Hoboken, New Jersey.

Silber, W. (1991). "Discounts on Restricted Stock: The Impact of Illiquidity on Stock Prices." *Financial Analysts Journal* 47 60–64.

Sornette, D. (2003). *Why Stock Markets Crash*. Princeton University Press, Princeton, New Jersey.

Sornette, D. (2009). "Dragon-Kings, Black Swans and the Prediction of Crises." *International Journal of Terraspace Science and Engineering* 2 (1) 1–18.

Sornette, D., and R. Woodard. (2009). Financial Bubbles, Real Estate Bubbles, Derivative Bubbles and the Financial and Economic Crisis. Preprint. arXiv:0905.0220.

Strogatz, S. (2004). *Sync: How Order Emerges from Chaos in the Universe, Nature, and Daily Life*. Hachette Books, London.

Stutzer, M. (1996). "A Simple Nonparametric Approach to Derivative Security Valuation." *The Journal of Finance* 51 (5) 1633–1652.

Taleb, N. (2007). *The Black Swan*. Random House, New York.

Taleb, N. (2012). *Antifragile*. Penguin (UK), London.

Thurner, S., J. Farmer and J. Geanakoplos. (2012). "Leverage causes fat tails and clustered volatility." *Quantitative Finance* 12 (5) 695–707.

Till, H., and J. Eagleeye. (2006). "Commodities – Active Strategies for Enhanced Return." In *Intelligent Commodity Investing*. Till, H and J. Eagleeye, editors. *Risk Books*. (pp. 471–490)

Twain, M. (1883). *Life on the Mississippi*. James R. Osgood & Co, Boston, Massachusetts.

Wilmott, P. (2013). *Paul Wilmott on Quantitative Finance,* 2nd edition. John Wiley and Sons, Ltd., Chichester UK.

Zou, J., and E. Derman (1999). Strike-Adjusted Spread: A New Metric for Estimating the Value of Equity Options. Goldman Sachs Quantitative Strategies Research Notes.